I0458804

# Israelites Unite or
## _Self-Destruct_

How Jewish civil wars resulted in Temple Destructions

**WOE TO US THAT WE DIDN'T
HEED THE WISE WORDS**

**Asher Elkayam**

WORKBOOK PRESS
RECOMMENDED

Copyright © 2025 by Asher Elkayam

All rights reserved.

No part of this book may be reproduced in any form or by any electronic or mechanical means, including information storage and retrieval systems, without permission in writing from the publisher, except by reviewers, who may quote brief passages in a review.

This publication contains the opinions and ideas of its author. It is intended to provide helpful and informative material on the subjects addressed in the publication. The author and publisher specifically disclaim all responsibility for any liability, loss or risk, personal or otherwise, which is incurred as a consequence, directly or indirectly, of the use and application of any of the contents of this book.

WORKBOOK PRESS LLC
187 E Warm Springs Rd,
Suite B285 Las Vegas NV 89119 USA

Website: https://workbookpress.com/
Hotline: 1-888-818-4856
Email: admin@workbookpress.com


Ordering Information:

Quantity sales. Special discounts are available on quantity purchases by corporations, associations, and others. For details, contact the publisher at the address above.


Library of Congress Control Number:

ISBN-13:      978-1-965732-80-9   Paperback Version
              978-1-965732-81-6   Hardback Version


REV. DATE: 10/17/2025

# Israelites
# Unite or
# *Self-Destruct*

How Jewish civil wars resulted in Temple Destructions

## WOE TO US THAT WE DIDN'T HEED THE WISE WORDS

Asher Elkayam

# CONTENTS

Dedication . . . . . . . . . . . . . . . . . . . . . . . . . . . . . . . . . 1

Permission to Use Biblical Images . . . . . . . . . . . . . . . . . . . 3

Israelites: Unite or Self-Destruct . . . . . . . . . . . . . . . . . . . 5

**Chapter One: The Schism Between North and South . . . . . . . . 11**

(A clear departure from the biblical commandments) . . . . . . . . . . . . . . . . 11

Background to Monotheism in the Holy Land . . . . . . . . . . . . . . . . . 11

Temptation of The Kings . . . . . . . . . . . . . . . . . . . . . . . . . 13

Following the Death of King Solomon . . . . . . . . . . . . . . . . . . . . 14

Dissension and hostility . . . . . . . . . . . . . . . . . . . . . . . . . . 14

How Did Jeroboam Come to Power? . . . . . . . . . . . . . . . . . . . . . 15

Disobedient Kings And Disintegration of faith . . . . . . . . . . . . . . . . . 16

**Chapter Two: Unnatural Succession in the Kingdom . . . . . . . . 17**

Might Makes Right . . . . . . . . . . . . . . . . . . . . . . . . . . . . 17

Jehu and Elimination of the house of Ahab . . . . . . . . . . . . . . . . . . 18

Jehu as Perceived by Prophet Hosea . . . . . . . . . . . . . . . . . . . . . 19

Athaliah's wicked ways and the Survival of the Judean Kingdom . . . . . . . . . 19

True Prophets Versus Jezebel and her False Prophets . . . . . . . . . . . . . 24

**Chapter Three: Rise And Fall of Faith Following King David . . . . 27**

The Good And Bad Kings of Judah . . . . . . . . . . . . . . . . . . . . . . 27

How Kings David and Solomon impacted future generations . . . . . . . . . . 29

Kings Uzziah And Hezekiah . . . . . . . . . . . . . . . . . . . . . . . . 29

King David, Jerusalem, and the three Faiths . . . . . . . . . . . . . . . . . 30

How Faith Weakened Following King Solomon's Death . . . . . . . . . . . . . 31

How Temptations Overcame Wisdom . . . . . . . . . . . . . . . . . . . . 32

Concluding Faith as a Basis for Victory . . . . . . . . . . . . . . . . . . . 34

**Chapter Four: How Biblical Laws Were Ignored . . . . . . . . . . . 36**

The Mount of Blessing and the Mount of Curse . . . . . . . . . . . . . . . . 36

Follow the Word of God and Prevent Injustice . . . . . . . . . . . . . . . . . 37

The Message of Hope and Happiness . . . . . . . . . . . . . . . . . . . . . 38

Then Come the Bad News . . . . . . . . . . . . . . . . . . . . . . . . . 38

The Warnings Get More and More Severe . . . . . . . . . . . . . . . . . . 39

The Warnings Caution About Submission to The Enemy . . . . . . . . . . . . 39

The Warnings Are Becoming Frightening . . . . . . . . . . . . . . . . . . . 40

Prediction that the Israelites Could Bow to Other Gods . . . . . . . . . . . . . 40

And Now, an Agricultural Disaster . . . . . . . . . . . . . . . . . . . . . . 40

The Stranger Turns into the Master . . . . . . . . . . . . . . . . . 41

The Warnings of Moses Are Similar to Those of Jeremiah . . . . . . . . . . . . . 41

Predicting The Exile of The Israelites . . . . . . . . . . . . . . . . 42

Observe God's Words and Avoid the Predicted Tragedies . . . . . . . . . . . . . 42

Moses Makes Sure There is no Objection to a Sacred Covenant . . . . . . . . . . . 43

There Will Be No Collective Punishment . . . . . . . . . . . . . . . . 43

Secret Things Belong to God . . . . . . . . . . . . . . . . . . . . 44

Redemption . . . . . . . . . . . . . . . . . . . . . . . . . . . 44

Choose Life . . . . . . . . . . . . . . . . . . . . . . . . . . . 44

**Chapter Five: King David's Kingdom –A Path to Follow . . . . . . . 46**

King David, Although Imperfect, Chosen Best . . . . . . . . . . . . . . . 46

King David, The Passionate And The Compassionate . . . . . . . . . . . . . 47

King David, a Forgiving Father . . . . . . . . . . . . . . . . . . . . 47

David, A True Friend to Jonathan, King Saul's Son . . . . . . . . . . 49

The Power of The High Priesthood in Biblical Times . . . . . . . . . . . 49

How The True Prophets Followed The Path of King David . . . . . . . . . . 50

The Disappearance of The Northern Tribes . . . . . . . . . . . . . . . . 51

How the House of Judah was saved . . . . . . . . . . . . . . . . . . 52

**Chapter Six: The Warnings and Predictions of the Prophets . . . . . 54**

The Admonitions of Prophet Hosea . . . . . . . . . . . . . . . . . . 54

Prophet Hosea Denounces Perversion . . . . . . . . . . . . . . . . . 54

Harlotry Had Replaced The Basic Commandment . . . . . . . . . . . . . 55

The Message of Jeremiah: Warning and Hope . . . . . . . . . . . . . . 57

Ezekiel's Accusations on Idolatry And Adultery . . . . . . . . . . . . . 58

Ezekiel's Accusations as Are Graphic And Powerful as Follows: . . . . . . . . . 59

Isaiah's Lament And Warning . . . . . . . . . . . . . . . . . . . . 61

A Milder Isaiah on Adultery and Perversion . . . . . . . . . . . . . . . 62

The Minor Prophets Come With A Major Warning . . . . . . . . . . . . . 63

Amos . . . . . . . . . . . . . . . . . . . . . . . . . . . . . 63

Micah . . . . . . . . . . . . . . . . . . . . . . . . . . . . . 64

Nahum- . . . . . . . . . . . . . . . . . . . . . . . . . . . . 64

**Chapter Seven: The Humiliation of Judea by Roman conquerors . . 66**

The Conquest of Judea by Foreign Nations . . . . . . . . . . . . . . . 66

How Hellenization divided the Jewish Nation . . . . . . . . . . . . . . 66

Roman Dominance as a Result of Jewish Disunity . . . . . . . . . . . . . 66

Rome And Herod . . . . . . . . . . . . . . . . . . . . . . . . . 67

Loss of Sanctity in Judea . . . . . . . . . . . . . . . . . . . . . . 69

Disunity Causes Tragedy . . . . . . . . . . . . . . . . . . . . . . 69

## Chapter Eight: Metamorphosis from Biblical Times to 70 CE . . . . 71

(From biblical rules to Hasmonean to Herodian and Roman rules) . . . . . . . . . 71

From Chosen Kingship to Brutal Power Grab . . . . . . . . . . . . . . . . . . 71

Destruction of the First Temple . . . . . . . . . . . . . . . . . . . . . . . . . 71

The Hasmoneans as The last Pure High Priests . . . . . . . . . . . . . . . . . 71

The Seleucid Empire And Judea . . . . . . . . . . . . . . . . . . . . . . . . . 72

The Jewish Struggle to Fight Hellenization . . . . . . . . . . . . . . . . . . . 73

The Successors of Hasmonean Dynasty . . . . . . . . . . . . . . . . . . . . . 73

Political Deterioration Begins in the Holy Land . . . . . . . . . . . . . . . . . 74

Rivalry Between Brothers and Advent of Pompeii . . . . . . . . . . . . . . . . 74

Civil Wars And Thirst for Power . . . . . . . . . . . . . . . . . . . . . . . . . 75

While in power . . . . . . . . . . . . . . . . . . . . . . . . . . . . . . . . . . 75

The Ruling of Judea by the Herodian Dynasty . . . . . . . . . . . . . . . . . . 75

Roman Rulers: From Pontius Pilates to Gessius Florus . . . . . . . . . . . . . 76

The Dissension That Brought The End of Jewish Independence . . . . . . . . . . 77

The Murder of Ananus The High Priest And The Intensified Chaos . . . . . . . . 77

## Chapter Nine: Sins And Crimes Committed On Both Sides . . . . . 79

The Six sins . . . . . . . . . . . . . . . . . . . . . . . . . . . . . . . . . . . 80

Sins And calamities Predicted by Biblical Prophets . . . . . . . . . . . . . . . 82

Both Sides Are to Blame . . . . . . . . . . . . . . . . . . . . . . . . . . . . . 83

## Chapter Ten: The Roman Empire: Cruel And Eccentric . . . . . . . 84

Murder and Poisoning in the Roman Empire . . . . . . . . . . . . . . . . . . . 85

Unusual Roman Cruelty . . . . . . . . . . . . . . . . . . . . . . . . . . . . . 86

The Importance of The Senate And the Praetorian Guard . . . . . . . . . . . . 88

Evil Roman Procurators in The Holy Land . . . . . . . . . . . . . . . . . . . . 89

Under Fadus, Tiberius and Cumanus . . . . . . . . . . . . . . . . . . . . . . . 91

Florus. The Most Cruel Procurator . . . . . . . . . . . . . . . . . . . . . . . . 93

## Chapter Eleven: Civil Strife Amid Roman Domination . . . . . . . . 97

The Treachery of Ptolemy: Murder of two Sons of Simon . . . . . . . . . . . . 97

The Success of Hyrcanus I . . . . . . . . . . . . . . . . . . . . . . . . . . . . 98

Aristobulos II replaces Hyrcanus I . . . . . . . . . . . . . . . . . . . . . . . . 98

Alexander Jannaeus Takes Over The Kingdom . . . . . . . . . . . . . . . . . . 99

Alexander Jannaeus And Cleopatra . . . . . . . . . . . . . . . . . . . . . . . . 99

Queen Salome Alexandra . . . . . . . . . . . . . . . . . . . . . . . . . . . . . 100

The Return and Dominance of the Pharisees . . . . . . . . . . . . . . . . . . . 100

Death of Salome And Sibling Rivalry . . . . . . . . . . . . . . . . . . . . . . 100

Aristobulos Retreats to The Antonia Fortress . . . . . . . . . . . . . . . . . . 101

The Importance of The Antonia Fortress . . . . . . . . . . . . . . . . . . . . . 101

The Pig that triggered the War . . . . . . . . . . . . . . . . . . . . . . . . . . 101

The Opportune moment for Roman Intervention . . . . . . . . . . . . . . . . .102

## Chapter Twelve: Josephus: A major Witness to Destruction . . . . .104
The Eloquence of Josephus . . . . . . . . . . . . . . . . . . . . . . . . . . . .104
How Josephus Describes The rival Factions . . . . . . . . . . . . . . . . .106
Agrippa II . . . . . . . . . . . . . . . . . . . . . . . . . . . . . . . . . . . . .107
Was King Agrippa a Friend of the Jews? . . . . . . . . . . . . . . . . . . . .108
The Passionate Speech of Agrippa to The Rebels . . . . . . . . . . . . . . . .108
Rejection of Agrippa's speech . . . . . . . . . . . . . . . . . . . . . . . . . .109
The Peace Loving Versus the Belligerent . . . . . . . . . . . . . . . . . . . .110
Religious Leaders Appointed by The Romans . . . . . . . . . . . . . . . . . .111
Josephus as an Indispensable Source of Information . . . . . . . . . . . . . . .112

## Chapter Thirteen: Hellenization And The Herodian Dynasty . . . .114
How Josephus described The Gradual Transformation of Judea . . . . . . . . . . .114

## Chapter Fourteen: How Did Herod Eliminate the Hasmonean Dynasty
. . . . . . . . . . . . . . . . . . . . . . . . . . . . . . . . . . . . . . . . . .119
Herod The Edumean . . . . . . . . . . . . . . . . . . . . . . . . . . . . . . .119
Herod Influenced by Power Thirsty Father Antipater . . . . . . . . . . . . . . .120
Antipater And Judea's Loss of Sovereignty . . . . . . . . . . . . . . . . . . .120
How Judea Changed For The Worse . . . . . . . . . . . . . . . . . . . . . . . .121
A Mixture of Hate And Admiration . . . . . . . . . . . . . . . . . . . . . . . .122
The Conflicted Personality of Herod . . . . . . . . . . . . . . . . . . . . . . .122
Josephus on the Death of Mariamme . . . . . . . . . . . . . . . . . . . . . . .123

## Chapter Fifteen: Sadducees Versus Pharisees . . . . . . . . . . . .125
How The Pharisees Regained Power . . . . . . . . . . . . . . . . . . . . . . .125
Even before Herod, king Yannai pursued the Pharisees . . . . . . . . . . . . . .126
The Split in Judea and Beginning of Civil War . . . . . . . . . . . . . . . . . .127
Survival of Faith Despite Hellenization . . . . . . . . . . . . . . . . . . . . .127

## Chapter Sixteen: Jerusalem, From Fame to Humiliation . . . . . .130
Jerusalem as The Center of World's Attention . . . . . . . . . . . . . . . . . .130
The Conquerors of Jerusalem since 586 BCE . . . . . . . . . . . . . . . . . .131
How Roman Protection Turned Into Domination . . . . . . . . . . . . . . . . .132
The Good News Before The Bad News . . . . . . . . . . . . . . . . . . . . . .133
Analyzing The Forces That Played a Role in The destruction . . . . . . . . . . .133
The Main Characters Around The Demise of Jerusalem . . . . . . . . . . . . . .135
The Mourning on the Two Temples . . . . . . . . . . . . . . . . . . . . . . . .136
Prophet Jeremiah's Mourning . . . . . . . . . . . . . . . . . . . . . . . . . .136
The Bitter Words of Josephus on The Demise of Jerusalem . . . . . . . . . . . .137
The Final Blow That Ended The Jewish Independence as Witnessed by Josephus . . .138

**Chapter Seventeen: Comparing Israel of today to Historic Israel . .141**

Are We Better off Today? . . . . . . . . . . . . . . . . . . . . . . . .141

The Knesset, The Only Israeli Parliament . . . . . . . . . . . . . . .142

The New Israeli Rules on Limiting The Israeli Supreme Court . . . . . . . . . .142

Political Divisiveness is Inevitable in Most Democracies . . . . . . . . . . . . .144

Times editorial article (may 5, 2023) . . . . . . . . . . . . . . . . . .144

The BBC View on Israel Judicial System -July 24 2023 . . . . . . . . . . . . . .145

Unusual Criticism of Israel by Silvain Cypel . . . . . . . . . . . . . . . . . . . .145

And This is Our message in French to Mr Cypel: . . . . . . . . . . . . . .147

Israel And The American Jews . . . . . . . . . . . . . . . . . . . . . . . . . .148

The Assassination that shocked the Jewish World (And the US president too). . . . .149

Conclusive Difference Between Ancient Israel and Modern Israel. . . . . . . . . .151

A last Word on Democracy in Israel . . . . . . . . . . . . . . . . . . . .151

**Chapter Eighteen: Summarizing The Complexities of Jewish Struggles**
**. . . . . . . . . . . . . . . . . . . . . . . . . . . . . . . . .153**

Partial Tolerance of Greek Culture . . . . . . . . . . . . . . . . . . . . .153

How Sadducees Were Close to Hellenism . . . . . . . . . . . . . . .154

How The Descendants of Simon Changed Course . . . . . . . . . . . . . . .156

Temporary Victory of the Pharisees. . . . . . . . . . . . . . . . . . . . .156

The Regretful King Yannai, Author of Baseless Hatred . . . . . . . . . . . . .157

Relative Peace Under Salome Alexandra . . . . . . . . . . . . . . . . . . . .159

Religion Used as a Pretext For Domination . . . . . . . . . . . . . . . . . .160

**Chapter Nineteen: The Thriving of Jewish Culture Under Duress. .162**

(Ironically, Jewish Culture Grew Under The Nose of the Occupiers) . . . . . . . .162

The House of Hillel And The House Shammai . . . . . . . . . . . . . . . . . .162

Yohanan Ben Zakkai . . . . . . . . . . . . . . . . . . . . . . . . . . . . .162

Pirkey Avot or The Saying of the Fathers. . . . . . . . . . . . . . . . . . . .163

The Importance of Pirkey Avot in Jewish Rituals. . . . . . . . . . . . . . . .165

Who's Who in Pirkey Avot?. . . . . . . . . . . . . . . . . . . . . . . . . .166

**Chapter Twenty: How Unity achieved Success . . . . . . . . . . .177**

The October 7 Israel Tragedy That Necessitated a Unity Government. . . . . . . .177

How Unity Can Achieve Success. . . . . . . . . . . . . . . . . . . . . . .179

The Talmud, a Harbinger For Jewish Unity. . . . . . . . . . . . . . . . . . .179

**Back to Ancient Israel . . . . . . . . . . . . . . . . . . . . . . . .188**

**Bibliography . . . . . . . . . . . . . . . . . . . . . . . . . . . .192**

**Historical Highlights From Abraham to the Destruction of the Second Temple . . . . . . . . . . . . . . . . . . . . . . . . . . . . . .199**

# DEDICATION

This book is dedicated the memory of my three departed brothers, Albert, Jacques and David whose memory keep me strong and forever hopeful . Bother David recently died on March 30, 2024.

To my beloved parents Solomon and Sima Elkayam who always encouraged me to acquire knowledge and who instilled in me a profound faith in God.

To the late David and Lee Renbaum, my sister's parents -in- law and to Danny Cohen, a close relative of the family who departed from us at the age of 91.

This book is dedicated to all my beloved family members, here in the US and overseas, including my talented children Ron and Alona, my beautiful wife Cheryl and my dear sister Tsippi and brother- in- law Michael and children Steven, Mark and wife Stephanie and their children David and Sarah and a new arrival to Steven and Valerie, beautiful Zoey.

To my cousins and nephews in Tel Aviv, including Shlomi and Vered and children Guy and Bar.

To my dear niece in Chicago, Esti and husband Guy and children Dana and Roy - To my dear niece Titi and daughter Annie and all family members in Paris , France.

To my numerous relatives in Nofit (in the suburbs of Haifa), including Ofir, Sigal Yair and Sharon and their  beautiful children including Or, Lyr, Avi , Gili, Yonatan, Hilah and the beautiful newly born children of Tal and Gal..

To my other relatives in Nofit including Eitan, Dorit, Tal, Gal, Madeleine, my sister in law in Israel and her blessed and numerous grandchildren.

To my relatives in Jerusalem including my nephew Yaron and his mother Jacqueline and nieces Maya, Iris and husband.

To my best friends in Israel:Dr Adam Ackerman and Naomi Ackerman and to my best friends in the US, Pinhas and Dr Rachel Joseph, David Soudry, an avid fan on the history of Moroccan Jewry and to all friends and loved ones in the US and all over the world, including Chuppa and Mary from New York City.

My apologies if I ever missed anyone.

# PERMISSION TO USE BIBLICAL IMAGES

The illustrations accompanying this project were artfully done by Gustave Dore and they are copied hereby with the permission from Paul Abramson, the official figure of www.creationism.org.

Mr. Abramson's authorization letter to this author included the following:

Dear Mr. Elkayam,

Thank you for your message. Congratulation on your works. I hope that they are interesting and helpful for folks.

'Yes, I do give you permission to use (full or cropped) the Dore Images on my web site. I ask that you include 'Used with permission from www. creationism.org' somewhere in your publication, to identify where you obtained the images from.

Best Wishes,

Paul Abramson www.creationism.org

# ISRAELITES: UNITE OR SELF-DESTRUCT

**(How Jewish civil wars resulted in Temple Destructions) Forward**

The following project will highlight the main events which caused the destruction of the first and second Temple of Jerusalem in the 586 BCE and 70 CE More recently, in the year 70 CE, Titus, the Roman general, appointed by Vespasian his father, brought an end to the existing Temple in Jerusalem. Three years later, in 73 CE, the last rebellion against the occupying Roman army took place in the Holy Land but it was quashed when the last rebels retreated to the fortress of Masada near the Dead Sea. The remaining rebels including men, women and children committed suicide so they would not fall in the hands of the Romans.

The Jewish rebellion which took place in the first century CE (between 66 and 70CE) was described in details by Jewish historian and rebel, Josephus Flavius. He was one of the military commanders who initially fought the Romans but realized in the process that it was futile for the Jewish rebels to fight the mighty Roman army. He ended up joining the Roman army as an advisor and became the protege of Roman General Vespasian who was selected by Roman soldiers in Egypt to become the new Emperor of Rome.

In minute details Josephus described the events of Jewish civil battles between two major Zealot factions which led to the provocation of the Roman generals Vespasian and Titus and which brought to the total destruction of the Jerusalem and its Temple and the capture of the two chief rebels.

**This is how Encyclopedia Britannica describes part of those events**

> *Herod [king of Judea at the time] and his successors could not wipe out all resistance to Hellenism among the Jews. There were, of course, varying degrees of resistance. Herod's supporters sought to bridge the gap between the two cultures and thus have the best of both worlds; the Sadducees combined a strict adherence to the Mosaic Law with at least a partial acceptance of Hellenism; the Pharisees were sterner opponents of foreign culture but more flexible in their attitude toward Judaism; the Essenes and other groups hoped for a messiah to deliver them from Roman domination and restore an independent Jewish nation. The Zealots had the*

*most important influence on political events. They condemned anything foreign and insisted that force was the only weapon with which to combat it. At first only a minority, they grew powerful as Roman policy toward the Jews changed. The mad Caligula reversed the formerly tolerant Roman policy by attempting to install his own statue in the Temple, and only his timely murder saved the day. After Claudius' inauguration of the province in 44 AD, conditions worsened under a series of greedy and incompetent procurators, and in 66 AD revolt broke out... (Encyclopedia Britannica 1979, Vol 17:950-951)*

*The rebels were described as a force to be reckoned with. They managed to defeat the Roman soldiers multiple times. Nevertheless, their blind faith in God coupled with fanatic tenacity brought a disastrous end to the second Temple, to Jerusalem and to the end of a Jewish state in the year 70 CE.*

*The governor of [South]Syria [Herod Agrippa II] could not quell the uprising, and the [Roman] emperor Nero entrusted the campaign to the veteran commander Vespasian. With superior forces Vespasian slowly and effectively subdued Galilee and Judaea. When he was recalled to Rome to become emperor himself, he gave his army to his son Titus. In 70 Titus captured and completely destroyed Jerusalem with great slaughter. In 73 the last flames of revolt were put out at Masada, where the last rebels committed suicide rather than fall into Roman hands." (Encyclopedia Britannica 1979, Vol 17:950-951)*

This project will be concentrating on the conflict and rivalry among the Israelites early on in biblical texts and even before the advent of Prophet Jeremiah who witnessed the destruction of the first Temple.

We shall demonstrate hereby that, only unity between factions of the same state can save that state.

We shall also demonstrate that the laws given by Moses to the early Israelites were the ultimate guide for unity of a nation. Any deviation from those laws is shown to have brought chaos, destruction, despair and calamity.

It is our goal to demonstrate how things have changed for the better in modern times. Yet, opinions differ but no bloodshed prevails today in civilized societies.

Throughout history, the pride of Jerusalem has been its Temple. The first Temple was built by King Solomon and finished by the year 957 BCE. Following the Babylonian invasion of Jerusalem and he capture of its last king, 371 years later in 586 BCE, the Jerusalem Temple was sacked and its king deported to Babylonia.

More details will emerge about the reason for its destruction.

The two important personalities who witnessed the destruction of the first and second Temple, namely Prophet Jeremiah and Josephus Flavius, were ignored. Their advice, if followed could have prevented destruction.

Prophet Jeremiah was the crier and the predictor of the events that led to the first tragedy. He bemoaned the disastrous plot of the starving inhabitants of Jerusalem during the Babylonian siege. His graphic descriptions of the atrocities caused by the besieging Babylonians could be found in the book of Lamentations.

Josephus Flavius (Joseph Ben Mathatiahu, as pronounced in the Hebrew language) was a vivid witness to all the events that led to the second demise of Jerusalem.

His passionate warnings were rejected by the rebels.

We shall also examine the concept of leadership. By that, we shall examine the fact the original kingdom of the Israelites was established by God Himself through the biblical prophets as the biblical God is the spiritual, invisible supreme leader.

Moses did not persuade the Israelites to have a human king. Since the Israelites wanted a living leader to rule over them, not necessarily an invisible leader, an unintended crisis of leadership took place. The thirst for power of various kings led to absolute chaos and bloodshed in the Holy land.

Since the kingdom of King Solomon split in two, the kings of Northern Israel served as a bad example for the kings of the Holy Land. Because they have been accused of multiple crimes and inner fighting. their kingdom ended and was overrun by their neighbors as we see ahead.

While the Bible reports that they have done evil in the eyes of the Lord, their crimes can be judged in our modern era as severe ones.

Their weakness stemmed from ousting each other by murder in order to govern. Their culture and faith was far away from the faith instilled by the biblical precepts of Moses. Furthermore, their attitude towards the biblical prophets was to be desired.

The worst kings were those who emanated from the house of Ahab and father Omri. Ahab was married to Jezebel who had an evil influence on him.

After the death of king Solomon and the split of the land into the Northern kingdom and the Southern kingdom, the state of political affairs went from bad to worse.

Rehoboam (931-913), son of Solomon, took over the kingdom after his father's death.

His reign coincided with the return of Jeroboam (913-910 BCE), a former servant in the kingdom of Solomon. He returned from Egypt after the death of King Solomon, as he felt safe, and was crowned by the Northern Israelites to become the first king of Northern Israel.

When the inexperienced Rehoboam refused to cooperate with the northern ten tribes in relaxing their conditions such as paying taxes and improving work conditions, the kingdom split in two.

Rehoboam, son of King Solomon, is reported by the book of Kings, that he has failed to unite all the tribes of Israel as king David and Solomon did before him. Consequently, enmity began between him and Jeroboam.

The other Jeroboam (793-753 BCE) we call Jeroboam II, son of Yoash reigned over Israel for forty one year, including his co-regency with father (also called Yehoash) from 793 BCE to 782 BCE. He was considered one of the cruelest kings of Israel, next to king Ahab.

Yet, a certain spiritual power remained in the Holy land throughout the leadership of various prophets like, early on, Prophet Samuel (1071-1012 BCE) During King Saul's reign and before the advent of King David.

Nathan was the prophet during King David's reign (1010-970 BCE).

The warnings and advice to four Judean kings began in the year 740 BCE by prophet Isaiah.

Prophet Jeremiah was active between the years 626 BCE (during king Josiah 's reign) and 587 BC around the exile of the Israelites from Jerusalem.

Ezekiel prophesied in Babylon following the exiles of the Jews from the Holy Land.

Other important prophets, also called minor prophets: Hosea, Amos, Micah, Zechariah and several more minor prophets will be commented on later on in this project. They all preached about justice and the rule of law. Unfortunately, since the Israelites have switched from a divine leadership to a concrete leadership, good battled evil and evil battled good.

### The Bitter Sweet consequences of Hellenization

Over five centuries after the destruction of the first Temple, during the Roman occupation the Israelites, following several civil wars, chose to join the Pharisees as the religious rulers of the land, Jewish culture and knowledge began to thrive. Brotherly wars ceased under occupation and more and more academies opened the gates for peaceful learning.

Ironically the Hellenization of Israel proved that the majority of the inhabitants neglected power grub as it was in the case of the descendants of the Hasmonean and the Herodian dynasties.

Thus the Jewish culture survived for generations leading to the revival of Jewish religious practices which kept the Jewish tradition alive until today.

*The following chapters will describe, summarize and highlight the various kings and rulers of the Holy Land, their prophets, priests and biblical women who changed history.*

*We shall also arrive at the conclusion that unity with compromise can save a nation while internal strife brings destruction and tragedy.*

# CHAPTER ONE

## THE SCHISM BETWEEN NORTH AND SOUTH

**(A clear departure from the biblical commandments)**

This chapter deals with the first major fragmentation of the people of the Holy Land. It is without a doubt that this split between two kingdoms of the Israelites will have major consequences and historic transformation of the Jewish nation.

Based on biblical accounts, it is evident that the background for the splitting of the kingdom began during the final years of king Solomon.

Despite king Solomon popularity as a God-loving, faithful, prosperous and wise king, the kingdom housed hundreds of thousands of foreign inhabitants. Among them 70,000 unskilled workers and 80,000 stone cutters. That was besides 30,000 of skilled workers who were designed for building the first Temple.

Many of those people worshiped gods other than the God of Israel. Their habits and religious customs were different from those prescribed to the Israelites under Moses' Law.

The Canaanites and other existing tribes in Canaan where the Israelites settled bowed down and prayed to dozens of gods including Baal, El and Ashera. They never had a sense of Monotheism as the Israelites did.

### Background to Monotheism in the Holy Land

The original promise to Moses by God was to settle the freed Israelites from Egypt in the Holy Land and command them to destroy all foreign gods which already existed there. The Holy land, previously called Canaan, was described in the Bible as a land of sinful people who worshiped multiple gods.

As the worship of one god seemed to have been forgotten during the stay of the Israelites in Egypt, it was Moses who was commanded by God to bring the Israelites back to monotheism by accepting the Torah from Mount Sinai and relating to the Israelites the Ten Commandments and additional rules and warnings, including the new covenant with the Israelites (Exodus 20: 19-23).

We remind our readers that the Ten Commandments were written twice by God and handed down to Moses. When Moses brought down the first Ten Commandments from Mount Sinai, he was met with the sinning Israelites who began worshiping a golden calf. The second time he brought down the Ten Commandments it was after Moses asked for forgiveness on behalf of the sinning Israelites (Exodus 32 and 33).

Moses also wrote down God's additional instructions about building the tabernacle and the list of various offerings to erect it. The covenant also included the building of the lamp stand, the altar and all the sacred items needed for sacrifices such as the ark and the incense altar. It also included the making of the garments for the high priest and his attendants, such as the Ephod ( a linen apron used for divination) and breast peace for the high priest.

We can find references to the covenant in Exodus 19, 24 and 34 and Deuteronomy 27 and 28.

Monotheism was first revealed to Abraham in the 19th century BCE, some six hundred years before the arrival of Moses and the exodus from Egypt during the 13th century (1313 BCE)

God also revealed Himself to Isaac, the son of Abraham and to his grandson Jacob.

Going through the book of Genesis, we learn that forefathers Abraham, Isaac and Jacob were extremely faithful to the Lord despite the presence of other cultures in the Holy Land.

We also learn in Genesis 47, that when famine ravaged the land of Canaan, where Jacob lived, it was time for Jacob and his entire family to migrate to Egypt. With the help of Joseph, Jacob's son, who became the second in command to the pharaoh of Egypt, all twelve sons of Jacob and their families settled in the land of Goshen, in Egypt.

We learn that the offspring of those twelve sons came to represent the twelve tribes of the Israelites, from the tribe of Reuben to the tribe of Benjamin..

The Bible also tells us that, after the death of Joseph and his generation, there arose a new pharaoh who did not know Joseph. The new pharaoh became hostile to the descendants of the tribes of Jacob who became more numerous and powerful during their four hundred and thirty years of living in Egypt( Exodus 1). Hebrew sages concluded that the Israelites dwelt in Egypt for only two hundred and ten years.

The explosion of the Israelite population in Egypt became a menace to the new Egyptian pharaoh and the Israelites were forced to become slaves for hundreds of years until they were liberated by Moses.

It is obvious that the Israelites began to forget their religious habits and customs brought from the Holy Land and taught to them by the descendants of Jacob. It is also evident that they were forced to become familiar with the Egyptian way of life. However, that way of life became a burden to them since they were subject to hard labor while forced to build new cities, Pitom and Raamses, also called Ramses (Exodus 1).

It was not until Moses appeared to them and promised to deliver them from Egypt under Gods' protection that the Israelites began to return to the concept of Monotheism when they were liberated and then led to Mount Sinai where they received the Ten Commandments, the written Torah and the Oral Torah (1313 BCE).

Since the date of Exodus and the date of receiving the Ten Commandments is 1313 BCE, Moses did not wait long before he delivered the Ten Commandments.

According to Jewish tradition the festival of Passover which is celebrated in the 15th day of the Jewish month of Nissan marks the Exodus. Passover is also called the festival of Freedom (Hag-Haherut), and also named the Festival of Spring (Hag Ha-Aviv).

Seven weeks after the first day of Passover, Jews celebrate the festival of Shavuot (meaning the festival of Weeks). It is mostly called the festival of the Giving of the Torah. The reason it is called Festival of weeks is because the Israelites waited seven weeks from their exodus from Egypt in order to receive the Ten Commandments.

## Temptation of The Kings

Back to the kings of Israel. It seems that the original kings of the Holy land, especially the kings of Judah who followed the reign of kings David and Solomon, tried to eradicate all foreign worship such as Baal and Ashera from the land but they were not completely successful.

Even king Solomon succumbed to the temptation of foreign gods and it is obvious that his successors witnessed a transition from good to bad behavior (1 Kings 11).

> *And king Solomon loved many foreign women, in addition to pharaoh's daughter, Moabites, Ammonites, Edomites, Sidonians, Hittites. From the nations about which the Lord told the children of Israel,' do not consort with them and they should not consort with you because they would surely*

> *turn your hearts after their gods'. Solomon [however] held*
> *fast to them in love. He had seven hundred royal wives and*
> *three hundred concubines. His women misled his heart. And*
> *as Solomon got older... his heart was no longer perfect as*
> *the heart of David his father. So, Solomon followed Ashtoret,*
> *the goddess of Sidon, and Milcom [Molech], the abominable*
> *[god] of the Ammonites. And Solomon did evil in the eyes of*
> *God....(1Kings 11: 1-6)*

As we follow the story of the first kings of the Holy Land, we learn that faith in the Lord is jeopardized when foreign influence becomes omnipresent. Furthermore, the earthly pleasures overtake devotion to God.

## Following the Death of King Solomon

After the death of king Solomon, Rehoboam, son of Solomon, took over the kingdom by succession. The tribes of Judah and Benjamin remained in the south of the Holy Land while the rest of the tribes of the Israelites were located in the North of the land.

Rehoboam (931-913 BCE), became king after his father's death. He reigned in the Holy Land for seventeen years. He was forty one when he was crowned king of the Judah.

Unfortunately, Rehoboam did not follow the biblical principles of worshiping the God of the Bible. Under him, the land was subject to foreign gods (Asherim) and abominable practices forbidden by the laws of Moses. That practice already existed under king Solomon, his father.

Consequently. It is obvious that king Solomon, during his glorious and powerful years did not set a good example for his sons and successors.

Fortunately, the Torah and the instructions Moses gave to the Israelites were preserved by the priests and the true prophets of the land.

The Torah was there to serve as a spiritual constitution for those kings who chose to obey it. Those kings who did not observe the biblical principles dictated to Moses by God, reportedly suffered demises.

## Dissension and hostility

Following a forty year long thriving kingdom under King Solomon, a bitter fight within the Israelites took place, ending in the division of the Holy Land into two entities: the land of Israel in the North and the Land of Judah in the South. Jerusalem was the capital of Judah and Shomron (Samaria) was the capital of Northern Israel.

The territory of Judah (Judea), including Jerusalem, became under Rehoboam, son of Solomon and Samaria fell under the ruling of Jeroboam.

According to 1 King 12, when Rehoboam threatened to make life miserable for the northern population of the Holy Land. The Israelites of the north had no choice but to form their own kingdom under Jeroboam.

> *'Jeroboam and all the people of [Northern] Israel and they spoke to Rehoboam, saying, 'your father made our burden heavy and now [would you] lighten on us the hard work of your father and his heavy yoke on us and we will serve you'(1 Kings12:4)*

Rehoboam's response after multiple consultations was harsh as follows

> *"My father scourged you with whips; I will scourge you with scorpions' (1 Kings12:14)*

## How Did Jeroboam Come to Power?

Jeroboam was previously a servant under king Solomon's rule. He escaped from the Holy Land and returned after king Solomon's death. He was the first king of the kingdom of Israel (931-910 BCE). Although he was considered evil in his ways to his people he managed to keep the northern ten tribes together by establishing false altars for those Israelites who still wanted to sacrifice as it was the tradition in the Holy Land.

Hereupon, Jeroboam duplicated in Northern Israel the abomination of the golden calf. We recall that the sin of the golden calf occurred in the desert following the exodus(Exodus 32).

> *Jeroboam thought in his heart: "The kingdom will now return to the house of David. If these people go up to offer sacrifices at the temple of the Lord in Jerusalem, then the people would return to their masters to Rehoboam king of Judah and they would kill me [after] they return to king Rehoboam, king of Judah. And the king took advice and he made two golden calves and he said to them, 'it is too much for you to go up to Jerusalem, here are your gods, oh Israel who brought you out of Egypt... And he made a house [of worship] in high places and he nominated from around the people priests who were not from the house of Levi[the biblical original priests]... Kings 1, 26-32*

## Disobedient Kings And Disintegration of faith

Thus Jeroboam departed from the traditional way of worship by hiring priests from all walks of life and who did not represent the true priesthood as described in the Bible.

Furthermore, he managed to hold his people with a complete contempt to the laws of Moses, thus defying the biblical laws the Israelites were required to obey by the commandment of God.

In the Meantime, Rehoboam, son of Solomon, rallied some one hundred and eighty thousand men to fight Jeroboam and start a civil war in order to regain power of the dispersed tribes. According to the book of Kings (1 Kings 12), Rehoboam was urged by Shemayah the prophet to refrain from fighting his 'brothers' in Northern Israel. Therefore the king heeded the prophet's warning. It is also reported that Rehoboam strengthened his kingdom in the city of Shechem.

This is a good example of a king avoiding war at the urging of a prophet.

Nevertheless, reportedly, Rehoboam in the kingdom of Judah did not act any better than his counterpart Jeroboam in Northern Israel. They both established foreign worship in the Holy Land. The book of Kings reports that the people of Judah who followed Rehoboam triggered the anger of God. In the fifth year of his reign, the territory of Judah was invaded by Shishak, king of Egypt who emptied the treasures of the king's palaces as well as the gold and other precious objects from the temple (1 Kings 14).

Rehoboam reigned for thirteen years (930-913 BCE). Just as Jeroboam in the north, he did not leave a good impression in the history of the Israelites. His son Abijah was crowned king in his place.

Consequently, the ruling of the two first kings of the two different kingdoms of the Holy Land ( Israel and Judah), namely king Rehoboam and king Jeroboam, represented a clear departure from their predecessors: King Saul, King David and King Solomon, who governed more or less successfully over the entire Holy Land and reigned over a unified Israel.

The early split of the kingdom of Israel in the tenth century BCE, would serve as a harbinger to further splits in the Israelite nation and would end in the destruction of two Temples.

Fortunately, thanks to a faithful minority of the Israelites who never forgot their heritage the Jewish culture and the biblical commandments were safeguarded to become a source of strength for reunification of the descendants of the biblical Israelites.

# CHAPTER TWO

## UNNATURAL SUCCESSION IN THE KINGDOM

Unlike the kings who reigned in neighboring countries and around the world, most kings of Judah and most kings of Israel were appointed either by succession or by sacred anointment, with a few exceptions.

The first kings of Judah were chosen by God, anointed by a prophet and consequently approved by the people of the land. A great example is as in the case of king Saul, king David and king Solomon.

The above kings of Judah were guided by their spiritual leaders while receiving divine protection.

In contrast, according to 1 King 11, the kings of Israel in the north began their dynasty as a rebellion against the kingdom of Judah in the south. As seen earlier, Jeroboam the rebel, became the first king of the kingdom of Israel in the North while Rehoboam became the ruler of the kingdom of Judah, in the south. While his kingdom was won by succession and while he could have been a great king, his ignorance of his wise counselors made his kingdom split in two entities.

**Might Makes Right**

Through world history we learn that kingship and power were obtained mostly by force. Prehistoric invasions as in the case of the Vikings invasions of today's Great Britain, Roman invasions and its conquests of Asia Minor and Europe made the invader the governor of the land they conquered. Early Chinese invasions like the Xia, Shang and Zhou dynasties proved that invaders could impose their rule, being the masters of the land they conquered.

In ancient times, military power meant might and domination of one weak nation by a conquering one. Even in our twenty first century we read about rebellions and overthrow of existing governments. However, it does not happen as often as in past history.

In the Holy Land, most of the kingdoms, as reported by the Bible, were transmitted from father to son or blessed by a prophet. In a few cases, the kingdom of Israel was taken over by a military leader as in the case of the house of Omri. Omri was the father of Ahab who was the husband of Jezebel, mother of Ataliah. Ataliah married Jehoram of the kingdom of Judah in order to seek power in the south of the Holy land.

Marriage between two opponent nations for the purpose of reconciliation or conquest has been in existence in the Middle East. European history shows that this practice of intermarriage for reconciliation or conquest has also existed between France and Austria or between England and Spain and more countries in history..

### Jehu and Elimination of the house of Ahab

The acts of brutality, cruelty and savagery of the house of Ahab raised the eyebrow of the prophets and of a new leader in Northern kingdom, named Jehu. In 2 Kings, 9 and 10 we learn about Jehu.

Jehu was an officer within Ahab's body guards, a soldier of fortune, who became the eighth king of (Northern) Israel. He was known as the strong man who killed the killers. In this case it was Jehu who was responsible for the death of Jezebel who was responsible for the death of hundreds of Judah's prophets, also named God's prophets.

Jehu was initially inspired by the words of God as he was commanded to eliminate the house of Ahab and Jezebel who were evil as they turned the Israelites away from the Lord.

According to the book of Kings (2 Kings, 9), God who spoke to him, encouraged him to destroy, not only the house of Ahab, but also all worshipers of Baal including Ahab's false priests and the entire household of king Ahab and queen Jezebel.

Jehu exceeded his objectives while purifying the house of Ahab. However, he executed king Jehoram (king of Judah), husband of Ataliah.

Furthermore, and according to 2 Kings 10, Jehu went too far as he executed king Ahaziah, son of Ataliah who was in good relations with Jehoram.

> *"And when Ataliah, the mother of Ahaziah saw that her son was dead, she arose and destroyed all the royal seed [of Judah]. So Hehoshabah, daughter of king Yoram[ Jehoram], sister of Ahaziah, took Yehoash [Yoash], son of Ahaziah; she stole him from among the executed sons of the sons of the king [of Judah], together with his nurse in the room of the beds. They hid him from Ataliah and he was not killed. And he [Yoash, the infant] was with her [his nurse] for six years while Ataliah reigned over the land(2Kings11:1-3)..*

## Jehu as Perceived by Prophet Hosea

**As Jehu exaggerated in his killing evil and good rulers, reportedly his action did not go well with God who thought that Jehu exceeded the limit of his authority and his divine instructions.**

According to the book of Hosea, we read that Jehu was condemned by the prophet himself who accused Jehu of abusing power and engaging in a long killing spree.

As prophet Hosea put it, ' God will avenge the bloodshed of Jezreel on the house of Jehu.' (Hosea 1:4)

Was God contradicting Himself when he ordered Jehu to eradicate the house of Ahab? The answer is no. Jehu became a bloodthirsty killer even as he felt he was obeying God's order. By executing Ahaziah, king of Judah, he overstepped his boundaries. Although Ahaziah was evil enough to be punished, he did not belong to the house of Ahab. In fact, after king Ahaziah died he was buried in the city of David, which was a great honor for the Judean kings.

The other reason Jehu was considered evil despite his destroying the kingdoms of Ahab and Jezebel, was that he ended up adopting the golden calf worship started by Jeroboam.

Jehu was initially anointed by a prophet, a student of prophet Elisha, to become king of Israel (2 Kings: 9). That gave him the power to govern and do all things he was supposed to do in order to eradicate the Baal worship.

On the succession of power, most kings of Judah transmitted their power from father to son: King David to Solomon to Rehoboam and so on.

On the other hand, most kings of Northern Israel assumed power by eliminating their predecessors.

The only exception was in the house of Jehu. In this case the power was transferred from father to son. After king Jehu died, his son, grandson and great great son took the throne respectively. The names of the dynasty of Jehu are as follows: Jehu, Jehoahaz, Yoash (or Yehoash), Jeroboam II, and Zachariah. The House of Jehu reigned in Northern Israel for 102 years total.

## Athaliah's wicked ways and the Survival of the Judean Kingdom

Some examples of unnatural succession can be found in the case of Ataliah, the daughter of Ahab and Jezebel who, despite being part of the northern kingdom came to the kingdom of Judah (by marrying Jehoram king of Judah), supposedly to make an agreement with Judah and consolidate her influence and power.

After she married Jehoram, her goal was to eliminate the seed of the Judean royals who descended from the Davidic dynasty. She seemed to have inspired her husband Jehoram (Yoram) to kill all of his six brothers.

Her intention was to force herself on the kingdom of Judah and become the queen of Judah, with the intention to dominate the kingdom of Israel. As we saw above, the military leader Jehu intervened and made an end to the evil reign of the house of Ahab.

Thanks to Yehoyadah, the Priest (Cohen), the young Yoash was preserved as an infant to be crowned king at a young age. The crowning of the young king took place according to King David Judean tradition. That was a startling measure against the reign of Ataliah who finally found her death by order of the armed guard, under Yehoyadah.

> *"And the captains of hundreds did according to all Yehoyadah the Priest instructed them...and the Priest gave to the captains of hundreds the spears and the shields of King David...And the infantry stood, each man with weapons in his hand from the right side of the Temple to the left side of the Temple...And he [the Priest] brought out the son of the king [the young Yoash] and placed the crown[on the young king's head] and the [usual] testimony [found in the Torah scroll]; they [the royal and the priestly crowd and their defenders] declared him king and they anointed him and they clamped hands and [they] said, 'Long live the king'"...Ataliah heard the sound of the infantry and the people...and the trumpets... Ataliah tore her cloths and shouted, 'mutiny, mutiny'. Yehoyadah the Priest ordered the captains of hundreds...,' do not put her to death in the Temple of God'...she came out through the horses entrance of the palace and there she was put to death' 2 Kings 11:9-16*

In sum, unlike the crowning of the northern kings, the crowning in the tribe of Judah had to take place in the presence of a prophet and in accordance to rules of the holy Temple. The kingship of Judah is considered a sacred duty and the king must be anointed and given a holy scroll from the Torah which serves as a guide to ruling the nation with dignity and justice.

Not all kings of Judah adhered to their holy commitment.

Surrounded by their prophets and priests, the kings who did well heeded the words of the prophets. The evil kings, as reported in the book of Kings, ignored the warnings and even had their own so called false prophets, as in the case of Jezebel, mother of Ataliah.

In the next two illustrations, thanks to Gustave Dore's sense of imagination, the artist shows how the false prophets were eliminated and how the true prophets survived the battle of Jezebel against the true biblical prophets.

The end of Ataliah was also imagined by the artist who painted the circumstances of her death as reported in the book of Kings.

## "The Death of Jezebel" *by Gustave Doré*

*Doré Bible Illustrations* • Free to Copy
www.creationism.org/images/

2Ki 9:33 And he said, Throw her down. So they threw her down: and *some* of her blood was sprinkled on the wall, and on the horses: and he trode her under foot.

**"Death of Ahab"** *by Gustave Doré*

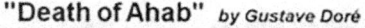

*Doré Bible Illustrations* • Free to Copy
**www.creationism.org/images/**

1Ki 22:35 And the battle increased that day: and the king was stayed up in his chariot against the Syrians, and died at even: and the blood ran out of the wound into the midst of the chariot.

"Slaughter of the Prophets of Baal" by Gustave Doré

Doré Bible Illustrations • Free to Copy
www.creationism.org/images/
1Ki 18:38-40 Then the fire of the Lord fell, and consumed the burnt sacrifice, and the wood, and the stones, and the dust, ... and they said, The Lord, he is the God; ... Take the prophets of Baal; let not one of them escape. ...

## True Prophets Versus Jezebel and her False Prophets

The kingdom of the Holy Land, which begun with King Saul (1038 1010 BCE), followed by King David (1010-970 BCE ) and King Solomon (970

BCE-931 BCE), split after the reign of the latter. That split will be analyzed in details in this project.

The early biblical kings listed above could not be crowned without the blessing of a prophet or a high priest of the land. This is why we shall stress the importance of the existing prophets and spiritual leaders during the reign of the kings of Israel and the kings of Judah. They all made an enormous impact on most kings. Their teachings often reached the evil kings of the kingdom to choose the right path to justice and faith in God. Unfortunately, not all the kings heeded the prophets' warnings.

While the prophets predicted the good and bad news of the land, the good priests (mainly in the kingdom of Judah) maintained the holy Temple in accordance with the biblical rules.

There were also substandard priests who defied the laws of the Bible. They were found mostly in the north of the land in the kingdom of Israel.

The good kings were surrounded by just and upright prophets and priests. A good example can be found in the presence of Nathan the prophet who served king David. When king David's son Adoniahu (Adonis) rebelled against the kingdom, it was Nathan the prophet who intervened in order to keep David's promise to have Solomon anointed and crowned king of the land.

Other prophets like prophets Jeremiah and Isaiah served as messengers of God in urging the Israelites to never lose faith.

Prophet Ezekiel spoke about his vision of the divine throne and prophet Daniel spoke about a cataclysmic future while emphasizing the faith in one God versus the existing gods of Babylon.

Those kings who were described as evil, as in the case of king *Ahab and his wife Jezebel* and her daughter queen Ataliah, were advised by what the bible calls false prophets and false priests.

On the other hand, prophet Elijah is described in the Bible as the one who fought against those false prophets by leaning on his faith in God.

In 1 Kings 18 and 19, we have an example of how the Israelites were saved from assimilation by prophet Elijah: We read about a serious confrontation between 450 false prophets of Baal and the only prophet of the Lord, Elijah. All his counterparts were slain by queen Jezebel while another prophet named Obadiah saved 100 of them.

Elijah ended up facing Ahab and his prophets and producing miracles by bringing fire and rain. Elijah's miracle enabled him to control the enormous crowd of Israelites gathered to choose between the Lord of Israel and Baal, the Canaanite god. When the Israelites saw that Elijah produced miracles, they believed in God and they obeyed prophet Elijah by slaying all the prophets of Baal.

Elijah is described in the Bible as a true messenger of God, a doer, a fighter for justice and the savior of the Israelites. He is recognized and venerated by all three religions: Judaism, Christianity and Islam.

Elijah's name is mentioned during the Passover Seder and other occasions such as during a Jewish ceremony on a Jewish circumcision day and during Saturday night blessing of the wine, indicating the end of the Sabbath and the beginning of a new week.

In Christianity, Elijah is compared by Jesus to John the Baptist.

The last book of the Hebrew Bible (Tannakh), the book of Malachi predicts that,

> ' *I will send you the prophet Elijah before the great and terrible day of the Lord...He will turn the hearts of the parents towards their children and the hearts of the children toward their parents...(Malachi 4)*

In the Qur'An, The story and the deeds of Elijah' are recounted in details as he is described as the true messenger of God, Allah. His Arabic name is Ilias

Besides the prophets and their sacred duties, the existing priests serving the righteous kings, observed and maintained biblical laws and principles. Unfortunately, not all kings and priests obeyed the laws of the Torah found in the Bible. Nevertheless, many kings, especially from the tribe of Judah, were able to uphold the biblical laws.

# CHAPTER THREE

## RISE AND FALL OF

## FAITH FOLLOWING KING DAVID

### The Good And Bad Kings of Judah

Biblical sources, including ample Talmudic literature, commenting on the Pentateuch assembled and written for five hundred years (from 200 BCE to 300 CE) tell us that faith leads to victory and independence.

The dynasty of the good kings of Judah, which began with king David, was championed by kings who followed the path of king David who had a firm and unconditional faith in God. The good kings of Judah who succeeded kings David and Solomon were Abijah(913-911 BCE), Asa (911-870 BCE, Yehoshafat (870-849 BCE), Uzziahu (767-740 BCE), Yotam, (740-732 BCE), Hezekiah (716-697 BCE) and Josiah (640-609 BCE).

While Josiah had the Holy Land and the Holy Temple purified from all foreign gods and foreign practices, he was killed by the Egyptian forces of king Necho II. According to 2 Kings 23:29,,' Necho slew him at Megido'.

The above named kings of Judah followed the path of king David during the totality of their reign while other kings of Judah to be named below did well at first, then faltered. King Yoash (Jeyoash-835- 795 BCE) reigned for 40 years. While he survived Athaliah's murder of the kings of Judah (see Chart I of the kings of Judah), he did well at first then he became evil towards the end of his life. King Amaziah, son of Yoash (796-767 BCE) did well at first then he changed course towards the end of his life. A remarkable king was king Josiah (640-609).

The following is an example of a good king who does well at first, then changes course. King Joash may serve as a good example to those kings who wanted to do as well as king David but circumstances made them change their ways of governing under the rules of the Torah.

In 2 Chronicles 23 and 24 we learn about the series of events following king Joash (Jeyoash) crowning and the death of Ataliah.

During prophet yehoyadah's service to king Joash, the kingdom of Judah functioned well by maintaining a proper observance of the laws of Moses. King Joash acted fervently in collecting money from all parts of Judah and Jerusalem in order to restore the Temple and reinforce it and bring it back to its original state.

> *The men in charge of the work [in the temple] were diligent...They rebuilt the temple of God to its original shape... When they had finished they brought the rest of the money to the king and with it were made objects for the Lord's temple [including tools for the] burnt offering and...other objects of gold and silver...( 2 Chronicles 24:13-14)*

*Then something unexpected happened right after the death of the high priest (Cohen Gadol) Yehoyadah.* It seemed that king Jeyoash did a complete U-turn in his ways of caring for the temple. He began to change his ways and to behave in a totally different way as he originally behaved during Yehoyadah's service to him.

After the officials of the kingdom of Judah spoke to him, they seem to have convinced him to change his mind about worshiping God in the holy temple. Instead they persuaded him to follow the false gods of Ashera (2 Chronicles 24: 17, 18).

The author of this chapter in Chronicles did not seem to describe a transition within the mind of king Jeyoash who seemed to switch from being a great king, in verse 13 and 14 to an evil king in verse 17 and 18 of 2 chronicles 24.

The transformation of king Jeyoash from good to evil did nothing but vexed the new prophet, Zachariah, son of Yehoyadah who warned the king and the elders of Judah about their sins in neglecting the words of the Lord in performing the holy sacrifices in Gods' temple. Prophet Zachariah also admonished those elders about their bowing to the foreign god, Ashera and its idols.

> *This is what Prophet Zachariah said to the king and his advisers '...This is what God says: why do you disobey the Lord's command....Since you have forsaken the Lords' command, He has forsaken you (2 Chronicles 24: 20)*

Unfortunately, prophet Zechariah's message was not well received by the elders and by the king himself who ordered him killed because of his warnings.

As in every case of defiance in the Bible, when a king neglects the laws of the Torah and bows to foreign gods, punishment ensues.

Indeed, the kingdom of Jeyoash was invaded by the Aramean army. His military leaders and officials were killed and his Temple and palace invaded and the plunder was sent to Damascus.

King Jeyoash was also wounded in the battle. He was finally killed by his own men who were angry that he killed the son of Yehoyadah.

Following the death of Jeyoash, his son Amaziahu (Amaziah) was crowned king of Judah at the age of twenty five. He reigned over the kingdom of Judah for twenty nine years (2 Chronicles 24: 23-27 and 2 Chronicles 25:1).

For a complete chart of the kings of Judah and the kings of Israel and the years they served, see charts of the kings of the Holy Land at the conclusion of this project.

## How Kings David and Solomon impacted future generations

King David is seen as the model king and the exemplary ruler and uniter of the tribes of Israel (in the North) and Judah (in the south).

Not only he was upright with the Lord most of his life, he was also a military strategist who rescued his people from so many enemies. Despite criticism about him as a man of many wars and an adulterer, he is admired all over the world for being a cunning military tactician, a superb speaker and a humble leader, a great poet and a precocious musician with multiple skills.

Most people who read his Psalms agree on the quality of his poetic style and his description of human strength and misery while relying on faith to be rescued spiritually and physically by the Lord.

The Psalms of David are read every single day in Jewish and Christian prayers. In fact, in Hebrew houses and hospitals, the Psalms are continually read in the presence of a sick or a dying loved one.

Despite his passionate attraction for the wife of his military general Uriah, he realized his mistakes and begged for forgiveness. After all, the Bible reports that God Himself forgave him because of his steady feeling of faith.

## Kings Uzziah And Hezekiah

In the book of Chronicles we learn how King David inspired two kings who reigned some two hundred years after his death- King Uzziah (767 BCE) and king Hezekiah (716 BCE).

King Uzziah (767 BCE) followed the path of King David by being faithful to God all his life. Although towards the end of his life he committed a sin by attempting to burn incense in the temple, which was strictly allowable to priests only, his life was spared by the Lord because of his previous good deeds King Hezekiah (716 BCE) followed the path of king David by organizing the orders of the Cohanim (priests) and the Levites, the priest helpers, from the tribe of Levi who performed the biblical sacrifices. The sacrifices were performed the same way it was done during king David's days.

Even the Passover festival was celebrated twice. First, King Hezekiah and his followers celebrated the biblical seven days of Passover. Then, the king allowed another seven days of celebration in order to instill the tradition of Passover celebration which was ignored by previous kings and Israelites ( 2 Chronicles :29).

Both King Uzziah (Uzziahu) and king Hezekiah (Hizkiahu) fortified the city of Jerusalem and the state of Judah in order to fend off any attack from foreign powers.

As some kings of Judah and most kings king of Israel were not always faithful to the Lord, king David remained the king to admire and revere.

Having conquered the surrounding territories of the Ammonites, the Philistines, the Arameans and the Amalekites, king David managed to create one solid state during his reign and unite the
Israelites.

*Since our project deals with unification as a basis for success it also deals with dissension among the Israelites who brought about the destruction of Jerusalem and its Temple.*

King David's success in battles and in spiritual matters allowed his son Solomon to become the second best king of Judah and Israel.

As the Bible report, under king Solomon, there was peace in the country for forty long years of prosperity It is evident that King David was not granted the high privilege of building a Temple for God, because of his past sin. Nevertheless, he was considered the favorite of all kings in the eyes of God, and in the eyes of the majority of the Israelites, according to the Bible.

## King David, Jerusalem, and the three Faiths

Since Jews and Christians quote the Psalms everyday in their prayers, they have made King David and his Psalms eternal. Is possible that the hopes expressed in the poetry of King David could mean something for one faith and mean another for another faith? Jerusalem is often mentioned and it seems to be a uniting factor between the faiths.

For Jews, Jerusalem is the holy city and the symbol of reunification of all Israelites and their pilgrimage to the Holy land.

For the Christians, Jerusalem is the city where Jesus preached and died before his last supper with his disciples.

Jerusalem is also an important city for Muslims (Moslems), who consider Jerusalem as a holy city.

Because of its long history, Jerusalem became the third holiest city for Muslims. In fact when Islam began to spread in the seventh century CE, Jerusalem was the first *qibla*, meaning the city towards which the Muslim prayers were directed when concentrating in prayer. It is also where the Dome of the Rock and Al Aqsa Mosque are located. Al Aqsa was built on the remnants of the destroyed temple of King Solomon and king Herod. As we see, Jerusalem unites the three world religions and King David is as well quoted and greatly revered in the Qur'An as *Malik Daoud* (King David).

## How Faith Weakened Following King Solomon's Death

The famous king Solomon (970-913 BCE) was not without fault. His strength, wisdom, popularity and building projects made him impose taxes all over the Holy Land and in the surrounding territories he controlled. After his death it was Rehoboam (931-913 BCE), his son, who became the king. He is described in the Bible as a weak and indecisive king. Since Rehoboam did not rely on the advice of the prophets of the land and because he imposed heavy taxes on the people of Israel there was a rebellion against him.

As seen earlier, it was Jeroboam the son of Nebath, former servant of King Solomon, who became king of the northern part of the Holy Land, called Israel.

This was the beginning of the schism between the kingdom of Judah and the kingdom of Israel. Faith in God and observance of the biblical laws of the Torah began to weaken since that unfortunate split between the two kingdoms.

We could not ignore the fact that King Solomon was at first devoted to God as his father David. After all, he was known to be the builder of the glorious, gigantic and lavish Temple in Jerusalem. However, because of foreign influence, including his marriage to the daughter of the pharaoh of Egypt and his association with the Queen of Sheba to the Holy Land and several other practices which were present in the land of Israel, King Solomon, toward the end of his life, deviated from the laws of God and Moses.

While surrounded by seven hundred wives and three hundred concubines 1 Kings 11:3), the Bible reports that King Solomon turned to other practices. He was reported to have followed the foreign gods of Shemoch, Ashtoret and Molech ( from Moab, Sidon and Amon).

Nevertheless, most of the kings of Judah were faithful to God. The biblical rules and principles were their guide for morality, justice and reverence to the Temple of Jerusalem. In addition, the prophets and the priests of the land were instrumental in attempting to inspire the kings of Judah to obey the laws of God. They were more convincing to the kings of Judah and less influential on the kings of the kingdom of Israel.

## How Temptations Overcame Wisdom

In the first two chapters of the first The Book of Kings in the Old Testament (Tannakh) we read about the ending reign of king David and the crowning of Solomon his son.

Between chapter 3 and chapter 10 of 1 Kings, we learn about the strength, the glory and the unusual wisdom of king Solomon.

However, on chapter 11 of the same book, we read about a sea change in the life of king Solomon which triggers the wrath of the Lord.

> *'As Solomon aged, his wives turned away his heart [from the Lord] to other gods and his heart was no more complete with the Lord, as was the heart of David, his father (1kings 11:4)*
>
> *'And the Lord said to Solomon, because this [foreign practice] was with you, and that you did not keep my Covenant and the laws which I commanded you, I will indeed tear the kingdom from you and I shall give it to your servant. However I shall not do so during your life time because of David your father. I shall tear it out from your son. (1 Kings 11:11-12)*

Nevertheless, King Solomon is described in the bible as the wisest of all men and as the ultimate builder of the sacred Temple. He is also described as the most successful of all kings, the richest and most talented in entrepreneurial tasks. Going through the biblical text and following the chain of events in King Solomon's history we learn that he had so many wives and concubines that his initial humility which was manifested before the Lord and before the children of Israel was somewhat diminished.

Furthermore, the fact that he had so many interactions with foreign governments and entities, such as Egypt, Lebanon and Ethiopia that his devotion to the God of Israel was somewhat reduced.

We learned that, initially, following King David's death, he was approached by the Lord who appeared to him in a dream and all what King

Solomon asked for was *wisdom* to know the difference between good and evil and be able to judge and control the people of the land.

Unfortunately, the illustrious Solomon, deviating from the biblical principles on which he was raised began to turn against God. The fact that other gods, considered foreign gods by the Bible, already existed in the Holy Land did not seem to advance the initial agenda King Solomon wanted to pursue. His original wish was to always follow the word of God and the laws of Moses to the letter.

Bible scholars wonder if the schism in the Holy Land following King Solomon's death was triggered by the behavior of the latter in his final years. Unlike King David who remained loyal to the Lord, King Solomon may have influenced his descendants to become pervert and enormously taxing on the people of Israel in the post Solomon era.

Throughout the books of Kings and the books of the Prophets we learn that foreign worship in the Holy Land never ceased to exist. It was up to the Israelites to overcome their temptations and follow the laws of Moses. Unfortunately many kings succumbed to perverting ways while other kings took the laws of the Bible seriously.

From here we learn that there was a *constant inner battle of conscience within the Israelites and their chosen kings.*

For those who believe in the Bible stories it is obvious that when the children of Israel did well in their observance of the Torah, they won over their enemies. On the other hand, when they strayed from the Torah they lost their battles. Their battles took place between themselves and between them and their enemies.

On the whole, history shows that the remnants of the exiled Israelites from Babylonia in the sixth century BCE and the second century CE, remained faithful to their faith and they even risked their lives in order to remain loyal to the Torah. The best example of this can be found during the Spanish Inquisition in the fifteenth century CE.

During the difficult days of the Spanish Inquisition, Jews had to choose between Christianity and Judaism. Those Jews who remained faithful were expelled from Spain. Those Jews who remained in Spain but observed Judaism in secret were called *Marranos* (pigs in the Spanish language). When discovered they were tortured to death.

Was it a miracle that Judaism survived despite all the 'do or die' orders issued by their oppressors. Besides the Spanish and the Portuguese who forced the Jews to convert to Christianity Jews were also faced the dilemma of conversion when Islam rose to power from 632 CE and up.

Ironically, the Inquisition was imposed on Jews and Moslems alike who resided in Spain. Jews had no other choice but migrate to the closest Moslem countries in North Africa. Most Jews settled in Morocco, Algeria and Tunisia, Italy and Greece.

Going back to biblical times it is reported that the kings of Judah were closer to the directives of King David who was upright with the Lord, most of his life. We understand that King David deviated at times by doing wrong. For example, when he sent his military leader to the battle front his intention was to marry the wife of that military. Uriah indeed perished in the battle against the Amonites (2 Samuel 11:5-27).

On the other hand, the wife of that military general, Bath Sheba, was to become indeed the mother of a most illustrious king in the biblical history. Solomon.

King Solomon was, according to the New Testament, nineteen generations away from Jesus who is revered around the Christian world (since king David was reported to be twenty generations away from Jesus).

### Concluding Faith as a Basis for Victory

We have summarized above the ups and downs of the Israelites and their kings and prophets. We have described glorious events and shameful episodes. We have also indicated how the nation of Israel was exposed to foreign cults and deities while given the Torah as an alternative to those foreign gods.

Unfortunately, the battle between good and evil (as defined by the Bible) was a long one. In biblical times, the Israelites were exposed to the Canaanites who worshiped several gods.

It was already announced by God to Moses, even before the arrival to the Promised Land, that the Israelites would be exposed to foreign cultures.

It was up to the Israelites and their leaders and kings to strictly follow the guidelines of the Torah lest they would be weakened and harassed by their enemies. It happened during a long and protracted battles against the Philistines. We learn through the book of Judges and from the book of Samuel that faith in the God of the Israelites is the secret for victory. In the book of Samuel we can read about the famous battle of Afek where the Israelites lost four thousand soldiers in the battle. Also the battle of *Mishmash* where the Philistines were won over by Jonathan, son of Saul and friend of the future king David.. So was the battle of the Valley of *Elah* where the young David battled Goliath. The first king of Israel was king Saul. He was killed on *Mount Gilboah*. So were his three sons when they battled the Philistines.

We also know the story of Samson and Delilah. While Samson remained a *nazir* (ascetic) and believed in the biblical God he was strong enough to battle the Philistines. However, when he was seduced by beautiful Delilah, daughter of the Philistines, he lost his hair and he drank wine. When he reveled the secret to Delilah that his strength came for his being ascetic, growing hair, abstaining from drinking wine, and believing in God, he was delivered to the Philistines. They imprisoned him and blinded him by piercing his eyes. When his hair grew long again he regained his powers and defeated the Philistines while assembled in their temple,

# CHAPTER FOUR

## HOW BIBLICAL LAWS WERE IGNORED

*In this chapter we shall focus on the rules which were heard in Mount Sinai and the warnings given by Moses to the Israelites.*

Those warnings were discovered early on by King Josiah (640609 BCE) when his high priest Hilkiah (Hilkiahu) discovered what it is believed to be the book of Deuteronomy (which was lost until then).

Some of those warnings were repeated by Prophets Jeremiah and Isaiah and even by Josephus to the rebels who fought the Romans occupiers between 66-70CE. Unfortunately those warnings were rejected prior to the destruction of the first Temple as well as that of the second Temple.

The reign of King Josiah brought a great blessing for the kingdom of Judah. Unlike his predecessors, he was lucky to be surrounded by righteous people like Hilkiah the high priest, the father of non-other than prophet Jeremiah.

During the reign of Josiah, a miracle happened which brought about a complete return of the Israelites to the observance of the Torah.

That important book was found while the Temple was being refurbished at the command of king Josiah. It revealed the most important warnings of Moses to the Israelites. The most important warnings given by Moses from God and intended for the Israelites can be found in chapters 27 and 28 in the book of Deuteronomy.

When king Josiah was informed of those warnings, he tore his clothes and he realized how the nation of the Israelites has been off the track in observing the word of God.

When that book was discovered, it was read over and over as it was taken seriously by king Josiah and by his priests and nobles.

The Following analysis and excerpts from the last book of the Pentateuch which shows how the Israelites, otherwise named Hebrews and Jews were rewarded or punished, based on their obedience to the rules of Moses

### The Mount of Blessing and the Mount of Curse

Moses, as instructed by God, has exposed the Israelites to two different choices: the blessing and the curse. It has been mentioned at least once before in the Bible. Now it is being emphasized, and it is predicting bad news should the Israelites stray from God's rules and instructions.

> *"And Moses commanded the people on that day, saying, 'when you will be crossing the Jordan [River] these are [the tribal representatives] who will stand on Mount Gerizim, in order to bless the people: Simeon and Levi, and Judah, and Issachar, and Joseph, and Benjamin. And these [tribal representatives] will stand On Mount Eibal for the curse: Reuben, Gad and Asher, and Zebulun, Dan and Naphtali . . . "(Deuteronomy 27:11-13)*

## Follow the Word of God and Prevent Injustice

Basic rules are given to refrain from doing certain things as follows in order to be in agreement with God. Avoidance of same will create balance of justice, compassion, and dignity between people. *Hereby here is a list of warnings mentioned by Moses.* Those warnings carry with them a message of curse, should the Israelites ignore them or fail to obey the rules. Those rules reemphasize the message of the Ten Commandments and make them even more explicit and clear to the Israelites. They center on the uniqueness of God, obeying His rules, honoring the father and mother. The rules go on and concentrate on helping the needy and the weak. There are serious warnings about sexual intercourse between family members and relatives. Justice and righteousness dominate the rest of the rules as follows:

And all the people shall say, Amen.
Cursed be he who lies with any animal. And all the people shall say, Amen.
Cursed be he who lies with his sister, the daughter of his father or the daughter of his mother. And all the people shall say,
Amen.
Cursed be he who lies "Cursed be anyone who makes a sculptured or molten image, [considered] an abomination by the Lord . . . And all the people shall respond, Amen.
Cursed be he who dishonors his father and his mother. And all the people shall say, Amen.
Cursed be he who trespasses the boundary of [the property of]. And all the people shall say, Amen.
Cursed be he who misguides a blind person on his way. And all the people shall say, Amen.

Cursed be he who perverts the judgment of the stranger, the fatherless, and the widow. And all the people shall say, Amen.

Cursed be he who lies with his father's wife, for he has uncovered his father's clothing with his mother-in-law. And all the people shall say, Amen.

Cursed be he who beats down his fellow neighbor in secret. And all the people shall say, Amen.

Cursed be he who accepts a bribe to slay an innocent person. And all the people shall say, Amen.

Cursed be he who will not enforce the terms of this teaching and observe them. And all the people shall say,

Amen."(Deuteronomy 27:15-26)

## The Message of Hope and Happiness

The message of hope and blessing is clear. It carries a sense of happiness and celebration once God's rules are followed. *Prosperity, wisdom, success, popularity, uniqueness, and military might of the Israelites are promised.* This message is an introduction to a warning but leaves the feeling that *the Israelites can be safe and successful if they choose the right path*, which is the path of God.

> "...*The Lord will give you abundance in excess for the fruit of your womb, the offspring of your cattle, and the produce of your soil in the land that the Lord swore to your fathers to give you. The Lord will open for you His good treasure: the skies to give the rain for your soil in time and to bless all the work of your hands. You shall lend to many nations and you will not borrow. The Lord will make you the head, not the tail; you will always be at the top and not at the bottom if you listen to the commandments of the Lord your God which I command you today, to keep and execute.*"(Deuteronomy 28:10-13)

## Then Come the Bad News

> *The bad news can happen if the Israelites "forget" the word of God and His instructions, as directed by Moses. It is clearly a choice between a blessing and a curse. Moses makes that very clear. Also, the warnings seem too steep for a new nation who has not yet settled in the Promised Land.*

> *"But if you do not listen to the voice of the Lord your God, to watch and do all his commandments and statutes whim, I am instructing you today all those curses will come upon you and they will overtake you:*
>
> *Cursed shall you be in the city and cursed shall you be in the field.*
>
> *Cursed shall be your basket and your kneading trough.*
>
> *Cursed shall be the fruit of your womb and the produce of your soil, the increase of your cattle and the flocks of your sheep.*
>
> *Cursed shall you be in your coming and cursed shall you be in your going." (Deuteronomy 28:15-19)*

## The Warnings Get More and More Severe

Is it to frighten the Israelites that Moses tells the outcome of not obeying God's laws and precepts? *Total destruction and annihilation are predicted if the Israelites transgress.* This is an opposite stand to the hopeful statements made earlier.

> *"The Lord shall send upon you destruction, tumult, rebuke in all the things you undertake until you are destroyed and disappear quickly as a result of your evildoing [because] of your forsaking me . . . The Lord will strike you with consumption, fever, and inflammation . . . and they will pursue you until you disappear." (Deuteronomy 28:20 and 22)*

## The Warnings Caution About Submission to The Enemy

*The past language of the Israelites always being victorious by the presence of God is changing now.* It is predicting a smashing defeat before the enemy. This is of course if the Israelites do not follow God's rules and laws as given to Moses.

> *"The Lord will have you beaten before your enemies. In one road you shall go after him [the enemy] and in seven ways you shall flee before him . . . Your carcasses shall become food for all the birds of the sky and all the beasts of the earth." (Deuteronomy 28:25-26)*

## The Warnings Are Becoming Frightening

*The warnings to the Israelites are becoming personal.* Not only may the nation, as a whole, be defeated if the Israelites do not observe God's rules and instructions, but now it is becoming personal. The possible defeat of the rebellious Israelites translates into personal tragedy of individual men and women. Moses warns of defeat in order to get God's points across to a nation who has been nothing but rebellious all these years.

> *"You shall betroth a wife and another man shall lie with her. You shall build a house, but you shall not dwell in it. You shall plant a vineyard, but you shall not redeem its grapes . . . Your flock shall be delivered to your enemies, with no one to help you. Your sons and daughters shall be delivered to another people . . . The fruit of your land and all your hard work's worth will be eaten by another nation . . . And you shall be nothing but oppressed and crushed . . . You shall be mad from the sight of your eyes [of what] you will see."(Deuteronomy 28:30-34)*

## Prediction that the Israelites Could Bow to Other Gods

Moses is predicting that the worse that could happen to the Israelites is they would end up bowing to other gods. *This is unprecedented. It has been as a warning before. Now it is almost becoming a prediction.* Maybe it is to scare the Israelites so they can begin to become the right people Moses wants them to be.

> *"The Lord will lead you, and the king you shall set over you, to a nation that you and your fathers did not know. And you shall worship there other gods [made] of wood and stone."(Deuteronomy 28:36)*

## And Now, an Agricultural Disaster

*In detail, Moses predicts the worse that could happen if the Israelites stray from God. This warning is about the crops and the food that the Israelites need in order to survive.*

> *"The field will produce much seed and you shall gather*

*little [crop] because the locust will consume it. You shall plant vineyards and you shall labor but you shall not drink of the wine or gather [the crop] because the worms shall eat it. You will have olives in all your boundaries, but you shall have no oil for anointment, for your olives shall drop off. You shall have sons and daughters . . . but they will go into captivity. All your trees and the fruit of your soil shall be owned by the locust. "(Deuteronomy 28: 38-42)*

## The Stranger Turns into the Master

*All along, the Israelites were instructed to treat the stranger as they would treat themselves.* In this case, if the Israelites stray from God and make Him angry, it is the stranger that will rule the Israelite.

*"The stranger in your midst shall rise above you higher and higher while you sink lower and lower . . . The Lord shall carry a nation against you from far, from the end of the earth, just as the eagle darts [through the air]. A nation, the language of whom, you shall not understand. An insolent nation who will not respect the elderly and will have no grace over the young. "(Deuteronomy 28:43 and 49-50)*

## The Warnings of Moses Are Similar to Those of Jeremiah

The predictions that Moses makes are similar to those that the Prophet Jeremiah made to his people long after the time of Moses. They are described in the book of Jeremiah. The suffering of the Israelites after the destruction of the Temple is described in details in the book of Lamentations. The books of Jeremiah and the books of Lamentations are, of course, separate from the Pentateuch. The Book of Jeremiah is part of the book of Prophets (*Neviim*) which was written long after the five books of Moses. The book of Lamentations is written in a third part of the Holy Scriptures, called *Ketubim (The Writings)*.

*"And he [the enemy] shall besiege you in all your towns until your high and fortified walls have come down . . . And you shall eat the fruit of your own body, the flesh of your sons and your daughters . . . in the siege and in the stress to which your enemy shall bring you. "(Deuteronomy 28:52-53)*

## Predicting The Exile of The Israelites

**Moses** predicted the exile of the Israelites from the land of Canaan even before the children of Israel settled there.

> *"The Lord shall scatter you among all the peoples from one end of the earth to the other, and there you shall serve other gods, wood and stone, whom neither you nor your ancestors have experienced. And among those nations you shall find no peace, and there shall be no rest for the sole of your foot. And the Lord shall give you there an anguished heart and eyes that pine and a languishing soul . . . The Lord shall send you back to Egypt in ships, by the route, which I told you, you should not see again. There you shall offer yourselves for sale to your enemies as male and female slaves, and there shall be no buyer."(Deuteronomy 28:64-65 and 68)*

### Observe God's Words and Avoid the Predicted Tragedies

Never before have we heard Moses speaking of every imaginable tragedy that could overtake the Israelites should they disregard the word of God. The last remarks Moses made pertained to a possible exile of the Israelites. But all those tragedies can be avoided. Moses warns the people of Israel, directing them in a two-way street: the blessing and the curse. *As always, we witness the power of the word.* The words have been frightening as well as soothing. The choice is in the hand of the Israelites.

To sum up, the rules above and their warnings were given in the land of Moab before the arrival of the Israelites to the Promised Land. Those rules are reported to be given over and above the Ten Commandments given earlier in Mount Horeb which part of Mount Sinai). In any case, the warnings about either rule are frightening.

*In the entirety of the five books of Moses, we cannot find so many frightening warnings and predictions, except on Chapter 28 in the book of Deuteronomy. ; all centered one after the other,*

Their intensity and awe can make some reader revere but tremble, fear but shake, read but not believe that God is able and willing to do all those things to His own chosen people, even though it is a warning, let alone a prediction.

Those awesome warnings lead to one good thing the Israelites must know: follow God's rules, and you have nothing to fear.

The Covenant with God Is for the Present and the Future. Moses now is facing the people, and he announces that all Israelites are entering into the covenant of the Lord. Everyone is present: the leaders, men and women, children, even the servants and the strangers are witnessing Moses' discourse. The covenant is not restricted only to the people present, but it carries on to future generations.

> *"And Moses called all Israel and said to them, 'You have seen all that the Lord did before your very eyes in the land of Egypt, to Pharaoh and to all his servants and to his whole country . . . And not with you alone do I make this covenant and this oath, but with those who are standing here with us this day before the Lord our God and with those who are not here with us this day."{Deuteronomy 29:1 and 13-14)*

## Moses Makes Sure There is no Objection to a Sacred Covenant

Moses is warning that if there is anyone who clings to other gods other than the Lord Himself, there is no security for the nonbeliever. God, although merciful, will not forgive the man or the woman who will worship the other gods.

> *"Perhaps there is among you some man or woman, or a family or a tribe, whose heart today is turning away from the Lord our God to worship the gods of those nations . . . The Lord will not want to forgive him; for then will the Lord's anger fume and His jealousy will rage against that man . . . and the Lord shall erase his name from under heaven."(Deuteronomy 29:17 and 19)*

## There Will Be No Collective Punishment

Those individuals or groups who sin and do not follow God's rules will be singled out and punished accordingly.

"The Lord will single him out from all the tribes of Israel unto evil, according to all the curse that is written in this book and God shall wipe his name out from under heaven."(Deuteronomy 29:20)

## Secret Things Belong to God

Moses warns the Israelites that God has mysterious ways of knowing the people who do and do not obey the covenant.

> *"The secret things belong to the Lord our God but the revealed things belong to us and our children forever . . ."{Deuteronomy 29:28}*

## Redemption

Even after sinning, God gives a chance to the people to redeem themselves and return to Him.

> *"And you shall return to the Lord your God and you shall hearken to his voice . . . you and your children . . . then the Lord your God shall return with your return [to God], and He will have compassion on you. He shall return, and He shall gather you from all the nations from which He scattered you there."(Deuteronomy 30:2-3)*

## Choose Life

Moses, through God, urges the Israelites to choose life and blessings. The message of hope and encouragement continues.

*The Above warnings and rules. defining reward and punishment. were applied to the right people according to their deeds. As Moses warned, those who followed the rules of the Torah succeeded while those who challenged the word of God were punished. Just as Prophet Jeremiah warned about the tragic destruction of Jerusalem in 586 BCE, Josephus also cautioned the rebels not to challenge the Roman Army. He described afterwards the horrors suffered by the rebellious Jews and by the rest of the subjugated population to those rebels in the year 70CE.*

*The Israelites who lived in the Holy Land during the existence of the first and the second Temple, knew well the precepts of the of the law of Moses.*

*Those who were not aware of the law were lectured and warned by their spiritual leaders and especially the existing prophets.*

*The laws of Moses are mostly rules of conduct between people and their fellow people, between man and woman, between rich and poor, and especially between powerful and powerless people.*

*When all the above commandments have been followed for the benefit of mankind they end up signifying that those laws of Moses are nothing more than a covenant between man and God Himself.*

*The warnings of Moses about reward and punishment were concentrated mostly in the last book of the Pentateuch. That book: Deuteronomy, was lost but was retrieved in the depository of the Temple by Hilkiah the High Priest under king Josiah (640-609 BCE). That notable discovery was done while King Josiah was having restorations and repairs to the existing Temple.*

# CHAPTER FIVE

## KING DAVID'S KINGDOM –

## A PATH TO FOLLOW

### King David, Although Imperfect, Chosen Best

Even as he was not without fault, king David was considered the best and the most faithful king in the history of Israel and the Israelites.

During King David's reign, the priests and military leaders played a crucial role in the life of the Israelites in the Holy Land.

For example, when king David was ill, one of his sons, Adoniahu (Adoniah), attempted to take over the kingdom by mobilizing various priests and military leaders to announce his 'new' kingdom.

For a short while, the priests, prophets and military leaders around Adoniahu gave the impression that a new king was going to reign in Israel. However, with the interference of King David's high priest and prophet, the situation was reversed and Solomon was anointed king (1Kings 1).

In biblical times, an anointed king by a spiritual leader spells trust and faith by all the inhabitants. The priests had the duty and the privilege to attend to all matters concerning the temple and all rituals of the land. The prophets had the sacred task to mediate between God and man.

In this case of king Solomon's anointment as a king it was Nathan the prophet who intervened on behalf of Solomon. Nathan was alerted by Solomon's mother Bathsheba who told the ailing King David that he once promised under oath that his kingdom would be given to his son Solomon.

When Bathsheba came to the king, followed by Nathan the prophet, and related the news to king David that Adoniahu rebelled against the kingdom and proclaimed himself king, king David, in his illness, upheld his promise. Solomon was finally anointed king by David's command (1 Kings 1).

The crowing ceremony of Solomon took place while attended by Nathan the prophet, Zadok the priest, Bathsheba, the mother of Solomon, military leader Benayahu Ben Yehoyadah and a multitude of people. Their presence enabled the crowning of king Solomon to be the legitimate king of Israel while simultaneously abolishing the declaration of David's rebellious son, Adoniahu (1 Kings 1:34).

Most of the kings of Judah followed the path of king David while most of the kings of Israel diverted from the teaching of the Torah.

Based on the biblical book of the Prophets, Kings and Chronicles, we are told that those leaders who followed the word of God were rewarded while those who diverted from the divine commandments were punished and consequently brought the end of the kingdom in the Holy Land.

We also deduct through the biblical texts mentioned above that the anointed kings, the prophets and the high priests had furthermore an enormous influence in politics through their spiritual power and their acceptance by the multitude. Their actions were considered legitimate in the eyes of the Lord as well as in the eyes of the people of the land.

## King David, The Passionate And The Compassionate

Besides being the ideal king, uniting and serving his people justly, King David was a compassionate father in forgiving his two sons who rebelled against him. King David had for his best friend Jonathan, the son of Saul, with whom a long history of cooperation took place between the two. Jonathan was aware of the animosity that king Saul, the first king of Israel, bore against the young David who excelled in battle.

As it is said in the book of kings

"And Saul with thousands [of enemies eliminated] and David with his tens of thousands" (1 Samuel 18:7)

Yet, Although Jonathan was faithful to his father Saul who was jealous of David, He was as faithful in friendship and unconditional love to David. He warned David about the looming danger that Saul sought to harm him.

## King David, a Forgiving Father

King David was known to be a forgiving father, even as his two sons Adoniahu and Absalom betrayed him by seeking the kingdom of Judah while king David was alive. King David, despite being described as an avid warrior and a man who broke the rule of decency by sending his main general to the front line and marry his wife, was forgiven by God according to the Bible. Yet, king David's blind faith in a supreme being is expressed in one hundred and fifty Psalms.

"Samuel Blessing Saul" *by Gustave Doré*

*Doré Bible Illustrations* • Free to Copy
www.creationism.org/images/

1Sa 9:21 And Saul answered and said, *Am* not I a Benjamite, of the smallest of the tribes of Israel? ... wherefore then speakest thou so to me?

King David was chosen to be the best king and leader of biblical Israel. Many kings of Judah followed the path of king David but, not all of them succeeded in surpassing the quality of man king David was.

## David, A True Friend to Jonathan, King Saul's Son

The friendship between the young David and Jonathan, King Saul's son was exemplary. Al tough Jonathan respected and feared his father Saul, his friendship to David was also of protective nature as we see in the quote ahead.

> *"And Saul spoke to Jonathan his son and all his servants about killing David while Jonathan, son of Saul, was in deep friendship with David. And Jonathan told David, saying:, 'my father is planning to kill you and now beware; in the morning go and dwell secretly in a hiding place...And Jonathan spoke favorably to his father Saul of David saying, 'let not the king sin against David his servant because he[David] did no wrong to you...why should you sin in [shedding] innocent blood by killing and his deeds were greatly to your benefit..'(1 Samuel 19:1-4)*

While Saul temporarily changed his mind about killing David, the war against the Philistines was raging on and David excelled in the battle against them. He was so successful that they fled from the battleground. David's success caused melancholy and anxiety in Saul's mind and he was ready again to get rid of David by thrusting his spear onto David while he was playing the harp but Saul missed as David dodged and the spear hit the wall. King David survived against all odds to eventually be anointed and become the best king of the Israelites.

## The Power of The High Priesthood in Biblical Times

The high priest of the land, had the dutiful power to stop anyone, even the reigning king from desecrating the rituals of the temple. One of the best examples of a high priest having more power than a king is found during the reign of King Uzziahu (Uzziah) of Judah.

King Uzziah (790-739)BCE, reigned for 52 years. Assyrian records show that he reigned for forty years (783-742). This is possible because he was a co-regent with his father Amaziah.

Uzziah was known to be a most popular king since king Solomon as he fortified the cities of the Holy Land, subdued the Philistines, the Arabians and the Edomites. He even had the Amonites pay him tribute (2 Chronicles:6-8).

In general, he kept the Holy Land safe and prosperous and relatively calm since the days of King Solomon.

King Uzziah decided in his later days to offer incense in the altar of incense which was strictly prohibited for anyone except for the high priest and his sacred attendants.

King Uzziah was faithful to the Lord most of his life. His fame in the land was as a result of being victorious over neighboring tribes and being a skilled builder, an entrepreneur and a military designer. He designed devices to shoot arrows and catapults to throw stones from towers (2 Chronicles 26:13-15).

As king Uzziah became famous and fearless and too sure of himself, he felt the spiritual need to approach the temple and burn incense in the altar, something that was not allowed. As a result of his action, he was stopped by Azzariah the high priest and eighty of his helpers. The Bible reports that, at that moment when King Uzziah decided to break the laws of the temple and that of the priests, he became a leper and was escorted out of the temple by Azzariah and his priests. He later died from his illness. The Bible justifies his illness and subsequent death as he defied the of incense burning, which was strictly limited to the high priest of the Temple.

He lived for another eleven years while his son Yotam(740-732) took over the kingdom (2 Chronicles 26: 16-23).

As we saw earlier in the transgression of king Uzziahu, the burning of the incense by the High Priest and his helpers in the Holy Temple was already forbidden in the Pentateuch. as we find passages supporting this sacred duty which was strictly limited to the person with the highest authority in the Temple (see Exodus 30:7, 8; Numbers 16:40; 18:7).

On the spiritual priestly power, we learn that some biblical priests had an enormous power in politics. Even a king was forbidden to perform a duty which was solely intended for a high priest. Unfortunately, not all priests performed their duties according to the rules of the bible. Most of the priests of the tribe of Judah were reported to be upright with God while the priest of (Northern) Israel did not.

On the whole, the Prophets of the Holy Land played a vital role in keeping the kings of Israel and their people to follow the right path.

## How The True Prophets Followed The Path of King David

After the death of King David and King Solomon, in the days of the first Temple, the biblical prophets who were considered the true prophets were challenged by what the Scriptures call false prophets Since the kings of Israel and Judah were influenced by their prophets and priests, a long battle between the biblical prophets who were considered the true prophets took place against the so called false prophets.

The false prophets were gathered in the Northern kingdom where most kings sinned and rebelled against the laws of Moses.

As we see further, the most cruel kings of the Israel kingdom were Ahab, Jezebel and Ataliah. In this case, queen Jezebel, Ahab's wife, commanded a vicious attack on the biblical prophets, in order to gain a political advantage over the Holy Land in a whole. Four hundred and fifty prophets were eliminated under Jezebel.

The intervention of the remaining true prophet in the Holy Land, prophet Elijah, came just in time to save the Israelites from worshiping the false god of Baal, which Jezebel attempted to impose on the Israelite nation.

Fortunately, and according to the Bible, Elijah was reportedly assisted by divine power in proving the false prophets were a detriment to the nation.

The believing Israelites who were convinced by Elijah who produced miracles in front of the false prophets helped eliminate the opposing prophets who were going to prevent them from worshiping the true God of Israel.

Thus the nations of Israel and Judah were saved from following the false gods of Baal, which were controlled by Jezebel.

Even after the death of Jezebel, the kings who ruled the nation of Israel in the North continued to sin while most of the kings of Judah in the south followed the path of King David.

During those biblical kings of Judah the inhabitants were called Israelites. After their exile to Babylonia and the destruction of the first Temple they were renames *Jews* as they emanate from the tribe of Judah and Benjamin who survived after the disappearance of the ten northern tribes.

In the books of Ezra, Nehemiah, Daniel and Esther the exiled Israelites who returned to the Holy Land thanks to king Cyrus were often called Jews.

## The Disappearance of The Northern Tribes

On the other hand the northern population of Israel did not survive even as it was initially saved by prophet Elijah. The evil kings of the North were defeated by the Assyrian and Northern Israel ceased to exist in 720 BCE.

Fortunately, the House of Judah survived as it was predicted and announced by prophet Hosea

## How the House of Judah was saved

Because of the atrocities and numerous sins we cited above found in the house Of Israel in the North. Prophet Hosea announced that the Lord was angry with them and they would disperse and disappear while the house of Judah will survive as it is quoted below

> *"...for, I will no longer have pity on the house of Israel, nor will I forgive them. Nevertheless, I will have mercy on the House of Judah and I will deliver them in the name of their Lord [I]. But I will not save them through [the use of] bow, sword, war, horses or horsemen.' When [Gomer] was done weaning Lo-Ruhamah, she gave birth to a son. The Lord said to him [to Hosea], 'Name him Lo-Ami [not my people], because you are no longer my people and I will no longer be there for you.'"(Hosea 1:1-9)*

*In sum, King David served in biblical times as the ideal king, a faithful and righteous human being. King David is still regarded by Jews and Christians alike as the best king of ancient Israel as well as the best military strategist and best unifier of the scattered tribes of Israel.*

*In conclusion, the impact of King David on generations after his death will continue to inspire the biblical Israelites and the exiled Jews for thousands of years*

## "The People Mourning Over the Ruins of Jerusalem" *by Gustave Doré*

*Doré Bible Illustrations* • Free to Copy
**www.creationism.org/images/**

Lam 1:8 Jerusalem hath grievously sinned; therefore she is removed: all that honoured her despise her, because they have seen her nakedness: yea, she sigheth, and turneth backward.

# CHAPTER SIX

## THE WARNINGS AND PREDICTIONS

## OF THE PROPHETS

### The Admonitions of Prophet Hosea

The warnings of the prophets to the kings and other leaders in the kingdoms of Israel and the kingdom of Judea served and as a check and balance for the actions of those leaders. Those warnings were often ignored and seldom heeded by some leaders as we see ahead.

As the prophets preached about the basic principles and commandments, they used their own language but they also used the divine message as they heard it from the Lord. Some of those prophets even used a rare language, which compared the entire Israelite community to a prostitute.

As this subject is difficult to teach to minor students, it is nevertheless clearly written in the Bible and it should be properly addressed.

The best explanation that can be given is that those accusations of adultery can be looked as a metaphor in order to shock the sinning Israelites and help them choose the moral path as written in the Biblical commandments.

The following is a clear interaction between the Lord and one of the Minor Prophets,

### Prophet Hosea Denounces Perversion.

*"The word of the Lord, which came to Hosea, the son of Be-eri, in the days of Uzziah, Yotam [Jotham], Ahaz, Hezekiah, kings of Judah, and during the days of Jeroboam the son of Yoash [Joash], king of Israel... The Lord said to Hosea, 'go and get yourself a harlot and children of a harlot because the land will surely be committing adultery...' So [Hosea] went and took for wife Gomer, the daughter of Diblaim. She conceived and she gave birth to a son. The Lord told him, 'name him Yzreel [Jezreel], because, very soon I will hold accountable the house of Jehu for the bloody acts which took place in [the land of] Jezreel and I will put a stop to the kingdom of the house of Israel. It will come to pass that, on that day, I will break the bow of Israel at the Valley of*

*Jezreel.' She [Gomer] conceived again and she gave birth to a daughter. The Lord told him, 'Name her Lo-Ruhamah [meaning no pity] for, I will no longer have pity on the house of Israel, nor will I forgive them. Nevertheless, I will have mercy on the House of Judah and I will deliver them in the name of their Lord [I]. But I will not save them through [the use of] bow, sword, war, horses or horsemen.' When [Gomer] was done weaning Lo-Ruhamah, she gave birth to a son. The Lord said to him [to Hosea], 'Name him Lo-Ami [not my people], because you are no longer my people and I will no longer be there for you.'" (Hosea 1:1-9)*

The comparison between sin and adultery is very clear. It is rare in the Bible that the Lord asks one of his messengers to become the 'fall guy' so that the Lord can make His point. The Lord, hereby is asking this prophet to marry a prostitute and then have children with her.

The Lord announces even the names of the children. Each name means something announcing the wrath of the Lord and the upcoming destruction of the sinning Israelites.

There is also a distinction between the sinning Israelites and the faithful Israelites, as we see below. As there were two kingdoms in the Holy land, one run by the kings of Israel, and the other by the kings of Judah, the Lord seemed more lenient towards the House of Judah, originally ruled by King David.

As seen before, King David was tolerated by the Lord because of his blind faith in God and his objection to the culture of idol worshiping in the land of Israel.

It is rare in the Bible that the Lord Himself asks a prophet to demean himself and marry a harlot. Obviously, the Lord was incensed with His people. He chose a concrete and living example the people could see and witness with their own eyes.

Hosea had three children and, as the Lord commanded. each of his children's names had a symbolic name to describe the moral behavior of the people.

## Harlotry Had Replaced The Basic Commandment

As Hosea continues to preach to the Israelites as inspired by the Lord, the accusations continue. Those who followed other gods have forgotten the true God, their maker and savior. The worship of foreign gods and sacrificing to them is an abomination to the Lord. Those who went astray have forgotten about the true covenant promising Israel to be a holy nation, a light to all the nations of the world.

The way the people and some of their kings conducted themselves seemed to be in contrast with the original promise made to Moses at Mount Sinai.

The following was the original divine promise to the Israelites

> *"In the third month after the children of Israel went out of Egypt...they came to the Sinai Desert and they camped there...facing the mountain. And Moses went up towards the Lord. The Lord called him from the mountain and said, 'You have seen what I have done in Egypt and I carried you over the wings of eagles and I brought you over to Me. And now, if you just heed my voice and keep My Covenant, you will become My best choice among all the people as I control the entire earth. You will then be for me a kingdom of priests and of holy people. These are the words you will say to the children of Israel.'" (Exodus 19: 1-6)*

Now Prophet Hosea is bringing more graphic accusations and descriptions of a life of whoredom that is the life of those Israelites who neglected the Lord.

> *"Fight with your mother, fight! Because she is not my wife;*
> *And I am not her husband.*
> *Let her remove her whoredom from her face*
> *And her adultery from between her breasts; Or else, I will remove her cloths, naked,*
> *And I will exhibit her as the day she was born.*
> *I will make her as the wilderness And I will place her in a desert- like land; And I will let her die of thirst.*
> *I will not have pity on her children,*
> *Because they are children of harlotry.*
> *Because their mother has committed adultery, The one who bore them has acted shamelessly. Because she said, 'I will follow my lovers,*
> *Those who provide me with bread and water, My wool and my linen,*
> *My oil and my libations.*
> *Therefore I will block your way with thorns And I will erect fences around it; She will not retrieve her paths.. She will go*

*after her lovers*
*But she will not reach them. She will seek them;*
*But will not find them.*
*Then she will say, 'let me return to my fist man,*
*Because I had it then better that I have it now.'" (Hosea 2:*
*4-7)*

Hosea, as other prophets below, attempted to make the Israelites realize their erroneous ways. It is a powerful metaphor intended to shock the people, as they seemed way out of line, according to the book of Hosea.

### The Message of Jeremiah: Warning and Hope

Prophet Jeremiah was a contemporary of prophets Zephaniah, Nahum, Habakkuk, Daniel and Ezekiel.

He mediated between the Lord and the people of Israel. During the reign of king Josiah of Judah he warned about the upcoming devastation of Jerusalem Temple and the nation of Judah. His prophecy materialized and the city of Jerusalem and its temple were devastated by the Babylonians in the year 586 BCE.

Jeremiah is also known for being the prophet who mourns on the people of Jerusalem. In the biblical book of Lamentations he describes in minute details the enormous suffering of the besieged Israelites in Jerusalem. The entire book of Lamentations is read and commented on during the fast of the 9th day of the Hebrew month of Av (also called Tisha B'Av). On that day, the observing congregants spend the entire day fasting, praying and concentrating on the devastation of Jerusalem.

In another instance, based on the Bible (also called Tannakh) the Lord calls out Jeremiah and asks him to deliver the following message to the sinning Israelites. Following grave accusations of the people, the Lord, through Jeremiah, gives another chance to the people to mend their ways and return to God.

*"...You have committed adultery, with many lovers. How*
*can you return to Me? - says the Lord. Lift your eyes and*
*see the bare heights, where have you not committed adultery?*
*On the roads you sat [and waited] for them [ lovers]...and*
*you defiled the land with your adultery and your evildoing...*
*You had the temerity of a harlot and you refused to accept*
*shame...You did wrong...' And it came to pass that the Lord*

*said to me during the reign of King Josiah (Yoshiahu), 'Have you seen what Israel, the apostate, did? Going up to every high mountain and under every green tree and committing adultery there? And I still said, after her doing all that, she will come to me; but she never returned; her sister, the betraying Judah saw it...she too went and whored... she defiled the land and she committed adultery with stone and wood...' And the Lord said to me..., 'go north and call out those words and say 'Return [to the Lord], oh apostate Israel, said the Lord, I will not be angry with you because I am kind...But you should realize your sin because it is against the Lord that you sinned while spreading your favors among strangers under every green tree and you never heeded me, says the Lord.'"*
*(Jeremiah 3: 2-13)*

In many other parts of Jeremiah we see how the accusations of the Lord take different turns as the people seem to have renounced the Holy Covenant.

*"For they have done an abomination in Israel and they have committed adultery with their neighbors' wives; and in my name they have spoken lies, which I have not commanded them. I am the One Who knows and I Am the witness, says the Lord." (Jeremiah 29: 23)*

*"For a long time you have broken your yoke, you have untied your bonds; And you said, 'I shall not worship. But on every high place and under a green tree you lay down like a whore.'"(Jeremiah 2:20)*

*"...For their crimes are numerous, their rebellious actions have increased...For this, how can I forgive you? Your children have forsaken Me. They have sworn by gods, which are not gods. Although I have fulfilled their needs, they committed adultery and they crowded the harlot's house."*
*(Jeremiah 5: 6-7)*

Despite Jeremiah's accusations, there is still hope to return to the Lord. The prophet brought the sad news but also delivered hope. We also learn in the book of Jeremiah that this prophet, as some other prophets, risked his life in order to bring the unpleasant predictions to the people.

## Ezekiel's Accusations on Idolatry And Adultery

Prophet Ezekiel was a contemporary of prophet Daniel and of King Zedekiah. He prophesied in the years before the destruction of Jerusalem.

In 586 BCE, he was exiled together with the Israelites to Babylonia. Earlier in the year 592 BCE he prophesied in the Holy Land where he announced serious accusations and horrifying predictions.

**Ezekiel's Accusations as Are Graphic And Powerful as Follows:**

> *"You were sure of your beauty and you used your name to commit adultery. You poured your favors on every passerby, whoever he was. You took some of your clothes and you made yourself tapestried high places and you committed adultery on them... You took your precious things out of my gold and out of my silver which I gave you and you made of them images of a male and you fornicated on them... You set My oil and My incense before them[ images and clothes]... You set before them [ images]... Then you took your sons and your daughters that I gave you and you sacrificed them for them [ images] to eat. You slaughtered my children and you gave them as offerings... In all your abominations and your adulterous acts you did not [even] remember the days of your youth while you were naked... woe to you, declares the Lord... You made yourself pride and you built yourself a high place in every street... and you spread your legs to every passerby and you increased your harlotries. You committed adultery with your neighbors, the children of Egypt... to make Me angry. I will [then] deliver you to the disposition of the Philistine women who are embarrassed by your evil acts. You also committed harlotry with the children of Ashur [the Assyrians] without you ever been satisfied... You increased your harlotries in the land of Canaan... and that too, did not satisfy you... [you committed] an act of a dominating harlot... by setting your mound in the corner of every street... you acted like the whore who did not ask for fees; the woman, who betrays her husband and takes in strangers instead..." (Ezekiel 16:15-32)*

Just as we saw in the book of Hosea, we see below another metaphor. The Lord calls the prophet Ezekiel again in order to hear about the lewd behavior of two women *Oholah* and *Ohalibah* who, in their youth, committed various acts of adultery with soldiers and noblemen from Egypt and Chaldea. They even sacrificed their own children in order to satisfy their foreign habits, which were vexing to the Lord. This is another symbolic episode depicted in the book of Ezekiel, similar to the story we recall in the book of Hosea, and which condemns entire communities in Judea and Israel. Ezekiel is instructed to bring the message of doom to those communities for their lack of faith in the Lord. Predictions are made on the destruction of Judah and Israel by foreign armies.

> *"And it came to pass that the Lord spoke to me, 'oh man! There were two women, daughters of the same mother. They committed adultery in Egypt. They whored while still young. There, their breasts were squeezed and their virgin nipples were massaged. And their names: Oholah, the older one, and Ohalibah, her sister. They belonged to Me. They gave birth to sons and daughters and their names were Samaria, for Oholah, and Jerusalem, for Ohalibah'". (Ezekiel 23: 1-4)*

Here is another accusation of Ezekiel as related through him by divine inspiration, pointing fingers at the Israelites in the North, and the Judeans in the south. Samaria is north of Judah. The Lord is so vexed that He paints a picture of the sinning people in graphic details and He sends the prophet Ezekiel to bring the message of doom to the Israelites.

> *"Oholah committed adultery while under My command. She lusted with her lovers, the Assyrians...dressed in blue, governors and deputies, handsome fellows, all of them horsemen...She became impure while she lusted with all their fetishes. She did not discard her whoring from Egypt because, in her youth, she slept with them. They massaged her virgin nipples and they poured their lust on her. Therefore I delivered her in the hands of her lovers, in the hands of the sons of the Assyrians...They captured her sons and her daughters and she was put to the sword...Her sister Ohalibah was aware of that and her lust was even greater than the lust of her sister. She also lusted after the Assyrians, governors and deputies... all of them young fellows mounted on horses... I saw how she turned to be impure...She went on with her whoring while she saw men sculptured on the wall, images of Chaldeans... sons of Babylon...As she saw them she lusted after them..." Ezekiel 23:5-15)*

With those powerful accusations, there is little else to say, except that, Ezekiel and other prophets used their power of the word in order to inspire their audience to follow a moral and ethical behavior.

They may have not meant that every man and woman in the land of Israel could be accused of harlotry. They spoke to the whole community of the Israelites as they aimed to describe the spiritual degradation of the people and they painted abominable scenes of lewd behavior the audience may have not wanted to hear about.

## Isaiah's Lament And Warning

Isaiah was a contemporary of Kings Uzziah, Ahaz and Hezekiah, kings of Judah. He began his ministry in the year 740 BCE, long before the demise of Jerusalem.

Isaiah was one of the greatest prophets, together with Ezekiel and Jeremiah. It is not coincidental that, at the time when people went astray, that there were always some luminaries such as those prophets who were reportedly sent by the Lord to shake up, stir up and awaken the fallen morality of the decadent people in the land.

While Isaiah accused the people in the crowded squares of Jerusalem, he also announced words of hope for better days to come.

> *"The vision of Isaiah, son of Amotz (Amoz), who prophesied over Judah and Jerusalem, during the days of Uzziah (Uzziah), Jotham (Yotam), Ahaz, Hezekiah (Hizkiahu), kings of Judah.*
>
> *Listen, Oh heavens and hear Oh earth For, the Lord Has spoken.*
> *'I have reared children and I have brought them up But they sinned against Me.*
> *An ox recognizes its owner... Israel does not recognize [Me].*
> *My people did not reflect.*
> *Oh, nation of sinners!*
> *People, heavy with inequity, Seed of evildoers,*
> *[You] corrupt children.*
> *They abandoned the Lord.*
> *They blasphemed the Holy One of Israel.*
> *They turned their back [on Me].*
> *Why are you looking for further punishment?*
> *Adding to your [existing] rebellion!*
> *Every head hurts.*
> *And every heart is sick. From foot to head, There is no safety.*
> *Your land is deserted!*

*Your towns burned by the fire Your land is being consumed,*
*Before you, by strangers....*

*The daughter of Zion remained*
*Like a booth in the vineyard; Like a lodge in a cucumber field,*
*Like a surrounded city.*
*Had not the Lord of Hosts*
*Left us any survivors,*
*We would have been*
*Almost like Sodom*
*[And we would have] looked like Gomorrah. (1 Isaiah:1-9)*

*How she became a prostitute!*
*The trustworthy city!*
*She used to follow the law to the fullest.*
*Justice [always] dwelt in her [midst].*
*And now [she has] murderers... (1 Isaiah 1:21)*

*Your leaders are rebellious;*
*And your friends are thieves; All, bribing lovers*
*And chasing after gifts.*
*They would not take a legal case of an orphan;*
*A grievance of a widow would not come to them."*
*1 Isaiah 1:23)*

## A Milder Isaiah on Adultery and Perversion

In some of his chapters, Isaiah describes some of the scenes Ezekiel was describing so clearly and bluntly. But we find that, Isaiah refers to some of the same scenes with a milder language and a bit less graphic.

*"On a high and elevated mountain, You set your couch.*
*There too, you have risen*
*In order to make sacrifices...*
*You made yourself a covenant with them [your lovers].*
*You loved sleeping with them...*
*You have increased your perfumes...*
*You never gave up...*
*But I, you never remembered...*
*You went downward to Sheol [the lowest point of self-respect]"*
*(Isaiah 57:7-11)*

We can make comparisons between Ezekiel and Isaiah. In this chapter Isaiah seems to describe some of the scenes Ezekiel described in the previous section. Whereas Ezekiel was instructed to paint adulterous scenes in minute details we see here a milder reaction to the lewd scene of the people Isaiah accuses of. Nevertheless, Isaiah was extremely aggressive in his accusations of the moral degradation of his people in his land.

> *"...You are indeed children of transgression;*
> *A seed of deception...*
> *Slaughterers of children in the rivers..."(Isaiah 57: 4-5)*

## The Minor Prophets Come With A Major Warning

As seen above, Hoseah, although considered a minor prophet, was as outspoken as the Major Prophets in connecting adultery to idolatry. Hosea can be compared in his language to Isaiah, Jeremiah and Ezekiel.

But the Minor Prophets where also helpful in their attempts to deliver the powerful divine message to the crowds.

## Amos

Prophet Amos was a contemporary of king Jeroboam II of the Northern Kingdom in the year 732 BCE. He also prophesied at the time of King Uzziahu (Azariah) of Judah in the year 767BCE.

Amos was a humble cowherd. He did not want to consider himself a true prophet although he acted as one, while announcing his divine predictions. His prophecies were so powerful that they frightened the priests of Jeroboam, the king of Israel. Amos predicted many calamities to befall several nations neighboring Israel and Judah. Israel and Judah were singled out because of their adulterous and immoral actions as they embraced foreign gods. Amos was even asked by Amaziah the priest to leave the kingdom of Israel and go to Judah. However, Amos replied:

> *"..., 'No, I am not a prophet and I am not a son of prophet.*
> *I am a cowherd ...And the Lord picked me while leading the*
> *herd and the Lord told me, ' Go and prophesy to My people,*
> *Israel. Now, hear the word of the Lord, you [Amaziah] who*
> *said to me, 'Do not prophesy about Israel and do not preach*

> *about the House of Isaac. Therefore, thus said the Lord,*
> *'Your wife will commit adultery in the city and your sons and*
> *daughters will fall by the sword...and you shall die on impure*
> *soil and Israel will indeed be exiled from its land.'" (Amos*
> *7:14-17*

## Micah

Micah, a minor prophet, predicted the destruction of Jerusalem and Samaria but also the restoration and purification from idolatry in the Holy Land after its destruction.

Prophet Micah was a contemporary of kings Jotham (Yotam), Ahaz and Hezekiah of Judah. He was also a contemporary of other prophets, namely, Isaiah, Amos and Hosea.

Micah prophesied between the years 737 BCE and 696 BCE.

Micah is quoted as protecting the poor and the deprived while denouncing the rich and accusing them with in injustice (Micah 2;10)

He also spoke against the abominations done in the land while describing the sinning Israelites, men and women in their lowest moral point.

> *"All her statues will be smashed and all her harlots'*
> *proceeds will be burned with fire. All her idols will become*
> *a wasteland...for they were gathered from the wages of*
> *prostitutes..."(Micah 1:7)*

Prophet Micah is best known by bible fans and bible scholars for his famous quote on human justice.

> *[the Lord] told you what is good. And what does the Lord*
> *requires from you [nothing] but doing justice and loving-*
> *kindness and walking humbly with your God (Micah 6:8)*

## Nahum-

Prophet Nahum was a contemporary of King Amon of Judah in 642 BCE.

Nahum, as other prophets before him, denounced the immoral acts and predicted the fitting punishment of the exiled people at Nineveh. This prediction was done outside of the Promised Land and within the exiled communities of the Israelites. He also predicted the destruction by the

Assyrian army of the city of Nineveh on the Tigris river.

*"Because of the numerous acts of her harlotries...the sorceress who attracts nations with her harlotries...I will lift up your garments over your face and I will show the nations your nakedness and to kingdoms I will show your shame. I will throw abominations on you. Those who will see you will withdraw from you..." (Nahum 3: 4-7)*

We have seen above the ugly reality as painted by the major and the minor prophets. Fortunately, with the severe warnings came messages of hope.

*In conclusion, all major and minor prophets who lived at the time of the reigning kings had a special mission in admonishing the evil leaders of Judah and notably those of the Northern Kingdom..*

While prophets existed all throughout the history of the Bible, the most powerful and outspoken prophets emerged when the Israelites were at their lowest level of morality. We have seen above how Moses addressed the sinning Israelites in the desert and how prophets Isaiah, Jeremiah, Hosea, Micah and Ezekiel courageously used powerful language in order to counter immorality and injustice.

The books of the prophets mentioned above have served as a check and balance for past generations and for future generations.

They will continue to represent a source of inspiration and education for spiritual leaders, men of faith and Bible lovers for hundreds and thousands of years to come.

# CHAPTER SEVEN

## THE HUMILIATION OF JUDEA

## BY ROMAN CONQUERORS

### The Conquest of Judea by Foreign Nations

Hundreds of years after the return of the Jews from exile in Babylonia to their promised Land where they experienced relative freedom and political independence, they found themselves in a new plot created by dominance of foreign powers.

In this case it was the Persian Empire which supplanted the Babylonian Empire. Following the defeat of the Babylonians the Greek dynasty, which began with Alexander the Great, dominated the Middle East until the arrival of the Romans and their conquest of the all neighboring countries surrounding the Holy Land.

### How Hellenization divided the Jewish Nation

The Greeks introduced their culture, otherwise called Hellenization by historians, to all the dominated states of its empire including the Holy Land.

In Judea, the Greek culture imposed on the Jews encountered a serious resistance as we see further.

Nevertheless, when forced on the local population Hellenization partially changed the culture of Judea by dividing the nation into hellenized Jews and religious Jews who were willing to fight the Greek conquerors in order to preserve the traditional Judaism as prescribed in the Bible.

### Roman Dominance as a Result of Jewish Disunity

The Roman Empire which began to dominate the Holy Land upon the arrival of Pompeii remained in control for about four hundred years (63 BCE- 313 CE)until the advent of the Ottoman Empire.

Since our project centers around dissent or unification within the Israelites, when Judea was under full domination by the Romans the Jewish priests were chosen by the ruling governors who were under the yoke of the

Roman Empire.

Rome also appointed the king of Judea, thus supplanting the High Priest who was also considered the all-powerful figure politically and religiously.

Because of the inner fighting within the Hasmonean High Priests in Judea, the Roman Emperors were bribed and convinced by the Edumean rulers of Judea to take control of the Holy Land. The Edumean dynasty began with Antipater.

## Rome And Herod

The most spoken about ruler of Edumean dynasty was Herod, son of Antipater. He turned out to be a cruel king who was more inclined to please the Roman regime than to give in to the Jewish population in matters of observing the laws of the Torah.

In one instance, Josephus reports that Herod had a golden eagle installed outside of the Temple of Jerusalem. The presence of the eagle represented his loyalty to the Roman legionaries. That, of course angered the multitude of the faithful in Jerusalem and guaranteed punishment for those who dared removing that golden eagle.

*Therefore, the priesthood during Roman times ceased to be what it used to be in biblical times.*

The following is an excerpt on How Josephus describes Herod as what we could call today a con man by bribing Roman Marc Anthony and convincing him that he was the right man for leadership over the territory of Judea

> *"And this was the principal instance of Antony's affection for Herod, that he not only procured him a kingdom which he did not expect, (for he did not come with an intention to ask the kingdom for himself, which he did not suppose the Romans would grant him, who used to bestow it on some of the royal family, but intended to desire it for his wife's brother, who was grandson by his father to Aristobulus, and to Hyrcanus by his mother,) but that he procured it for him so suddenly, that he obtained what he did not expect, and departed out of Italy in so few days as seven in all. This young man [the grandson] Herod afterward took care to have slain, as we shall show in its proper place. But when the senate was dissolved, Antony and Caesar went out of the senate house with Herod between them, and with the consuls and other magistrates before them, in order to offer sacrifices, and to lay up their decrees in the*

*capitol. Antony also feasted Herod the first day of his reign. And thus did this man receive the kingdom, having obtained it on the hundred and eighty-fourth Olympiad...." (Josephus, The Antiquities of the Jews, Book 14, chapter 14)*

Furthermore Josephus describes how power in Judea could be sold with money and goods and it can be decided by a foreign country, as follows

*"At this time Herod, now he had got Jerusalem under his power, carried off all the royal ornaments, and spoiled the wealthy men of what they had gotten; and when, by these means, he had heaped together a great quantity of silver and gold, he gave it all to Antony, and his friends that were about him. He also slew forty-five of the principal men of Antigonus's party, and set guards at the gates of the city, that nothing might be carried out together with their dead bodies. They also searched the dead, and whatsoever was found, either of silver or gold, or other treasure, it was carried to the king; nor was there any end of the miseries he brought upon them; and this distress was in part occasioned by the covetousness of the prince regent, who was still in want of more, and in part by the Sabbatical year, which was still going on, and forced the country to lie still uncultivated, since we are forbidden to sow our land in that year. Now when Antony had received Antigonus as his captive, he determined to keep him against his triumph; but when he heard that the nation grew seditious, and that, out of their hatred to Herod, they continued to bear good-will to Antigonus, he resolved to behead him at Antioch, for otherwise the Jews could no way be brought to be quiet. And Strabo of Cappadocia attests to what I have said, when he thus speaks: "Antony ordered Antigonus the Jew to be brought to Antioch, and there to be beheaded. And this Antony seems to me to have been the very first man who beheaded a king, as supposing he could no other way bend the minds of the Jews so as to receive Herod, whom he had made king in his stead; for by no torments could they be forced to call him king, so great a fondness they had for their former king; so he thought that this dishonorable death would diminish the value they had for Antigonus's memory, and at the same time would diminish the hatred they bare to Herod." Josephus, book 15, chapter 1)*

When Herod assumed power the status quo changed in Judea. The Roman conquerors and their proxy leaders (in this case, it was Herod) were more concerned on how to enrich themselves. Gold and silver represented what we know today as 'money talks'.

## Loss of Sanctity in Judea

The question remains: How could the holy kingdom of Judea have lost its sanctity to become subject to bribery, lust and murders.?

The answer may well be that, after the Holy Hasmonean dynasty ceased to exist, the descendants of the Maccabees lost their national pride and their sense of justice as it is prescribed in the biblical law and became enemies to each other.

Furthermore, because of their enmities and inner fighting, their rivalries became resolved by a foreign power, Rome, which found it convenient to deal with Herod the Edumean. The latter had no love for Judea and the Judeans as he was able to bribe Rome for his share of power.

When Rome controlled the Holy Land and its religious practices, it is no doubt that the Jews were seriously provoked. Their sacred laws and precious Temple were being desecrated, their dignity and freedom were at risk.

We could not blame the Jews for forming groups of resistance again the Roman occupants.

We could not blame even the Zealots for their actions against the legionaries.

What we are blaming is the fact that the various Jewish factions, extremists or Zealots did not act as one unit against the occupying forces. Instead, they rivaled each other.

We therefore condemn the fact that Jews hated Jews and caused unnecessary hatred that resulted in unnecessary murders as we explain in other chapters.

## Disunity Causes Tragedy

In reviewing the causes that led to the destruction of the second Temple of Jerusalem in the year 70 CE, much injustice has been done. The crimes committed by extremists against extremists and extremists against innocent people as witnessed by Josephus the historian are an abomination in itself. It may be considered as a transgression of biblical laws by all those who obey the biblical commandments.

*We also indicate that numerous crimes were caused by the occupying Roman army. The lack of regard for the Jewish customs by the Roman emperors and their assigned procurators of Judea may justify a war for independence and freedom of religion.*

*Whether one is a believer or secular, those crimes which preceded the destruction of the second Temple are in themselves serious transgressions according to national and international laws. Those crimes and other transgressions were committed by both sides: the Roman occupiers and the besieged Jews who were under Roman rule.*

The two Jewish rebellious leaders who battled each other and terrified the nation could have spared the second biggest historic tragedy in the life of the Jewish people had they tolerated the Roman rule as the sages did.

# CHAPTER EIGHT

## METAMORPHOSIS FROM BIBLICAL

## TIMES TO 70 CE

**(From biblical rules to Hasmonean to Herodian and Roman rules)**

### From Chosen Kingship to Brutal Power Grab

Looking back at the history of Judea, the kingdom of the Holy Land, which begun with King Saul (1038-1010 BCE), followed by King David (1010-970 BCE ) and King Solomon (970 BCE-931 BCE), split after the reign of the latter. That split will be analyzed in details in this project.

The early biblical kings listed above could not be crowned without the blessing of a prophet or a high priest of the land. This is why we shall stress the importance of the existing prophets and spiritual leaders during the reign of the kings of Israel and The biblical priests were descendants of Aaron.

The high priests were named Cohanim (plural of Cohen). One the last biblical priests from the seed of Aaron was Zadok the priest who served under king David. Also according to 1 Chronicles 6:315, the last high priest of Israel was Seriah, father of Jehozadak.

### Destruction of the First Temple

The Jerusalem Temple, originally constructed under king Solomon and destroyed by Nebuchadnezzar, in 586 BCE, was the Temple that was rebuilt by the exiled Jews from Babylonia. King Cyrus of Persia, who took over the Babylonian Empire, allowed the Jews to return to their homeland and rebuild their Temple some seventy years later although the Babylonian captivity ended in 538 BCE upon the victory of the Persians over the Babylonians.

### The Hasmoneans as The last Pure High Priests

When the kingdom split and the northern ten tribes were exiled there was no mention of priests from the seed of Aaron, the original Cohen, from the tribe of Levi.

Yet we learned that when the Greeks occupied the Holy land it was

Mattathias the Hasmonean High Priest, father of the Maccabees who organized a successful rebellion against the Greeks.

Mattathias was believed to be the descendant of the original biblical High Priest, Aaron, brother of biblical Moses.

In other words, after the death of Simon the Hasmonean, son of Mattathias and the last son of the Hasmonean dynasty, real high priesthood in the Holy land ceased to exist.

We noticed that Simon's son John (Yohanan) Hyrcanus I and John Hyrcanus II Simon's great grandson) were also the High Priests of the Holy Land. However, during their priesthood, the Holy Land began to lose its independence.

Simon's son, John Hyrcanus I (175 BCE- 104 BCE) ruled under the Greek occupation of the land, while John Hyrcanus II (103 BCE30 BCE) ruled Judea under the Roman Dominance.

When the descendants of Simon, the last Hasmonean ruled under the Hellenization of the land, real and pure high priesthood of the land ceased to exist as it was soiled by the interference of Herodian dynasty and the domination of Rome over all the countries of the Middle East, including Judea.

Details on How the Holy Land gradually lost its independence will be discussed in another chapter.

## The Seleucid Empire And Judea

Some two hundred years later, the Holy land was conquered by Alexander the Great in the year 332 BCE. Alexander used the Holy Land territory to subdue the Phoenician coast on his way to conquer Egypt and Babylonia. By the time of his death in in 323 BCE (at age thirty three) he had conquered a large territory stretching form the Middle East to India.

The successors of Alexander were unable to unite the Greek Empire. Upon his death, Ptolemy took control of Egypt. Two kingdoms were created: the Ptolemaic kingdom and the Seleucid Kingdom. Two other entities submerged after the death of Alexander: Macedon and Pergamon in Greece proper.

However Judea was involved with the Seleucid and the Ptolemaic Empires.

In 301BCE, the Ptolemaic kingdom in the south extended over the Holy land. Until then the land of Israel was relatively free until the *Selucids* in the north became in total control of the Holy land.

### The Jewish Struggle to Fight Hellenization

Hellenization began to take place as the Selucids built several cities and started to impose their customs and culture on the local population,

Antiochus III (223-187 BCE) won control of Judea and until then the Jews were permitted to follow their biblical traditions and customs.

However when the Seleucid Monarch *Antiochus IV* who succeeded Antiochus III, took control of the Holy land, he decreed a total Hellenization of the land of Israel and all the countries under the Seleucid rule.

That was the last straw that triggered the Maccabean revolt against the Selucids.

Following that revolt which lasted between 167 BCE to 160 BCE when Judah the Maccabee died.

### The Successors of Hasmonean Dynasty

Following the rise of the Hasmonean dynasty in Judea, Mathatias the Hasmonean was the High Priest (the Cohen) who sparked the Maccabean revolt (167-160 BCE) against the Seleucid Empire. His son was Judah the Maccabee who was the leader of the revolt. Judah's brothers were Simon, Jonathan, Eleazar and Yohanan.

The Maccabees under Mathatias, Judah and his brothers, defied the decrees of Antiochus IV to hellenize he Holy Land in the second century BCE.

The Hasmoneans under Mathatias were considered extremely faithful to the laws of Moses. Mathatias was also a practical leader, For example, he allowed fighting the Greek (Seleucid) occupants on the day of the Sabbath, in order to save the purity of the Temple.

Following the Maccabees victory over their occupants, the Temple of Jerusalem was purified and inaugurated. Hence the festival of *Hanukkah* (Hanukkah meaning inauguration).

Following his death *Jonathan his brother took over the battle for independence and later on he became the High Priest of the Holy Land (152-142 BCE)'*

*Simon, the other Maccabee brother* served as high priest between 142 BCE to 135 BCE. He enlarged the Holy land by conquering Medeba, Gerizim and Shechem.

## Political Deterioration Begins in the Holy Land

*From here on, we are going to 'witness' a serious deterioration and disintegration of the political system in the Holy land as the governing body, namely the High Priest who also was the ruler and in some cases the declared king as in the case of Aristobulos.*

Simon's son, with a hellenized name, *Aristobulos,* served as the High Priest between the years 104-103 BCE. He was the first in the dynasty to claim the title of king. His reign did not last long as he fell ill shortly after his brother Antigonus was killed by Aristobulos soldiers. Antigonus was commanded to appear before his brother Aristobulos the king without arms. At the command of Salome who reportedly hated Antigonus, Antigonus appeared with military gears and he was struck dead as reported above.

Next in line was *Alexander Jannaeus* (103 BCE to 76 BCE). His Hebrew name was *Alexander Yanai.* He was the brother of Aristobulos. He became the New Hasmonean king and High Priest.

Alexandra Salome first released him from jail and married him as per the Jewish law (Deuteronomy 25:5-10) of levirate marriage (*Ybbum*) according to which it is imperative for a man to marry his brother's wife after the death of that brother.

Alexander Jannaeus also enlarged the Holy land by attacking the Edumeans and invading Transjordan, He was considered cruel and he was responsible for the death of 6000 Pharisees who disagreed with his way of celebrating the festival of the Sukkot (Festival of the Tabernacles). That cruel act was enough to trigger a civil war between the Saducees and the Pharisees.

*Alexandra Salome*, his wife succeeded him and reigned between 76 BCE and 67BCE. She served as queen while her son Hyrcanus II served as a High Priest

*Aristobulos II* (67-BCE TO 63 BCE) was the younger son of Alexander Jannaeus and Alexandra Salome.

## Rivalry Between Brothers and Advent of Pompeii

When he was old enough to govern he proclaimed himself king of Judea and a battle between him and Hyrcanus II attracted the Roman Empire that succeeded the Greek Empire in the Middle East. Following a series of appearances by the envoys of the two brothers and that of the Sanhedrin, Pompeii, the Roman General opted for Hyrcanus II at the recommendation of Antipater the Edumean. Consequently, Aristobulos II's grievance before Rome was rejected by Pompeii who sent Aristobulos in captivity to Rome while allowing Hyrcanus II to continue to serve as the High Priest of the Land under Roman rule.

*Thus, Hyrcanus II* (63 BCE to 40 BCE), the older son of Alexander Jannaeus and Alexandra Salome' became the ruler of Judea in name only.

Originally, before Salome' death Hyrcanus was to be the High Priest while Aristobulos the head of the Judean army.

## Civil Wars And Thirst for Power

Consequently, following Salome's death the civil war between the major factions of the land continued until a foreign power intervened between the two.

The civil war and the thirst for power continued as followed within the Jewish factions:

*Antigonus* (40-37) was the son of Aristobulos II. He overthrew Hyrcanus II and he was responsible for mutilating him by having his ears cut off by the Parthians who were allied to Antigonus. That deliberate mutilation of cutting the ears of John Hyrcanus II meant that the latter could no longer serve as a High Priest because of his infirmity.

## While in power

After ruling Judea between 40-BCE to 37 BCE, during which, after he led several battles against Herod who obtained permission from Rome to be the new king of Judea.

Antigonus. While allied with the Parthians (in today's Iran) led several battles against Herod and his Roman allies. After a few victories and defeats against Herod's army, Antigonus, while defending Jerusalem ended up being defeated by the Roman Legions, thus sent by mark Antony and commanded by Roman general Sosius.

Antigonus surrendered to Sosius and was sent to Mark Antony in Rome where he was beheaded, thus ending the rule of the last Hasmonean over Judea and the advent of an Edumean king over the Holy land.

## The Ruling of Judea by the Herodian Dynasty

Now, we begin to witness a different kind of ruling the Holy land. king *Herod, son of Antipater the Edumean,* was also called king Herod the Great. He ruled over all Israel between 37 BCE to 4 BCE. He was a cruel and ruthless king who was responsible for eliminating all his suspected foes including his own two sons and several of his wives. He was also reported to have ruled to kill all the new born babies of Bethlehem. According to the new Testament, the Herod's decree to kill new born babies was aimed at killing baby Jesus.

He was named Herod the Great because, on the other side of his cruelty, he endeavored to rebuild the Temple of Solomon in order to please the crowds of the city who considered him most unpopular. He indeed brought the Temple to a luxurious and legendary level spoken about until today by many historians.,

*Herod Archelaus, was the* son of Herod the Great and older brother of Herod Antipas. He was appointed tetrarch of Judea, Samaria and Idumea (4BCE to 6 CE). That included the cities of Caesaria and Jaffa.

*As Herod the Great had many wives, Herod Antipas* was his son from one of Herod's wives named Malthace. He was appointed tetrarch over Galilee and Pera (4BCE to 39 CE)

*Herod Phillip II* was also the son of Herod the Great. His wife was Cleopatra of Jerusalem. He was appointed tetrarch of the Northeastern region of His father's kingdom and he ruled between the years 4BCE to 34 CE.

*Herod Agrippa I,* 37 CE -44 CE was the grandson of Herod the Great. He was also known as Herod II.

He was king over all the Holy Land from 41 CE to 44 CE.

*Herod Agrippa II* (48 CE to 70 CE). His official name was Marcus Julius Agrippa. He was the last ruler of the Herodian dynasty and tetrarch over the territories outside Judea such as Chalcis and the Northern territories. He was a pacifist who urged the rebelling factions against Rome multiple times to lay down their arms.

## Roman Rulers: From Pontius Pilates to Gessius Florus

In the meantime the main Roman rulers over the Holy land were Pontius Pilates (26 CE to 36 CE) Tiberius Alexander (46-48 CE)- Antonius Felix (52-CE- 59 CE) Porcius Festus (59 CE to 61), Gessius Florus (64-66 CE). As the 7th Roman procurator of Judea Florus was one of the most cruel rulers over the Holy land. He was reported to be partial towards the Greeks and openly antagonistic towards the Jews. He was considered most unselfish and trouble maker between Jewish factions in the Holy Land. Josephus reported that Florus entered the Jewish Temple and took seventeen talents of silver (a considerable value). This created a considerable tumult among the contributing Jews to the Temple. Josephus also reported that the Jews of Jerusalem began to beg for charity in order to replenish the stolen silver. Some Jews acted sarcastically while begging for Florus. When Florus found out he had thousands of Jews put to the sword. That also contributed to rebellion by the rebelling factions against Rome.

In summary, going back in history. the biblical priesthood from the seed of Aaron the High Priest, ceased to exist when the land of Israel became occupied by the Greeks and the Romans.

## The Dissension That Brought The End of Jewish Independence

The Hellenization of the Holy Land had a lot to do with the changing social structure which gave way to betrayals, killings and lust for power.

The biblical Israelites could not unite following the death of Solomon and the new Israelites from Judea who became known as Jews of the first century CE, under occupation, were torn between various cultural and religious currents.

One part of the Jewish population was hellenized and wanted peace with the occupying forces. Another part of the population was split between the Sadducees and the Pharisees (spoken about earlier).

The third religious group were the Essenes. Finally, the violent segment of the population were the rebels, who were themselves split into two main rival camps.

One important reason for the rebellion was that the rebels were composed of religious extremists who would not compromise for anything that contradicted the practice of Judaism.

The other part of the rebels was composed of converted Edumeans to Judaism and a multitude of Sicarii (cloak and dagger men) who stealthily who were successful to attack rival Jews as well as Roman soldiers in the land.

## The Murder of Ananus The High Priest And The Intensified Chaos

Ananus (also called Ananias) was the last upright priest who headed a rebellion against the Roman occupation. He was not considered a zealot. Sadly, he was killed in the year 68 CE by the zealots who sought to cease the ultimate power in the rebellion. As mentioned before, the zealots were not observing Jews who wanted the Temple purified of any foreign intervention.

On the contrary they had no scruples in assassinating the last genuine priest of the Temple in order to gain absolute power over the land. On this, Josephus lamented as the death of the last standing priest brought about the beginning of the end of the Holy Temple.

> *"I should not mistake if I said that the death of Ananus was the beginning of the destruction of the city, and that from this very day may be dated the overthrow of her wall, and the ruin of her affairs, whereon they saw their high priest, and the procurer of their preservation, slain in the midst of their city. He was on other accounts also a venerable, and a very just man; and besides the grandeur of that nobility, and dignity, and honor of which he was possessed, he had been a lover of a kind of parity, even with regard to the meanest of the people; he was a prodigious lover of liberty, and an admirer of a democracy in government; and did ever prefer the public welfare before his own advantage, and preferred peace above all things; for he was thoroughly sensible that the Romans were not to be conquered. He also foresaw that of necessity a war would follow,.." (Josephus, War of the Jews Book 4: chapter 5:2)*

That was the reason why the Israelites or Jews in more recent times could not unite and form one front to resist foreign cultures, Greek or Roman.

# CHAPTER NINE

## SINS AND CRIMES COMMITTED

## ON BOTH SIDES

Before we go over the sins committed by the Zealots as well as by the Romans we must state that the Zealots themselves were fighting each other. The camp of John of Gishala and Simon Bar Giora competed for the control of the city of Jerusalem and its glorious Temple. In the middle there was another group headed by Menahem who was considered the chief bandit who terrorized the peaceful population in order to gain power. All three groups acted separately while murdering those in Jerusalem who did not want to fight the Romans.

Menahem was known for being the head of the sicarii, the cloak and dagger bandits. In order to gain control of the Temple he ended up killing Ananias the priest who was a powerful figure in the community. Ananias and his son Eleazar headed a party of the faithful population. When procurator Florus acted cruelly with the population Ananias did not want the Romans to be represented any longer in the sacrificial rituals conducted in the Temple. That, of course, triggered another Roman violence.

In order to appease the Roman conquerors, the Temple priests used to make a sacrifice honoring the existing Roman Emperor. However, as indicated earlier, Florus the procurator was hated citywide because of his cruelty and disregard toward the people of Jerusalem.

Now, we have cited four different groups who acted separately and who did not want to be dominated by the Roman occupiers.

The less militant group against the Romans were the Sadducee aristocrats and the Pharisee sages who did not mind the Roman occupation.

The Sadducee group, although religiously and ideologically opposed to the Pharisees wanted to be left in peace. We mentioned earlier that a part of the Sadducee population adopted Hellenistic ways of life.

The Pharisee group, headed by Yohanan Ben Zakkai (to be discussed later), wanted to push education as a way of preserving Judaism and the biblical precepts for generations.

Consequently, we have five sections of the population who did not agree with each other while comprising three militant groups who committed baseless murders of the population.

Among the rebels and towards the peaceful population, countless murders took place which brought an unprecedented misery to the entire population of the city.

Paul L. Maier (author of Josephus, The Essential Works), paraphrasing Josephus, wrote the following on the plight of Jerusalem during the siege by the Romans

> *'Famine now raged in the city, and the rebels took all the food they could find in a house-to-house search, while the poor starved to death by the thousands. People gave all their wealth for a little measure of wheat and hid it to eat it hastily and in secret so it would not be taken from them. Wives would snatch the food from their husbands, children from their fathers, and mothers from the very mouths of their infants. Many of the rich were put to death by Simon [of Gishala[ and John [Bar Giora], while the sufferings of the people were so fearful that they can hardly be told, and no other city suffered such miseries. Not since the war began was there ever a generation more prolific in crime...*

If that was not enough, three years after the destruction of Jerusalem (70CE), there was another rebellion against the Roman led by Eleazar who was an associate of Menahem the sicarii leader.

This time, it was suicide which was a way of fighting the Roman conquerors. About one thousand rebels (including their wives and children) who fled to the fortress Masada, near the Dead Sea, were convinced by Eleazar to end their lives and not be slaughtered or sold as slaves by the Romans (73 CE).

## The Six sins

The sins committed by the Zealots of Jerusalem during the rebellion again Rome were sins that are considered crimes in modern times and should be prosecuted.

Most decent nations and people on earth respect the bill of human rights. The rules against those sins committed by Zealots against Zealots and Zealots against the innocent people of the Holy Land could be condemned by any civilized nation of the twenty first century.

By fighting each other in order to gain power, those Zealots violated the laws and the rules of Moses found throughout the Pentateuch.

*The first sin is the sin of suicide-* Although in the twenty first century we see suicide of a person as tragic and disturbing act, it is mentioned in the Bible as a major sin. Many Jews in their battle against the Romans chose suicide rather that fall victims of slavery.

The Bible quote is,' You should choose Life' (Hebrew transliteration: *Ubaharta Bahayeem).* This commandment is found in Deuteronomy 30, verse 19

*The second sin is the lack of self-love.* By that, we mean that the battling Zealots did not care about each other, nor did they care about themselves as long as they committed suicide or as long they knew they would be victims while fighting the Roman Army. Some historians attribute the suicide committed by the Zealots to national pride. Their determination to die as free people rather fall into slavery and hardship can be considered heroic. The Bible quote on this subject:

> *"You should watch out for your souls very much"(Deuteronomy 4, verse 15)- In other words, keep yourself very safe. The Hebrew transliteration is : Venishrmatem Meod Lenafshotechem.*

*The third and the next major sin was the killing of a fellow and innocent person*

The Zealots, by fighting each other did not observe the sixth commandment (Do not Kill). Eye witness Josephus reported multiple killings between factions.

*The fourth sin was ignoring the eighth commandment (do not steal), the Hebrew transliteration being,'Lo Tignov'* That commandment was also broken as they stole from each other. The leader of one faction, John of Gishala and his combatants, are reported to have committed multiple acts of thievery.

*The fifth sin was ignoring the ninth commandment (do not bear false witness on your fellow person*), the Hebrew transliteration is,'Lo Taaneh Bereakha Ed Shaker' was also ignored by the fighting partisans. The opposing rebels are reported to have denounced each other in order to attract combatants.

The sixth sin: You should not covet...(in Hebrew transliteration:Lo Takhmod)

The Zealots  transgressed by not honoring the tenth commandment. In order to achieve their power they allowed themselves to covet the possessions of their fellow men and women as they terrorized the well -to -do population in the Holy Land by forcing them to give up possessions and food. The ten commandments can be found in Deuteronomy 5, verses 6-18.

**Sins And calamities Predicted by Biblical Prophets**

The above mentioned sins bring us to the principle of universality, which is to : *love your fellow person as you love yourself.* They may or may not have anything to do with religion, Nevertheless, they are mentioned in the Pentateuch as the rules to be observed by the Israelites. That principle exists in every civilized society, including ancient Chinese and ancient Middle Eastern cultures.

Finally, the warnings against the above transgressions and other sins were clearly enumerated in chapters 27 and 28 in the *book of Deuteronomy and the book of Jeremiah as written in details in previous chapters of this book.*

Whether one is a believer or a non-believer in the Tannakh (otherwise called the Old Testament), the fact remains that hose warnings are spelled out in the book of Deuteronomy.

In the book of Lamentations, Prophet Jeremiah described and narrated the tragedy of the first Temple. Over six hundred years later, Josephus narrated the events that led to the demise of the second Temple.

Both tragedies have been verified and proven through archaeological research and through Babylonian archives, also called: Babylonian Chronicles.

According to *Inside Science* and concerning the siege of Jerusalem by the Babylonians in 586 BCE..

> *"the story of the siege[of Jerusalem] is supported by Babylonian scribes, who wrote...on cuneiform tablets hardened in ovens, according to Laurie Pierce, a lecturer in Mideast studies at the University of California, Berkeley.... Israeli and American archaeologists have found evidence just outside of Jerusalem's old city that apparently supports the Biblical description [of the destruction of Jerusalem]...In an area called Mount Zion, which is also known as Western Hill, they found the remains of a home of someone the Bible calls 'Big Man' of one of those probably sent to exile...In and around the ruins [of the house] the archaeologists found an ash layer mixed with half a million shards or pieces of pottery, arrowheads typical of the Babylonian arsenal and a piece of gold and silver jewelry—all typical at that time.*

*Pottery shards and ash are usually found in the trash but [archaeologist] Gibson pointed no one keeps arrowheads and Jewelry in a trash bin. Someone probably left in a hurry... Many of those who were forced to leave Jerusalem rose through the Babylonian bureaucracy, and some created a banking network in a flourishing economy [according to archaeologist Pierce, quoted from Inside Science]...*

## Both Sides Are to Blame

While writing about the Roman provocation of the Jewish people it is no doubt that the Jews were seriously provoked. Their sacred laws and precious Temple were being desecrated, their dignity and freedom were at risk.

We could not blame the Jews for forming groups of resistance again the Roman occupants. We could not blame even the Zealots for their actions again the legionaries.

What we are blaming is the fact that the various Jewish factions, extremists or Zealots did not act as one unit against the occupying forces. Instead, they rivaled each other.

We therefore condemn the fact that Jews hated Jews and caused unnecessary hatred that resulted in unnecessary murders as we explain in other chapters.

*In conclusion of crime and punishment about the destruction of the second Temple of Jerusalem in the year 70 CE, the crimes committed by extremists against extremists and extremists against innocent people as witnessed by Josephus the historian are an abomination in itself. It may be considered as a transgression of biblical laws by all those who obey the biblical commandments.*

*We also indicate that numerous crimes were caused by the occupying Roman army. The lack of regard for the Jewish customs by the Roman emperors and their assigned procurators of Judea may justify a war for independence and freedom of religion.*

*Whether one is a believer or secular, those crimes which preceded the destruction of the second Temple are in themselves serious transgressions according to national and international laws. Those crimes and other transgressions were committed by both sides: the Roman occupiers and the besieged Jews who were under Roman rule.*

# CHAPTER TEN

## THE ROMAN EMPIRE: CRUEL

## AND ECCENTRIC

Although many crimes were committed by Jews against Jews and Jews against Roman occupiers, one can imagine that those Jews who stuck to their faith were miserably provoked several times by the Roman occupiers as Josephus reports in his book on *The Jewish Antiquities*

It is no wonder that the cruelty of some procurators in the Holy Land triggered armed resistance. The rebelling factions, although religious to the point of extreme zealotry, reached their breaking point and desperately fought the Romans to the death although they were no match to an organized and disciplined army and the Roman legionaries.

As cruelty gives rise to cruelty, we are going to indicate some of the known atrocities which took place in Rome proper even before the famous war against Rome by the rebelling Jewish groups who fought to the death in order to save their Temple.

Before we analyze the condescending treatment of Jews by some Roman procurators, we need to understand that those procurators came from a very unstable political regime.

According to most historians and based on the timeline of the Roman emperors who governed Rome since its inception, only 25% of Roman emperors died of natural causes. This also suggests that 75% of Roman emperors were murdered or committed suicide.

We know how Julius Caesar, himself, who is considered the most illustrious leader of Rome was murdered by the Senators of Rome (namely Cassius and Brutus), even before Rome became an Empire.

In fact, Julius Caesar's victories over Gaul, Britannia and parts of the Middle East territories have contributed to replacing the Republic of Rome with the Empire of Rome.

As Julius Caesar delivered a vast empire he was known to be a forgiving person to his enemies. He considered mercy to his foes to be '*our new method of conquering...*'

After his death, political chaos erupted in Rome. The new chiefs of state, the emperors, became murderers or victims of murder.

As Roman emperors were murdered, either by their predecessors or by their adversaries as we see ahead in some of Josephus and other historians' assessments of government leading to Nero. Nero was the emperor when the Jewish rebellion was taking place(between the years 66CE and 70CE).

## Murder and Poisoning in the Roman Empire

*The following passage, written by Josephus gives the reader the notion on how complex, treacherous, fragile and uncertain was the life of some emperors such as Claudius and Nero.*

*Now Claudius Caesar died when he had reigned thirteen years, eight months, and twenty days; and a report went about that he was poisoned by his wife Agrippina. Her father was Germanicus, the brother of Caesar. Her husband was Domitius Aenobarbus, one of the most illustrious persons that was in the city of Rome; after whose death, and her long continuance in widowhood, Claudius took her to wife. She brought along with her a son, Domtitus, of the same name with his father. He had before this slain his wife Messalina, out of jealousy, by whom he had his children Britannicus and Octavia; their eldest sister was Antonia, whom he had by Pelina his first wife. He also married Octavia to Nero; for that was the name that Caesar gave him afterward, upon his adopting him for his son...But now Agrippina was afraid, lest, when Britannicus should come to man's estate, he should succeed his father in the government, and desired to seize upon the principality beforehand for her own son [Nero]; upon which the report went that she thence compassed the death of Claudius. Accordingly, she sent Burrhus, the general of the army, immediately, and with him the tribunes, and such also of the freedmen as were of the greatest authority, to bring Nero away into the camp, and to salute him emperor. And when Nero had thus obtained the government, he got Britannicus to be so poisoned, that the multitude should not perceive it; although he publicly put his own mother to death not long afterward, making her this requital, not only for being born of her, but for bringing it so about by her contrivances that he obtained the Roman empire. He also slew Octavia his own wife, and many other illustrious persons, under this pretense, that they plotted against him.(The Antiquities of the Jews, book 30, chapter 8)*

As we continue to follow up on Roman rulers we learned that besides Nero, Caligula was considered the most cruel of all emperors and Elagabalus the most unfit of all emperors.

## Unusual Roman Cruelty

In her Introduction in the book "Twelve Caesars", Mary Beard mentioned emperor Alexander Severus whose remains were discovered in Lebanon in 1837. Emperor Severus and his mother were killed by the Praetorian Guard for bribing the German troops to surrender after he invaded Germany.

His cousin was emperor Elagabalus who was killed by the Praetorian Guard while hiding with his mother. But that is not all. Mary Beard stated that his *'legendary excesses outstripped even those of Caligula and Nero, and whose party trick of smothering his dinner guests to death under piles of rose petals...'*

Galabalus is considered by historians to be among the worst emperors. He was ridiculed by historians for acting as a deity and by forcing members of the government to participate in religious rituals celebrating his deity.

While Caligula is on top of the list for the most cruel emperors, Galabalus is seen as the weirdest and the most awkward leader in Roman history. The Praetorian Guard, after killing him, replaced him with his cousin Severus Alexander. mentioned above.

Nero stabbed himself to death after the Senate condemned him in 68 CE.

Galba took over and he was himself stabbed to death in 69 CE by the Praetorian Guard. Allegedly, his head was taken to Otho.

Otho was a military commander who was defeated by another military commander whose name was Vitellius. The latter took over the empire in the same year (69 CE). He was also murdered by Vespasian soldiers.

We notice here that three emperors were assassinated by their own troops in the same year after the death of Nero.

Vespasian's reign represented a departure in the Roman Empire.

His government lasted 10 years and he died as a result of diarrhea.

Jason Novak, author of *'Et Tu Brute?'* wrote that he died of fever.

Vespasian was a great general and military tactician and, at times, he showed some compassion for the besieged Jews of Jerusalem. After he destroyed several cities inside the Holy land and slew the rebels within, he was chosen to become the next Roman emperor by the Roman garrison stationed in Egypt. His son Titus took over and Jerusalem and its Temple were destroyed under him while the majority of the city's inhabitants were killed or sold as slaves.

Jason Novak, mentioned above, is the author of an illustrated compendium of all emperors of Rome from the first emperor Augustus to the last one named Romulus Augustulus.

Mr. Novak painted Roman history via cartoons, which made it easy and fun for all readers of any age to understand the tragedy of the Roman emperors.

Since we are dealing with the tragedy of Jerusalem and its destruction by the Roman occupiers, let us see how the Roman emperors in Rome did some half a century before the destruction of Jerusalem and over a century after the destruction of Jerusalem and its Temple.

As we indicated earlier, we noticed that three Emperors ruled, and died in the same year, 69, CE, just one year before the destruction of the Jewish Temple: Galba, Otho and Vitellius.

Galba was murdered by the Praetorian guard. Otho stabbed himself to death in the heart as he was beaten by Vitellius who proclaimed himself emperor and was murdered by Vespasian soldiers.

As Anarchy reigned in Rome, Vespasian left the Holy Land in a hurry during those tumultuous times to become the next emperor after Vitellius.

Another tragedy occurred to two emperors over a century after the Romans conquered Jerusalem: In the year 193 CE, emperor Pertinax was assassinated by the Praetorian Guard.

Pertinax was a son of freed slaves who only reigned for a few months. After him, in the same year 193 CE,

Didius Julianus, who actually purchased his emperor title, was killed by a soldier from the Praetorian guard.

Titus, who subdued Jerusalem and all its inhabitants, was poisoned by Domitian in 81 CE. The latter was stabbed in the groin in 96 CE. Nerva died of fever in 98 CE.

Here is a rare exception of death by disease. Trajan died by stroke after a rebellion in Mesopotamia in 117 CE.

Hadrian died of Tuberculosis in 138 CE. Antonius Pius died of fever. Jason Novak stated that he died after he gorged on cheese in the year 161 CE. Lucius Verus died of a stroke.

Marcus Aurelius died in his sleep in 180 CE. Some sources claim that he died following a plague. He was considered a Stoic philosopher. He was the last emperor of the Pax Romana, which was an exception in the history of Rome where relative peace dwelt in the Roman empire.

Most of the Roman emperors were not so lucky as ending their life via natural death. He was one of the last five emperors of Rome who were considered good emperors.

After him, Commodus, his son ruled Rome until he was strangled to death by a champion wrestler In 192 CE.

The list of Roman emperors is not exhaustive because we are dealing with the rebellion in the Holy Land. The reason we have enumerated the twenty emperors who ruled Rome before and after the destruction of the Jewish Temple was to show how most of the Roman emperors around the rebellion in Jerusalem were cruel and inhuman.

*As we see here, corruption and murder was also a way of life among the emperors.*

In his introduction on *Evil Roman Emperors*, Phillip Barlag begins with this:

> *'Absolute power corrupts absolutely' and he continues describing the story of Rome which '...begins and ends with wicked rulers...These monstrous men reflect the darkest parts of our own psyche...What is striking about all these people, both individual people and the institutions we discuss, is they all found different ways to be awful. In a way, they were all innovative in finding new ways to manifest the darkest elements of the human soul...In the fifty-year span between 235 and 285 CE, at least two dozen people claimed to be emperors. They didn't not rule long but that doesn't mean they should be overlooked. Being evil or awful takes no time at all. It can also get you killed in a hurry. Some rulers from this period would possess far impressive resumes if they have not been assassinated young... '*

As we continue to follow up on Roman emperors before and after the tragedy of the Holy Land, we noticed that Augustus, the very first emperor or Rome, was victim of poisoning by wife Livia in the year 14 CE.

Tiberius was smothered to death by Caligula in the year 37 CE and Caligula was stabbed some thirty times by the Praetorian guard.

## The Importance of The Senate And the Praetorian Guard

As we cited so many murders in cold blood and poisoning of several emperors, we also noticed that the Praetorian guard and the Roman senate had as much or more power of decision than the Roman emperors themselves.

As Phillip Barlag puts it so beautifully in his introduction:

> *'The Senate and the Praetorian Guard were not individual people, but they ruled and projected power. They held away over life and death, with the power of their institutions behind them to enforce their will. All too frequently, members of these groups used that power for nefarious aims and in direct opposition to the interests of the Roman state itself'*

But, have we ignored the Roman soldiers and legionaries throughout the empire? Absolutely not.

*It looks like the Roman army was the only stable institution when it comes to discipline. Discipline also spelled ruthlessness, cruelty and total destruction of the enemy. However cruel, the army had a say on how a new emperor should be elected as in the case of Vespasian.*

For example, after the chaos of the year 69 CE, mentioned above, it was the garrison of the Roman army in Egypt which allowed Vespasian to be the next emperor of Rome after Vitellius.

## Evil Roman Procurators in The Holy Land

We now see how some of the Roman procurators became cruel and indifferent to the Jewish people and their religious cause.

Besides the sins committed by the Jewish rebels we must also take into account the sins of the occupying forces which triggered so many riots in the land. Those Roman sins are actual provocations which created a clash of culture between Jews and non-Jews.

Here is one typical event where Pontius Pilates insisted in introducing Caesar's effigies into the Jerusalem and its Temple.

The same type of provocation occurred in the preceding century at the time of the Maccabees who rejected foreign statues and images introduced by Antiochus Epiphanes into the Jewish Temple. As we know the Maccabees fought the Seleucid and won.

Here is how Josephus describes the determination of the Jews to fight the intentions of Pontius Pilates to the point they were willing to die rather than agree to have those effigies remain in Jerusalem. When Pilates realized how determined and serious were those Jews about their faith he rescinded his decision to introduce those images to Jerusalem.

> *"But they threw themselves upon the ground, and laid their necks bare, and said they would take their death very willingly, rather than the wisdom of their laws should be transgressed; upon which Pilate was deeply affected with their firm resolution to keep their laws inviolable, and presently commanded the images to be carried back from Jerusalem to Caesarea (The Antiquities of The Jews, Book 18, chapter 3)"*

Similarly, and earlier in time around 40 CE, Emperor Caligula wanted to have his image installed inside the Temple of Jerusalem.

While emperors Julius Caesar and Claudius, before him, respected freedom of religion and allowed the Jews to freely worship their God, Caligula wanted to depart from that point of view and wished to be acknowledged as god in the Temple of Jerusalem. The reaction to his desire to do so came, not only from thousands of protesting Jews who reacted in horror, but also from Petronius, governor of Syria (who was ordered by Caligula to march on Jerusalem). Reaction also came from Agrippa I (Herod Agrippa's grandson) who implored the emperor not to go ahead with his plan. As expected, Caligula was convinced and changed his mind.

Following so many provocations between two opposing camps the rebellion against Rome was ripe enough to take place in the years 66 CE to 70 CE

Already in 58 CE, Felix the procurator decided to have Jonathan the High Priest killed. Jonathan, who was considered a good High Priest in the Holy Land was not too happy that Felix was mingling in Jewish affairs. So the Roman solution was murdering Jonathan.

Josephus reports that Felix hired the *Sicarii,* the cloak and dagger men who were also Jewish militants who opposed Roman occupation.

> *Felix also bore an ill-will to Jonathan, the high priest, because he frequently gave him admonitions about governing the Jewish affairs better than he did, lest he should himself have complaints made of him by the multitude, since he it was who had desired Caesar to send him as procurator of Judea. So Felix contrived a method whereby he might get rid of him, now he was become so continually troublesome to him; for such continual admonitions are grievous to those who are disposed to act unjustly. Wherefore Felix persuaded one of Jonathan's most faithful friends, a citizen of Jerusalem, whose name was Doras, to bring the robbers upon Jonathan, in order*

*to kill him; and this he did by promising to give him a great deal of money for so doing. Doras complied with the proposal, and contrived matters so, that the robbers might murder him after the following manner: Certain of those robbers went up to the city, as if they were going to worship God, while they had daggers under their garments, and by thus mingling themselves among the multitude they slew Jonathan and as this murder was never avenged, the robbers went up with the greatest security at the festivals after this time; and having weapons concealed in like manner as before, and mingling themselves among the multitude, they slew certain of their own enemies, and were subservient to other men for money; and slew others, not only in remote parts of the city, but in the temple itself also; for they had the boldness to murder men there, without thinking of the impiety of which they were guilty. And this seems to me to have been the reason why God, out of his hatred of these men's wickedness, rejected our city; and as for the temple, he no longer esteemed it sufficiently pure for him to inhabit therein, but brought the Romans upon us, and threw a fire upon the city to purge it; and brought upon us, our wives, and children, slavery, as desirous to make us wiser by our calamities. (The Antiquities of the Jews, Book 20, chapter 8)*

## Under Fadus, Tiberius and Cumanus.

More provocations under some procurators who had no love for the occupied Jews. A lot of unnecessary killings and beheading occurred. A lot of calamities and tragedies took place within the Jewish population even before the siege of Jerusalem and the Roman attack of the city.

As Josephus wrote about Fadus, Tiberius and especially Florus who was considered one of the major instigators of the war between the Jews and the Roman occupiers.

*Now it came to pass, while Fadus was procurator of Judea, that a certain magician, whose name was Theudas persuaded a great part of the people to take their effects with them, and follow him to the river Jordan; for he told them he was a prophet, and that he would, by his own command, divide the river, and afford them an easy passage over it; and many were deluded by his words. However, Fadus did not permit them to make any advantage of his wild attempt, but sent a troop of horsemen out against them; who, falling upon them unexpectedly, slew many of them, and took many*

> *of them alive. They also took Theudas alive, and cut off his head, and carried it to Jerusalem. This was what befell the Jews in the time of Cuspius Fadus's government...Then came Tiberius Alexander as successor to Fadus...When that feast which is called the passover was at hand, at which time our custom is to use unleavened bread, and a great multitude was gathered together from all parts to that feast, Cumanus was afraid lest some attempt of innovation should then be made by them; so he ordered that one regiment of the army should take their arms, and stand in the temple cloisters, to repress any attempts of innovation, if perchance any such should begin; and this was no more than what the former procurators of Judea did at such festivals. But on the fourth day of the feast, a certain soldier let down his breeches, and exposed his privy members to the multitude, which put those that saw him into a furious rage, and made them cry out that this impious action was not done to approach them, but God himself;...(The Antiquities of the Jews : book 20, chapter 5, item 1)*

The result of that incident was catastrophic: the Procurators sent his soldiers who frightened the multitude who fled back to the inner city, trampling on each other through narrow passages, and, as Josephus reported, some twenty thousand Jews perished in the process.

In another instance there was one major provocation which was triggered by one of the Roman soldiers who tore sacred laws of Moses as we read from eyewitness Josephus:

> *...one of the soldiers seized the laws of Moses that lay in one of those villages, and brought them out before the eyes of all present, and tore them to pieces; and this was done with reproachful language, and much scurrility; which things when the Jews heard of, they ran together, and that in great numbers, and came down to Caesarea, where Cumanus then was, and besought him that he would avenge, not themselves, but God himself, whose laws had been affronted; for that they could not bear to live any longer, if the laws of their forefathers must be affronted after this manner...Antiquities of the Jews, Book 20, chapter 5, item 4)*

That incident was settled in favor of the Jews when the procurator had that soldier who desecrated the laws of Moses beheaded. Thus, total sedition was prevented.

Furthermore, we witness under Florus, the worst provocations took place. This procurator was considered the most inhuman and most cruel of all procurators that reigned in Judea. No wonder that Josephus considered Florus to be the reason for the major war between Jews and Romans. This is what we learned from Josephus.

## Florus. The Most Cruel Procurator

This is what we learned from eye witness Jesphus about the cruelty of Jesphus, which pushed the Jews to rally against him.

> *Now Gessius Florus, who was sent as successor to Albinus by Nero, filled Judea with abundance of miseries. He was by birth of the city of Clazomene, and brought along with him his wife Cleopatra, (by whose friendship with Poppea, Nero's wife, he obtained this government,) who was no way different from him in wickedness. This Florus was so wicked, and so violent in the use of his authority, that the Jews took Albinus to have been [comparatively] their benefactor; so excessive were the mischiefs that he brought upon them. For Albinus concealed his wickedness, and was careful that it might not be discovered to all men; but Gessius Florus, as though he had been sent on purpose to show his crimes to everybody, made a pompous ostentation of them to our nation, as never omitting any sort of violence, nor any unjust sort of punishment; for he was not to be moved by pity, and never was satisfied with any degree of gain that came in his way; nor had he any more regard to great than to small acquisitions, but became a partner with the robbers themselves. For a great many fell then into that practice without fear, as having him for their security, and depending on him, that he would save them harmless in their particular robberies; so that there were no bounds set to the nation's miseries; but the unhappy Jews, when they were not able to bear the devastations which the robbers made among them, were all under a necessity of leaving their own habitations, and of flying away, as hoping to dwell more easily anywhere else in the world among foreigners [than in their own country]. And what need I say any more upon this head? since it was this Florus who necessitated us to take up arms against the Romans, while we thought it better to be destroyed at once, than by little and little. Now this war*

*began in the second year of the government of Florus, and the twelfth year of the reign of Nero. But then what actions we were forced to do, or what miseries we were enabled to suffer, may be accurately known by such as will peruse those books which I have written about the Jewish war.(Antiquities of the Jews, Book 20, chapter 11, item 1)*

Josephus extends his accusation of Florus who was the major cause of the Jewish rebellion in his other book : *The War of The Jews.*

As if it was not enough, more calamities were brought upon the Jews who did not expect Florus to be so cruel and so provocative. After he ordered money taken out of the temple and as some Jerusalem citizens made a mockery of his behavior by going around town and begging for money in a sarcastic way, Florus felt provoked and commended his army to punish a great number of Jews of Jerusalem.

Florus ordered to murder indiscriminately adults, children, clergy and even infants to satisfy vengeance and hate. et alone adults and people of the clergy.

The following are three segments from the War of the Jews describing in vivid details how the Jews were first provoked in Casarea and later on in Jerusalem where a carnage of innocent people took place under the command of Florus

*Now on the next day, which was the seventh day of the week, when the Jews were crowding apace to their synagogue, a certain man of Caesarea, of a seditious temper, got an earthen vessel, and set it with the bottom upward, at the entrance of that synagogue, and sacrificed birds. This thing provoked the Jews to an incurable degree, because their laws were affronted, and the place was polluted. Whereupon the sober and moderate part of the Jews thought it proper to have recourse to their governors again, while the seditious part, and such as were in the fervor of their youth, were vehemently inflamed to fight. The seditions also among the Gentiles of Caesarea stood ready for the same purpose; for they had, by agreement, sent the man to sacrifice beforehand [as ready to support him;] so that it soon came to blows...*

*Moreover, as to the citizens of Jerusalem, although they took this matter very ill, yet did they restrain their passion; but Florus acted herein as if he had been hired, and blew up the war into a flame, and sent some to take*

*seventeen talents out of the sacred treasure, and pretended that Caesar wanted them. At this the people were in confusion immediately, and ran together to the temple, with prodigious clamors, and called upon Caesar by name, and besought him to free them from the tyranny of Florus...and while everyone was sorry for what he had done, and denied it out of fear of what would follow: that he ought, however, to provide for the peace of the nation, and to take such counsels as might preserve the city for the Romans, and rather for the sake of a great number of innocent people to forgive a few that were guilty, than for the sake of a few of the wicked to put so large and good a body of men into disorder..*

*...Florus was more provoked at this, and called out aloud to the soldiers to plunder that which was called the Upper Market-place, and to slay such as they met with. So the soldiers, taking this exhortation of their commander in a sense agreeable to their desire of gain, did not only plunder the place they were sent to, but forcing themselves into every house, they slew its inhabitants; so the citizens fled along the narrow lanes, and the soldiers slew those that they caught, and no method of plunder was omitted; they also caught many of the quiet people, and brought them before Florus, whom he first chastised with stripes, and then crucified. Accordingly, the whole number of those that were destroyed that day, with their wives and children, (for they did not spare even the infants themselves,) was about three thousand and six hundred...(The War of The Jews, Book 2, chapter 14, items 5 and 6)*

Concluding this chapter on Roman cruelty we can see how the Jews of Jerusalem and other towns were deliberately provoked and humiliated under Florus who took the pleasure to have thousands put to the sword under his command.

It is no wonder that Jesephus estimated that the actions of Florus had to bring about the rebellion against the Roman occupiers.

Brutality began with the emperors and other leaders of Rome. Barbarity extended to assigned procurators in the Holy Land.

Roman cruelty resulted in Jewish cruelty of the zealots against the occupiers and against other zealot factions. While the pacifist Jews wanted to settle their claims by complaining to the existing authorities, the extremists Jews took to the streets to achieve justice on their own

In one sentence, mayhem reigned simultaneously in Rome and the Holy Land. Its inhabitants paid with their lives due to Roman disregard for human life. The Jewish rebels, who fell victims to Roman cruelty, were also guilty of crimes and injustice against their own brothers and sisters.

# CHAPTER ELEVEN

## CIVIL STRIFE AMID ROMAN DOMINATION

As mentioned before, the political trouble in the Holy Land began with the last Hasmonean rule over Judea (Judaea):

Simon the High Priest was the last Maccabe brother, son of the High Priest Mathatias, who was killed by Ptolemy, his brother -in-law.

### The Treachery of Ptolemy: Murder of two Sons of Simon

Ptolemy was the Seleucid governor of Jericho. At that time, thanks to Simon, the Holy Land was semi-independent as it was recognized by Demetrius II, the Seleucid king who freed Judaea from paying taxes.

The territory of Judea including the Hasmonean dynasty was even recognized by the Roman Senate in 139 BCE.

Ptolemy, who married Simon daughter, had in mind to supplant the Hasmoneans and take control of Jerusalem and Judea,

He invited Simon, the venerable High Priest of Israel to a lavish banquet in Jericho. His invitation was nothing but a treachery. And while Simon and his two sons were enjoying themselves to a point where they became drunk, Ptolemy gave signal to his hiding armed men to kill Simon and his two sons.

Fortunately, the remaining son of Simon, John Hyrcanus, was alerted about Ptolemy's intention to kill him while he was at the time in the city of Gezer.

While extremely saddened for hearing about the killing of his father Simon and his two brothers, John Hyrcanus mustered his armed forces and instructed them to be ready to repulse and battle the forces of Ptolemy.

When Ptolemy's men arrived at the city of Gezer they were eliminated by the forces of Hyrcanus as Ptolemy fled the scene. Therefore john Hyrcanus was saved for the time being.

As indicated before, after the death of the last Hasmonean, son of Mathatias, murder and treachery began to be omnipresent within multiple contenders for the rule of Judea'..

As Hyrcanus sought to get back at Ptolemy for killing his father Simon and his two brothers, he besieged Ptolemy with his powerful army and Ptolemy threatened to kill the mother of Hyrcanus (who presumably was present at the banquet). John Hyrcanus found himself in a tough spot so he refrained from attacking Ptolemy.

In the meantime Ptolemy attempted to invade Jerusalem but he was repulsed by the populace who already declared John Hyrcanus as the High Priest and the commander in chief of the Holy Land. Ptolemy fled the scene after killing Hyrcanus' mother.

The treachery of Ptolemy is mentioned in Dante's 'The Divine Comedy' as Dante underlined treachery in killing beloved guests as a horrible act which deserved hell.

## The Success of Hyrcanus I

Hyrcanus became militarily successful as he enlarged the borders of the country and he even helped queen Cleopatra of Egypt whose son Latyrus rebelled against her. Hyrcanus offered her his two generals, Hilkiah and Hananiah to help her in eventual battles.

Despite his being in command of a powerful army, Hyrcanus reportedly was easy to be convinced by Sadducee advisers who switched him from the Pharisee camp to the Saducee one.

Therefore he became hostile towards the Pharisees as he was often ill advised by the Sadducees.

Beside his quick temper and his gullibility. Hyrcanus was a great High Priest and under him the land did not experience any further invasions from neighboring forces.

## Aristobulos II replaces Hyrcanus I

Hyrcanus I had three sons: Aristobulos II. Antigonus and Alexander Aristobulos II succeeded his father Hyrcanus I and conquered Tyre and Sidon in the north and converted its population to Judaism by circumcision just as his father Hyrcanus converted the people of Edom.

It is rare in history that Jewish rulers force conversion on occupied populations and this could be one of the reasons that the purity of Judaism began to weaken as we shall examine further in the case of the Antipater and Herod the Edumite rulers who changed the status quo by ending up controlling the Jewish rulers.

As related earlier treachery and deceit became a norm when it came to seize power or to have some ruler killed.

In this case, Aristobulos' wife, Queen Alexandra (Salome), who was heading the Court, did not like Antigonus (son of Hyrcanus I and brother of Aristobulos II) had Antigonus killed by Aristobulos' men, supposedly by order of the king.

Since Aristobulos II wanted to find out if Antigonus was loyal to him he ordered his guards to have Antigonus come to him unarmed and without military gear. Unfortunately, he was told by deceit, via the queen and her associates in the Court, that the king wanted to see him in his military cloths.

The above information on the death of Antigonus is based on a combination of sources, namely the Talmud and Josephus, Antigonus was executed in 104 BCE after he proved to be a valiant soldier and the conqueror of Samaria.

Aristobulos, who loved Antigonus could not bear the death of his beloved brother and became gradually sick and perished in the process.

## Alexander Jannaeus Takes Over The Kingdom

The remaining son of Hyrcanus I, Alexander Jannaeus (103 BCE to 76 BCE) took over the reign as he *proclaimed himself king of Israel,* against the Hebrew tradition which dictates that a king of Israel must be anointed by a prophet (as in the case of Kings David and Solomon and other kings of Judah).

However, just like his father Hyrcanus I, Alexander conducted several campaigns and aggrandized the frontiers of Israel by conquering more territory. Hamat and Gedera were subdued and especially Gaza in the south was burned and destroyed with its temple Apollinus and its priests.

## Alexander Jannaeus And Cleopatra

Alexander made peace with queen Cleopatra of Egypt and he helped her with her enemies, especially Latyrus her son who was challenged by the army of Egypt which was commanded by two famous Jewish generals: Hananiah and Hilkiah.

Despite his bravery and his assumed holiness, as he purified the city of Gaza from foreign worship, Alexander was a cruel despot. He did not act as a High Priest should act in the Holy Land. His ferocious battles against his own people, the Pharisees, caused insurmountable pain, murder of tens of thousands of innocent Pharisees and confusion within the Holy Land. Before his death he confessed to his wife Alexandra all his sins in having killed so many Pharisees and he even suggested to have peace with the Pharisees.

In the Hebrew tradition an observant Jew must repent before his death and repay to the best of his ability any money owed.

## Queen Salome Alexandra

Salome Alexandra took over the kingdom of Judea (76BCE-67BCE) after the death of Alexander Janneus. Her Hebrew name was Shlomtsion the Queen.

She married Alexander Janneus after the death of her first husband Aristobulos I. According to the levirate rule in the Jewish Court the surviving brother must marry the wife of his deceased brother, In this case it was Aristobulos who died and therefore Alexandra became the wife pf Alexander Janneus shortly after the death of her first husband.

She was the sister of the head of the Sanhedrin, Simeon (Simon) Ben Shetah, who is spoken about in Pirkey Avot (Saying of the Fathers) and the Talmud. As head of the persecuted Pharisees, he was compelled to flee the Holy Land and only return when Alexandra was free to deal with him following Alexander Janneus 's death. She tried to protect the Pharisees from Alexander Janneus' cruelty toward them. However she reportedly had a limited political role during the persecution of the Pharisees.

She was therefore do deal freely with the Pharisees after the death of her husband Alexander Janneus. Alexander spent most of his adult life in wars and after he conducted so many campaigns and have over 50,000 innocents Pharisees killed he died of malaria in the year 76 BCE. The day of his death was declared a holiday in the land of Israel.

## The Return and Dominance of the Pharisees

When the persecuted Pharisees returned to the Holy Land they were able to re- establish the Sanhedrin and Simon Ben Shetah as their head of the Court.

In fact, under her reign, the Pharisees became the ruling class of the Holy Land.

Queen Alexandra took charge and had the Sadducee move out of Jerusalem as they feared reprisal from the Pharisees.

Queen Salome (Hebrew Shlomtsion), had two sons with Alexander Jannaeus: Hyrcanus II and Aristobulos II(notice the hellenized names).

Salome named Hyrcanus II as the High Priest, being the elder son. He was to become king of Judea after his mother's death.

## Death of Salome And Sibling Rivalry

Following Salome's death (67 BCE), the two brothers began fighting each other for the kingdom of Judea.

Aristobulos II, who was a disciplined, yet ruthless leader, won the battle of Jericho against his brother Hyrcanus II who was taken prisoner.

Following a ransom agreement between Aristobulos and Hyrcanus, the latter released the throne to his brother Aristobulos.

## Aristobulos Retreats to The Antonia Fortress

Following that defeat, Antipater, the Edumite convert to Judaism, who was Hyrcanus II's adviser, offered his troops to fight Aristobulos II. Since Hyrcanus II was considered a weak leader, Antipater took over the command of the army and pushed Aristobulos II's army who retired to the Fortress of Antonius or Antonia Fortress, overlooking the Temple area.

*That fortress had a long history of resistance. Whoever controlled the fortress could control the Temple Mount.*

## The Importance of The Antonia Fortress

Before we relate what else happened between the two brothers Aristobulos II and Hyrcanus II we need to underline the importance of the Fortress named after Mark Antony and rebuilt by Herod, but originally built by the Hasmoneans.

During the rebellion of the Jews against the Roman occupation in the years 66CE to 70 CE, that fortress served as a serious bastion against the Roman legionaries who at first could not take it. Only after the fortress was occupied by the Romans after a terrible carnage of the rebelling Jews that the destruction of Jerusalem and its temple was imminent.

When Aristobulos was defeated by the troops of Antipater, he withdrew to the Antonia Fortress where he found a relative safety. However, his defeat coincided with the advent of Pompeii who, with the help of Antipater, began to subject Judea to the Roman rule. Aristobulos was sent to Rome where he died there. John Hyrcanus II remained the High Priest of the land but with limited power as Judea lost its traditional independence.

## The Pig that triggered the War

As indicated, Aristobulos II retreated to the Antonia Fortress as it was initially built by HyrcanusI the Hasmonean for the convenience of the High Priests in preparing for the Temple service and wearing the proper sacred garments to enter the Temple as prescribed in the Bible.

As the war was raging between the two brothers Hyrcanus II and Aristobulos II, the daily sacrifice continued in the Temple. However the besieged Jews of Jerusalem needed animals for the daily sacrifice. Antipater, who was an Edumite convert but not an observant jew convinced Hyrcanus to send a pig for daily sacrifice instead of a sheep. We note that the daily sacrifice of pure animals was agreed on between the two opposing armies until that pig was introduced to the Temple. That was a sacrilege that could not be tolerated.

To that, Josephus the historian lamented and predicted the Jewish civil war just as Prophet Jeremiah predicted the destruction of the First Temple and lamented about it in the book of Lamentations.

We recall that, earlier in history, the Temple was desecrated by Antiochus Epiphanies, one thing that triggered the battle of the Hasmoneans and the Maccabees to battle the Greek garrisons and after they beat them, purified the Temple and celebrated the inauguration which is called today Hanukkah.

That animosity between the two brothers, one that observed the daily sacrifice and the other who deliberately introduced a sacrilege to the Temple became an invitation to Rome, under General Pompeii to be involved in the affairs of Judea.

## The Opportune moment for Roman Intervention

Amid the battling parties, the religious governing group in Israel maned the Sanhedrin remained neutral and did not get involved in political matters, The two warring camps and the neutral Sanhedrin sent each one a delegation to the Roman general Pompeii to rule between them. Earlier, since 70CE, Pompeii had led the Roman army against Spain, Greece and the Parthians (today's Turkey and Iran) and he stopped in Syria in 64 BCE.

Pompeii, being an astute and ruthless general, knew that it was better not to invade the Holy Land because the fighting Jews such as the Maccabees had a reputation of being fierce against the Greek invaders However, he was waiting for the opportunity to conquer Judea, which was a strategic territory between the north (Syria) and south (Egypt).

The pleading of the three Jewish delegations that came to him offered that opportunity.

Then, in 63 CE, Pompeii responded to Hyrcanus. He invaded Jerusalem, beat Aristobulos and exiled him to Rome after massacring some 12,000 Jews who defended the Temple.

He destroyed the walls defending Jerusalem, re-established Hyrcanus as the High Priest and allowed him to remain the king *in name only* and most of all he imposed high taxes on the Jewish state.

By now, it became evident that the governing of Judea is controlled by Rome. A few years later, in 57 BCE, Pompeii named the governor of Syria, Gabinius, to govern the affairs of Judea.

Following those events, Pompeii went back to Rome, expecting to become the next emperor. He ruled until 48 BCE. However, his rival was Julius Caesar who was considered a great general after he conquered Gaul, Britannia and Germania (France, Great Britain and Germany of today).

While the Senate backed Pompeii and forbade the crossing of the Rubicon River, which Julius Caesar crossed in order to invade Rome, Pompeii and the Roman senators fled Rome. Caesar pursued Pompeii all the way to Egypt only to find himself surrounded by the troops of Pompeii in the city of Alexandria.

In the meantime Hyrcanus in Judea, was convinced by Antipater to switch sides from Pompeii to Julius Caesar. Under those circumstances, Hyrcanus sent 3000 Jewish soldiers who helped Julius Caesar break the siege of Alexandria. In return, Julius Caesar canceled the harsh taxation on Judea and allowed the walls of Jerusalem to be rebuilt and fortified. Hyrcanus remained the High Priest of Judea under Caesar but not a king any longer. However the power of governing Judea was given by Caesar to non-other than Antipater, who was not a real native of the Holy Land and who did not care about Jewish life. His son Herod the Great would prove to be the most cruel ruler of Judea, us the ruling of Judea by the Hasmonean dynasty ended and was given to non-Jewish rulers named procurators who did not care about the Jewish population, its rituals and other customs.

# CHAPTER TWELVE

## JOSEPHUS: A MAJOR WITNESS

## TO DESTRUCTION

### The Eloquence of Josephus

This chapter deals with the social and the political structure of Judea as stated by Josephus Flavius. He was originally called in his Hebrew name Yoseph Ben Mathatiahu (The son of Mathatias). He was, not only a great historian but also a great spiritual and military leader. The importance of his work is that, besides writing in details the history of the Hebrews, he also interacted with the intellectuals and the military leaders of his time.

Many historians have been quoting the books of Josephus and his descriptive details on the tragedy he witnessed.

Josephus is seen by historians as the best source of evidence to the events leading to the end of the Jewish state in the year 70 CE.

As a military general who initially battled the conquering Romans and defending the city of Jotapata (Yodfat), he surrendered to the Roman General Vespasian as he came to the conclusion that his army was no match against the Roman legions.

## "The People Mourning Over the Ruins of Jerusalem" *by Gustave Doré*

Doré Bible Illustrations • Free to Copy
www.creationism.org/images/

Lam 1:8 Jerusalem hath grievously sinned; therefore she is removed: all that honoured her despise her, because they have seen her nakedness: yea, she sigheth, and turneth backward.

What is also most valuable in his superb style of describing details, he was a living witness to hundreds of events within the Hebrew community during the Roman occupation of the Holy Land. Josephus was born in Jerusalem in the year 37 CE and died in the year 100CE.

During his childhood and especially during his manhood he witnessed a spiritual and physical devastation of the Holy Land. Having been a precocious scholar he analyzed the enmity between various factions in the Jewish society. *The Sadducees and the Pharisees* were the main factions in the land. In between, there were members of the *Essene sect* who had a mystic philosophy.

## How Josephus Describes The rival Factions

The Essenes were separate from the Sadducees and the Pharisees. Although they were spread around the Holy Land, a great number of them settled in the desert part of Jordan, especially in the Qumran area. In 1948, the Qumran Scrolls were discovered, revealing their acetic way of life. While choosing a simple life of poverty they followed the rules of the Bible to the letter. However their spiritual leaders including their priests observed celibacy. The other group of Essenes preferred marriage as the only way to prolong their lineage. The stress caused by the occupation of the Holy Land by the Roman Empire resulted in the creation of minority extremist groups which ended up controlling the rest of the population. Among them were the *Zealots and the Sicarri,* the evil spirited individuals who brought the end to the social, religious and political entity of the land.

Within the above three factions the Jewish population at the time of Josephus was divided into five different groups. The peaceful part of the population was headed by the priests and the well to do people who were opposed to confronting the Roman army. It is also reported that the majority of the population did not want war with the occupying forces. However, a good number of that peaceful population was controlled by the violent opposing cells. The rebels were headed by J*ohn of Gishala* (Yohanan from Gush Halav)The *Sicarii* were headed by and Eleazar. Sicarii is a Roman word deriving from the word *sica* meaning knife. Those people settled scores by murdering their opponents via a stealth way and disappearing in the crowd. Their opponents were merely peaceful.

**Menahem was one of the Sicaarii and Zealot leaders who objected to the occupation of the Masada fortress near the Dead Sea when it was occupied by the Roman legionaries.**

**With his band of robbers and Sicarii he managed to overthrow the Roman soldiers, slaughter them all and take control of the fortress.**

**Furthermore he managed to conquer the Antonia Fortress in**
**Jerusalem by overpowering the soldiers of Agrippa II**

## Agrippa II

Agrippa II was the grandson of Herod the Great and the last ruler in the Herodian dynasty as well as the last king of Judea under the Roman control. According to various sources in history including a branch of the Talmud called *Sotah*, he was well liked by a sizable portion of the general the Jewish population.

He interacted well with the priests and the Levites of the Temple in their daily sacrificial duties.

However, the facts lead us to the conclusion that he was partially responsible for the destruction of the Jewish Temple.

Just before the great rebellion Agrippa II made an emotional speech before the zealots who were ready to attack the Roman garrison. He emphasized the futility in fighting the disciplined Roman soldiers. He also told them after he consulted the Jewish leaders, the Temple priests and the Sanhedrin and that there was no way the Zealots would be victorious because God will not be with them this time.

Agrippa II was deeply involved in the Jewish rebellion against Rome by attempting to crush the rebels and save the rest of the population from annihilation.

King Agrippa II was in sort an adviser to the invading Roman military leaders. He was in constant contact with Vespasian and his son Titus, both ruthless generals who wanted to eliminate all Jewish rebels.

Although Vespasian was someone lenient towards the local population and was reluctant to annihilate a total population of a city, Titus, his son and his advisers were in the opinion that it was strategically better to kill all the inhabitants of a rebel city even as the majority of the population wanted peace with the Romans. A great example can be found in the city of Taricheae, today's the city of Gamala in Israel. It is heartbreaking to read how an entire population of the city of some forty thousand people was crushed by the Roman legions.

Josephus reported that over six thousand young men of the city were chosen to be sent to the slave hard labor while the remainder of the population including women and children were to be sold as slaves. It was even more heartbreaking to learn that twelve hundreds of those who were considered 'useless' were put to the sword.

King Agrippa II was instrumental in encouraging Vespasian and Titus, the two leading military authorities in the Holy Land, to go and attack rebel cities such as Taricheae and Jotapata was another rebellious city that was destroyed.

Jotapata (Yodfat) and other small cities and villages were burned to the ground and their inhabitants slaughtered or sold as slaves. Agrippa II himself took a fair amount of slaves among the Jewish population.

## Was King Agrippa a Friend of the Jews?

The short answer is no. He was certainly a client of the Roman Empire. A Jew himself, he always wanted peace between Jews and Romans. However, his actions in advising the Roman militarily to attack rebel cities gives an impression of selfishness and power grabbing on his part. The fact that he implored the rebels not to resist the Roman occupation could be interpreted as his reason to remain a friend of the occupying regime while keeping his kingdom intact. In some instances, according to Josephus he lent hand to the attacking forces under Vespasian and his subordinates against the Jewish partisans.

## The Passionate Speech of Agrippa to The Rebels

Agrippa tried his best to discourage the rebels from getting ready to fight the Romans.

He told them that they have no chance of overcoming the powerful army of Rome which extends from Persia to the Euphrates to most of Asia and Europe and includes even India, Gaul, Spain and the British islands.

He warned them not to seek vengeance against a powerful empire with a mighty navy as opposed to the Zealots who have none.

He also emphasized that they are breaking their own religious rules as Providence is not on their side.

He also predicted that if they tried to challenge the Roman legionaries they will bring a national disaster in have their city, Jerusalem and the rest of the country and the Temple burned to the ground.

Agrippa made a very long address- For simplicity we chose his most convincing words as follows:

> *...You are the only people who think it a disgrace to be servants to those to whom all the world hath submitted. What sort of an army do you rely on? What are the arms you depend on? Where is your fleet, that may seize upon the Roman seas?...how can you then most of all hope for God's assistance, when, by being forced to transgress his law, you*

*will make him turn his face from you? and if you do observe the custom of the sabbath days, and will not be revealed on to do anything thereon, you will easily be taken, as were your forefathers by Pompey...Have pity, therefore, if not on your children and wives, yet upon this your metropolis, and its sacred walls; spare the temple, and preserve the holy house, with its holy furniture, for yourselves; for if the Romans get you under their power, they will no longer abstain from them, when their former abstinence shall have been so ungratefully requited...*

*(Wars of the Jews, Book2. Chapter 16, Part 4)*

## Rejection of Agrippa's speech

After his speech, Agrippa and his sister wept. Nevertheless, neither king Herod (before him) nor him could pacify the rebels who were determined to fight to the death to stop the Roman regime in its occupation of the Holy Land.

Unfortunately he was ambushed by Eleazar who appointed himself as the captain of the Temple. Eleazar and his militants, together with a group of Sicarii burned the palaces of Agrippa II and that of his sister Bernice in the vicinity of the Temple.

Despite his wise advice and his emotional address to the rebels and his warning of an imminent calamity, the rebels, headed by Eleazar and his helpers rejected his advice. Angered by the mistreatment they received from the Florus the cruel procurator, they decided to stop making sacrifices for the Romans as it was the custom to appease the occupiers. While refusing to pay the due taxes to the governing procurator, they also decided not even to accept any sacrificial animal destined for the Roman foreigners. King Agrippa exhorted them to continue to pay the taxes and make the customary sacrifices, He even implored them to be patient until the replacement of the unfit Florus

*...Moreover, he [Agrippa] attempted to persuade the multitude to obey Florus, until Caesar should send one to succeed him; but they were hereby more provoked, and cast reproaches upon the king, and got him excluded out of the city; nay, some of the seditious had the impudence to throw stones at him. So when the king saw that the violence of those that were for innovations was not to be restrained, and being very*

*angry at the contumelies he had received, he sent their rulers, together with their men of power, to Florus, to Caesarea, that he might appoint whom he thought fit to collect the tribute in the country, while he retired into his own kingdom.*

*And at this time it was that some of those that principally excited the people to go to war made an assault upon a certain fortress called Masada. They took it by treachery, and slew the Romans that were there, and put others of their own party to keep it. At the same time Eleazar, the son of Ananias the high priest, a very bold youth, who was at that time governor of the temple, persuaded those that officiated in the Divine service to receive no gift or sacrifice for any foreigner. And this was the true beginning of our war with the Romans; for they rejected the sacrifice of Caesar on this account; and when many of the high priests and principal men besought them not to omit the sacrifice, which it was customary for them to offer for their princes, they would not be prevailed upon... Hereupon the men of power got together, and conferred with the high priests, as did also the principal of the Pharisees; and thinking all was at stake, and that their calamities were becoming incurable, took counsel what was to be done... and invited them to make war upon them, and brought up novel rules of a strange Divine worship, and determined to run the hazard of having their city condemned for impiety, while they would not allow any foreigner, but Jews only, either to sacrifice or to worship therein.,. (War of the Jews, Book2, chapter 16, item 5)*

There is no accurate account on the death of king Agrippa II. Because of conflicting reports it safe to say that he died some twenty years after the rebellion. The year of his death varies between historians who claim he died between 92 CE and 95 CE.

## The Peace Loving Versus the Belligerent

Josephus gave us some details on those extremist groups who were ready to give up their lives in the rebellion. What is more they were not united. They began opposing each other, seeking domination.

It is without a doubt that the Roman cruelty towards the rebels did not mitigate their determination in confronting the well-disciplined Roman soldiers.

The Roman procurators and governors at the time were mostly interested in the financial tribute they were collecting from the Jewish population. The majority of Hebrews of the land, otherwise called the Jews by Josephus, wanted their religious and personal freedom.

Among the Sadducee and the Pharisee groups there were those who wanted peace with the Romans while hoping for a tranquil way of life even under foreign control. However, the extremist groups among them, called Zealots, did not want anything to do with the Roman occupation, knowing well they were no match against the mighty Roman army.

The hostile groups were headed by two evil leaders: the first extremist group was headed by Simon. His Hebrew name was *Shimon (Simon) Bar (the son of)Giora*. The second vicious group was headed by John. His Hebrew name was *Yohanan from (the city of ) Gush Halab (named Gishala* by Josephus). John was described by Josephus as the head of a ruthless and remorseless gang of rubbers (which could be compared to the historic Mafia).

Shimon (Simon) was a cunning leader with no scruples who convinced the Edumites to join him in fight the Romans.

Edum or Edom is the country west of the Jordan River. It neighbors the Holy Land and it is located in today's Jordan. Simon terrorized his own people, including spiritual leaders such as members of the High Priesthood, in order to achieve his goal of establishing power in the Holy Land.

## Religious Leaders Appointed by The Romans

Adding to the social fracture, religious leaders were appointed by the Roman regime. Consequently, it created a chaos among the majority of the Jewish population who wanted to follow the biblical laws of Moses.

Thus, the liberty to practice religion was only partial. We notice from the books of Josephus that the Roman emperors such as Pompeii, Vespasian and Titus, did not initially mind that the Jews were 'free' to practice their religion.

The Romans, just like the Greeks before them, were eager to impose their culture on the Hebrew population by exposing Roman statues and other forms of political and cult domination.

The other challenge the Hebrews of the land faced was that the Roman procurators and the Roman soldiers often showed enmity to the populace. We are reminded here that the Roman legions in general (all throughout the vast Roman Empire) had an immense influence on their civilian leaders.

Vespasian who was a good military strategist and who subdued most of Judea left abruptly Judea in order to fill the position of Emperor. Following Nero's suicide in 69 CE, Vespasian became the fourth man to govern Rome in a single year where three emperors ruled Rome: Galba, Otho and Vitellius.

As indicated, Vespasian was the preferred choice to rule Rome by the Roman army stationed in Egypt in the year 69 CE.

He was replaced by Titus who finished the job in destroying Jerusalem and its Temple in the year 70 CE

Furthermore, the Roman control on the Jewish way of life was the main contributor to the rebellion

## Josephus as an Indispensable Source of Information

The writings of Josephus were grouped in one big and voluminous book containing over nine hundred pages. The small characters of the book in pages divided in two columns for each page could easily fit a two thousand page history book if it were typed at the normal 13 or 14 size type.

Being so profuse in his descriptions, Josephus did not neglect any details of the events he himself witnessed.

After he summarized the Old Testament, he proceeded in describing the horrors which took place among the Hebrews of the land, leading to the devastating of Jerusalem, its temple and other cities in the Holy Land.

The horrors did not only occur among the Jews but also within the Romans soldiers when they were fighting the Jewish militants under the evil leaders Simon and John, mentioned above.

The populace at large did not have any appetite for war and its people were reluctant to face the terrible force of the Roman legions. The king of Judea at the time was Agrippa. Based on Josephus, he did not seem to exert a political clout on the warring parties. However, king Agrippa is quoted by Josephus to have made long speeches of appeasement to Jewish communities nationwide in order to prevent a confrontation with the Romans.

Josephus, in his abundant writing and precise wording describing the minute details of the sedition against the Romans educates the reader on the interactions between factions and between them and the Romans and more.

When Josephus describes the events around him, he writes in length about the people and their emotions. He talks about the geography and the precise location of the event. His description of the various parts of the Jerusalem temple and all its walls and their precise location within the temple compounds seem to perfectly concur with today's archaeologists and historians according to Dr Ackerman. Dr Adam Ackerman is a bestselling author and a specialist on Jerusalem history since its creation and erection by King David.

Commentaries on the writing of Josephus (written by commentators at the end of his writings) state that Josephus, in his voluminous book about the history of the Jews, was written for the Romans and the Greeks. In fact it was written in Greek. Yet, we find lengthy passages about every single aspect of Judaism and its different facets. Josephus amplified his description of the Zealots, the Sadducee sect, the pharisees, the robbers, the violent elements of the time, the burden of occupation, the famine, the civil war, the sedition and the rebellion.

Josephus never neglected to describe any aspect of the social life in the Holy Land during the first century of the first millennium in the Holy Land. Yet, regretfully, and maybe purposely, there was not enough description and details on the birth of Christianity. Could Josephus, a genuine High Priest(not assigned by the Roman occupiers) and a devoted Jew, could he have preferred to ignore the burgeoning of Christianity around him? It was precisely, during his rebellion against the Roman legions that Christianity began to flourish according the New Testament.

Yet, we find one reference to James, the brother of Jesus, and another reference to John the Baptist. After careful research we find critics on both sides of the commentaries about the burgeoning Christianity.

We shall not go into details about the pros and the cons of the matter except that we find in the New Testament several quotes from the Torah, the Talmud, The Sayings of the Fathers (Pirkey Avot) which were studied and championed by the wise men of the Holy Land during the rebellion leading to the destruction of the second Temple in the year 70 CE.

The New Testament includes multiple references to prophet Isaiah and other prophets of the original Hebrew Bible, which brings closer both faiths, Judaism and Christianity. With this, we conclude that the morality found in the New Testament drew a significant inspiration from the Tannakh, otherwise called the Old Testament. a positive effect on its readers and believers.

# CHAPTER THIRTEEN

## HELLENIZATION AND

## THE HERODIAN DYNASTY

**How Josephus described The Gradual Transformation of Judea**

The following outlines will touch on events which took place before the demise of Jerusalem and the Jewish rebellion against the occupying Roman forces in Judea. Some of those events were witnessed by Josephus himself.

While Josephus narrated the events witnessed in his lifetime, he also cited historical events which described the bravery of Jewish fighters who previously sacrificed their lives some two hundred years before his time in order to maintain and safeguard their religion and belief in the biblical God.

The events that Josephus depicted during the rebellion were documented thanks to the fact that he was permitted by his occupiers to have access to any documentation which was rescued from the destructive fires which consumed the Temple and its compounds in the year 70 CE.

Therefore the following statements will be brief and informative. They count historical events describing Judea as a free nation fighting for its freedom only to end up losing that freedom to occupying forces.

The transformation of Judea from a free country to an enslaved one took place gradually when outside forces began to dominate and supplant the priestly power of Judea.

That pure priestly power which governed Judea politically and religiously ceased to exist upon the advent of the Herodian dynasty in Judea.

We chose for simplicity and clarity to enumerate facts and events which took place from the time the Jews regained political power under Judah the Maccabee until they lost their military power and their and political freedom under the Roman occupation.

**Josephus was a descendant of the Hasmonean dynasty.** That was the dynasty of Judah the Maccabee (Judas Maccabeus), son of the great Matthias the High Priest who died in 165BCE. Judah, before his death, managed, together with his brothers and followers, to fight and subdue the Greek garrisons who occupied the Holy Land in the year 167 BCE. His victory prompted the purifying and inauguration of the Temple. Inauguration in Hebrew means *Hanukkah*. Hence the festival of eight days of Hanukkah has been celebrated for hundreds of years by Jewish observers and non-observers for hundreds of years since the Maccabean revolt and victory in 160 BCE.

Before the Roman dominance of the Middle East, Syria was controlled by the Greeks and it is important to note that Antiochus Epiphanes IV was one of its leaders who sought to impose his pagan way of life upon the Jewish population of the Holy Land.

Antiochus IV is described by various historians as one who wanted to hellenize the Seleucid Empire. In 167 BCE, he captured Jerusalem and, among other oppressive rules on the Jewish population, he wanted to offer the sacrifice of a pig on the Jewish altar to his god Zeus. He was also called Epimanes because that word translates (from the Greek language) as the word *mad*. He was considered mad because he was obsessed with Hellenism and that was the reason that he wanted to impose his beliefs on the Jewish population.

When Antiochus IV imposed his cult on the Jewish priests inside the Jewish Temple, that abomination went too far and it triggered a serious revolt in the land against him and his mighty army.

Although part of the Jewish population was drawn to Hellenism, the priestly sect of the Hasmoneans headed by Mathatias, called for a unified rebellion against the Greek garrisons.

The revolt, which lasted from 167 BCE to 160 BCE, began in the rural city of Modiin, near Jerusalem, and was headed by Judah Maccabeus, the son of Mathatias. It ended in beating the Greek garrisons and in the celebration of the inauguration of the Jewish Temple.

In various battles against the Greek occupiers, Judah's brothers (Johanan, Jonathan and Eleazar), valiantly battled and died in defeating the enemy.

Josephus was notorious in citing predictions of the biblical prophets and connecting them to the events of the day. For example the victory of the Maccabees over the Greeks was predicted by prophet Daniel (according to Josephus).

After establishing a victory in the Holy land, Judah Maccabeus became the high priest of the land by replacing his father Mathatias the Hasmonean. During Judah's leadership the descendants of Antiochus made peace with the Jews and began to respect their laws. Although, The Jews gained independence in 160 BCE, the Greek Empire remained more or less united until the victory of Rome over the Greeks in the year 30BCE.

To summarize, the Greek conquest of the Middle East began with Alexander the Great in 323 BCE and ended when Egypt was conquered by Rome.

Following the fall of Antiochus Epiphanes IV, Judah Maccabeus made an alliance with the emerging Roman Empire, even before they invaded Egypt. Thus, Judah and the reign of the Hasmonean dynasty in the Holy Land witnessed the transition from the Greek dominance to the Roman occupation.

Egypt was first conquered by Alexander the Great who fought and won over the Persian Empire (between 332 BCE and 331 BCE). Alexander was tolerant towards religious practices of the occupied territories, including Judea. That tolerance changed after his death as we have seen above in the case of Antiochus IV and the rebellion against him by the Hasmoneans and the Maccabees.

Following Alexander's death, the Greek Empire was run by the Ptolemaic Dynasty that ruled over the Near East for 300 years.

Concerning the Maccabees, Simon was the last Maccabee. His son was John Hyrcanus I(175 BCE-104 BCE) from the Hasmonean Dynasty who became the new High Priest and king of Judea(134104 BCE). He was a God -fearing man and he switched from being a Pharisee to being a Sadducee.

It was also reported that John Hyrcanus I made several expeditions to Syria and conquered several cities. He repelled the invasion of Judea by the Syrian general King Antiochus VII.

In 135 BCE, the brother-in-law of Hyrcanus I, Ptolemy, the governor of Jericho, assassinated his father Simon the Hasmonean in 175 BCE.

Josephus and other historians of ancient Israel report that the first time in history a whole non- Jewish nation was converted to Judaism. John Hyrcanus was the first Jewish leader who forcibly converted the nation of Edom (also called Idumea) to become Jews by circumcision.

Whether those who converted to Judaism were real practicing Jews, that was another matter. We shall relate below the advent of the Herodian dynasty which began with the ruling of Antipater, father of Herod the Idumean.

Josephus also spoke about the ancient capitals of the Holy land. Before Jerusalem, Sephoris was the temporary capital of the Holy Land. Its inhabitants were reported to be loyal to the Roman occupiers.

Josephus was himself a high priest. As related earlier, the high priest in the Holy Land maintained also the political power over the land.

He was not only the high priest of the land, but also a strategic military leader, He secured cities in the Galilee, including Sephoris, Tiberias. He was opposed by other Galilean leaders. However, he ended up uniting the Jews of Galilee.

Now Aristobulos I succeeded Hyrcanus I upon his death (104 BCE) and ruled Judea for one year (104-103 BCE). As the new high priest he took the liberty to proclaim himself king of Israel.

While the Sadducees and the Essenes of Israel did object to his self-proclaimed kingship, the Pharisees were angered by his self-elevated rule. They were furious because he was not of the Davidic line, not being a descendant of King David, the favorite king of Ancient Israel.

After his sudden death it was Alexander Janneus 103 BCE to 76 BCE. Following Alexander Janneus, it was Alexandra the mother of the future high priest Hyrcanus II who ruled Judea between 76 BCE to 67 BCE.

In the year 66 BCE, it was the year that Antipater the Idumean convinced Aristobulos II to fight his own bother Hyrcanus II, but Aristobulos was stopped by the emerging Roman general Pompeii who restored Hyrcanus II to the priesthood while sending Aristobulos II, his brother, to Rome, where he died thereafter. It was without a doubt that Antipater, Herod's father, had a lot to do with the departure of Aristobulos and the re-installment of Hyrcanus II.

Antipater had direct access to Rome as he recognized its dominance over the Middle East. At first, he was loyal to Pompeii who was involved in installing Hyrcanus II and exiling his brother Aristobulos II to Rome. When war erupted between Pompeii and Julius Caesar in Egypt between 49 BCE and 48 BCE, it was Antipater who came to the rescue of Julius Caesar with neighboring troops under his Commandment. Consequently, Antipater was awarded Roman citizenship by Julius Caesar, Caesar also appointed Antipater as the first procurator of Judea, since Judea ceased to be ruled by Jewish rulers and high priests.

Here we see how Rome got involved in being the mediator between two brothers (Hyrcanus II and Aristobulos II).

In the year 40 BCE, it was Antigonus, Aristobulos' son and the nephew of Hyrcanus II, who managed to have Hyrcanus II castrated so he could no longer remain the high priest of the Holy Land and he [Antigonus] ruled Judea between the years 40 BCE to 37 BCE.

Antigonus was the last Hasmonean king of Judea under the rule of the neighboring Parthians who were part of the Roman Empire..

With the interference of Herod the Idumean, son of Antipater, Antigonus was executed by order of Herod, who wanted to do away with the Hasmonean Dynasty and remain loyal to Rome.

In reviewing the political status of independent Judea under the Hasmonean dynasty we record that independent Judea lasted between the Maccabean revolt (167-160 BCE) and ended upon the arrival of Pompeii to Judea in 63 BCE.

We are noticing here that after the death of Simon the Maccabee, his descendants took Greek names such as Hyrcanus, Aristobulos and Janneus. We see here how Greek culture (Hellenism) penetrated the Holy Land and became the reason for Jewish resistance to foreign domination.

# CHAPTER FOURTEEN
## HOW DID HEROD ELIMINATE THE
## HASMONEAN DYNASTY

### Herod The Edumean

Herod was an Edumite or Edumean. The Edumites were not Jews but many of them converted to Judaism (through circumcision) under the former High Priest Hyrcanus II. We also learned from Josephus and other historians who quote Josephus that Aristobulos I, who was also a warrior, forcibly converted the Itureans to Judaism. The Itureans dwelt north of Judea in today's Lebanon.

Herod, son of Antipater, was born in 73 BCE. He reigned over Judea under Roman occupation of the Holy Land. He had a dominating power over the political and the social plight of Judea. He reigned in the years 37-4 BCE.

Herod was a controversial figure. He was a blood -thirsty person on one hand and a great builder on the other hand. Based on accounts by Josephus, Herod was a powerful but also an inconsistent leader. For example, he worked hard to save the Holy Land from famine by importing corn from Egypt. On the other hand, he was cruel to his own family and hundreds of innocent Jews. The New Testament reports that he was responsible for killings thousands of newborn children under two in order to attempt to kill the newborn Jesus.

He is notably known for building the New Temple of Jerusalem on the ruins of the first Temple destroyed by the Babylonians in the year 586 BCE.

Since he had no religious sensitiveness for the Jewish population who enjoyed the Temple of Jerusalem, Herod also erected other buildings sacred to the Romans and the Greeks. He made a donation for the Apollo temple in Rhodes. For the Romans he built Caesarea and Sebaste and other venues to please Romans and Greeks in Judea.

As a tyrant and power- thirsty monarch, Herod murdered his own wife Mariamme and her two sons Alexander and Aristobulos.

Herod's oldest son, Antipater II (he had with another wife), was also executed. As a power hungry monarch, his suspicion of his own family members caused him to order the killing of anyone he suspected.

Herod's descendants were Herod Antipas, Herod II, Herod Archelaus, Antipater II, Philip, Aristobulos IV, Salome, Herod IV and more including Phazael. (all those were descendants of Herod).

Besides building Caesarea and Sebaste he reinforced other cities of the Holy land. Caesarea is an important city in Israel to this day. As he oversaw the rebuilding of the Jewish Temple, he added so much reinforcement and luxury to it that it became legendary among Hebrews and non- Hebrews in Judea and abroad.

## Herod Influenced by Power Thirsty Father Antipater

Herod was immensely influenced by his father Antipater. As indicated before, Antipater played a role in convincing Aristobulos I to wage war against his own brother. His scheme worked well for him as he was a friend and a sympathizer of the Roman Empire.

Upon rivalry between the two Hasmonean brothers, Pompeii of Rome became an arbiter between them. We see here one of many conflicts which were resolved between Judeans by foreign powers. Naturally, the foreign powers took advantage as was the case when the first temple was destroyed by the Babylonians (586 BCE). In this case, it was Antipater, the Edumean, who incited Aristobulos to fight his brother.

## Antipater And Judea's Loss of Sovereignty

*As a consequence, Judea lost its sovereignty in the year 63 BCE as follows*: Pompeii invaded Jerusalem in the year 63BCE but did not plunder the Temple. Pompeii's intervention was prompted by the fight between the Hasmonean heirs, Hyrcanus II and Aristobulos II who asked Pompeii to arbitrate between them. That intervention ended the independence of Judea as a sovereign state. Pompeii's conquest of Jerusalem did not interfere with the religious structure of Judea except that Pompeii favored Hyrcanus II(during his fight against Aristobulos II) and restored him as the high priest of Judea. Aristobulos was sent to Rome and died there. He was buried in Judea by order of Antonius.

Now Herod, the son of Antipater, was pronounced king of Judea by Pompeii. As such, he ruled Judea with an iron fist. He made sure that no one he suspected could continue to live.

Herod 's cruelty in spilling blood and imposing heavy taxes upon the population caused him to be summoned by the Sanhedrin to appear for his crimes.

When Herod stood trial before the Sanhedrin, his trial was canceled by Sextus of Syria who liked Herod. That trial was also delayed by Hyrcanus himself

We can witness here the weakness of the high priest Hyrcanus whose power was reduced by the Roman presence. Rome controlled Syria and the surrounding states neighboring Judea.

When Herod seized power in Judea with the help of the Romans, Judea was already divided between the Sadducees and the Pharisees. Before Herod, and even before the rebellion against Rome, the Jews under Hyrcanus I, who was appointed by Rome as the favored high priest in Judea, were permitted to practice their own religion. As mentioned earlier, Hyrcanus was favored over Aristobulos. Caius, on behalf of Rome, allowed the Jews to fortify the walls of Jerusalem. The tribute they paid to the Romans and the high priest was waived on the seventh year of the *Shemitah* (it was the year of rest for the land, as per the Bible, when it was forbidden to plow and cultivate the soil).

The Roman decrees exempted the Jews from performing military service. The Jews were also exempt from working or fighting on the Sabbath day.

## How Judea Changed For The Worse

When Herod ruled Judea, he exerted considerable influence over the high priests of Judea.

Josephus wrote abundantly about Herod who dominated Judea for 33 years. Herod, vassal of the Roman Empire, ruled Judea, Samaria, the Galilee, Perea and Idumea.

When he died in the year 4BCE, his kingdom was divided among three of his sons: Herod Archelaus ruled Judea, Samaria and Idumea for ten years.. However Roman emperor Augustus appointed Quirinus to replace Archelaus who was accused by the local population of mismanagement and consequently banished to Gaul (Vienna).

Consequently, the province of Judea became under direct Roman rule. Another son of Herod, Herod Antipas was appointed tetrarch upon the Galilee territory and Perea until he was exiled to Spain by command of emperor Caligula. He died in the year 39 CE. The third surviving son of Herod, Phillip (son of Cleopatra by marriage to Herod) ruled over the remainder of the territories of the Roman Empire in the Middle East until his death in the year 34 CE. He was known for strengthening the buildings of the ancient capital of Judea, Sephoris and his new capital, Tiberias, named after emperor Tiberius.

In reviewing the Herodian dynasty, which started with Antipater, the father of Herod, we can only learn of multiple acts of cruelty within the Herodian dynasty as Herod was responsible of killing several members of his family including two of his sons and his wife, Mariamme, who was the sister of Hyrcanus II, then high priest of Judea.

As Hyrcanus II seemed to have a feeble control over Judea even as he was challenged by the appointment of Herod over Judea by Mark Anthony. In the year 40 BCE, Hyrcanus' nephew, Antigonus, challenged his uncle by cutting off his ears in order to disqualify him for the serving as the high priest of the land. Consequently, Hyrcanus II fled to Babylonia and after four years in Babylonia, he returned to Jerusalem, upon Herod's invitation, and was welcomed by the people of Jerusalem, Since he paused a threat to Herod, the latter had him killed six years later in the year 30 BCE.

**A Mixture of Hate And Admiration**

Herod's rule in the Judea constituted a mixture of hate and admiration from among the population of Judea. When Herod engaged in the gigantic project of rebuilding the Temple of Jerusalem, attracted the admiration of the majority of the Jews of Jerusalem and the Holy Land.

Consequently, it is hard to forget his monumental enterprises. However, his acts of cruelty, greed, thirst for power mentioned above, and his sick state of mind. could well stand in his way to be remembered as the great and just king of Judea. His ambitious building projects were to satisfy the occupied Jews as well as their Roman occupiers.

He also built for himself the fortress of Masada and his own Herodium, which was a superb palace which can still be visited nowadays in the west bank of the Jordan River, not far from the city of Bethlehem.

**The Conflicted Personality of Herod**

We learn (among other quotes) this special quote of from Sepher Yosippon (Translated to English by Steven B. Bowman) on Herod the Great but also Herod the 'not so Great'. His conflicted personality was responsible for him, while being a great military leader, a wonderful builder, but also an insecure despot. He not only was responsible for eliminating thousands of innocent people but also members of his family, including the love of his life: Queen Mariamme.

*The day came when Mariamme, the queen, had a quarrel with the king's sister Shlomith...and the queen vilified her and her family. Shlomith denounced her to the king [Herod] saying, 'When you were with Augustus, my husband Joseph lay with Mariamme, the queen' But the king dd not believe her for he knew his wife was a virtuous woman of long standing. But because of the hatred she had for him the king took these words a little to heart, and summoning his wife he asked her, ' Tell me please what is this hatred that you feel towards me without cause, for you do not love me as before while I love you above all women. I swear to you that. From the day I knew you I have felt no lust for another woman but you'. Mariamme said, 'if you have loved me as you say, who has heard the love of someone who loves yet kills; if love why kill? Why did you command Joseph to kill me on the day you went to Augustus?'*

*When the king heard this, he was greatly shaken; he stopped hugging her and shouted,"Surely the word I have heard is true!Here is the sign that Joseph did not reveal my secret unless he had lain with her! The king left the palace and slept in another house (Sepher Yosippon, p.203).*

As indicated above, Herod was a man of excess and super passion, passion that could harm and destroy but also love to the point of self-destruction. In the following quote, by the same author mentioned above, we find a typical expression of an exaggerated feeling for a wife that he loved so much that he ironically had her killed out of insecurity and jealousy

*Herod regretted killing his wife, the king's anger changed to passion, and the king, yearning exceedingly for his wife Marianne, recalled her name constantly as if she were still alive. He commanded her servants to make her a perpetual feast and to arrange a chair for her at the king's side, as when she lived. The king fell seriously ill...;he could not suffer the longing and [he] nearly died from longing...'(Sepher Yosippon, p.205).*

### Josephus on the Death of Mariamme

*And thus died Mariamme, a woman of an excellent character, both in chastity and in greatness of soul; but she*

*lacked moderation, and had too much of combativeness in her nature. Yet she had more than can be said in the beauty of her body and in the dignity of her bearing in the presence of others. And this was the principal source of her failure to please the king and to live with him harmoniously. For she was pampered by the king out of his love for her, and under the expectation that he could never be harsh to her, she took too much liberty with her speech. She was most afflicted by what had been done to her relatives, and she freely spoke of all they had suffered by him, thus provoking both the king's mother and sister till they became her enemies, and even, at last, did Herod himself also, the only one from whom, mistakenly, she expected never to suffer any harm(Antiquities 15.7.6)*

The Herodian dynasty, which began with Antipater, Herod's father, was a major contributing cause for disrupting the sanctity of Judaism which ended up causing a major rebellion. That sanctity, initially soiled by the Roman occupier and their inadequate procurators, was a major reason for a Jewish rebellion.

The rebels comprised a mixture of religious fanatics and Edumean-influenced forces. We recall that the Edumean Antipater, Herod's father, has an enormous influence on the Hyrcanus II, who was the High Priest. The Edumeans, who originally converted to Judaism, could not be compared to practicing Jews who were raised on the Torah from a young age.

King Herod inherited his father's philosophy and belief. As the Herodian leaders catered to the Roman leaders, the priesthood of the Holy Land weakened more and more to the point of being replaced by Roman sympathizers like Antipater and his son Herod.

*The leadership of the Holy land, which was led by the original dynasty of the Hasmoneans, led by High Priest Mathatias and his son Judah the Maccabee and his brothers, ceased to exist with the arrival of the Herodian dynasty.*

# CHAPTER FIFTEEN

## SADDUCEES VERSUS PHARISEES

### How The Pharisees Regained Power

As we continue to paint the discord between factions in the Holy Land, even before Herod took over the kingdom of Judea (as chosen and backed by Rome), there was Alexander Janneus(103 BCE to 76 BCE), son of Hyrcanus I, son of Simon (Shimon) the Maccabee and great grandson of Mathatias the Hasmonean High Priest.

His name was pronounced Yannai in the Hebrew and in the Talmudic language. Josephus reports that he was extremely cruel. In his disdain for the Pharisees he ordered the crucifixion of 800 pharisees and the slaughter of their wives and children while he was feasting with concubines. Josephus also reported that Herod was an enemy of the Pharisees.

It is unfortunate to learn how the descendants of the Maccabees, found themselves facing civil unrest and war. John Hyrcanus used to be a Pharisee but because of his Greek influence he separated from the Pharisees and joined the Sadducees. The Sadducees represented the aristocratic class of the land. They were also Roman sympathizers. Hence we see the split of the Jewish population between two rival

sects.

Alexander Yannai was crowned king of Jews at the age of 23 and, a hellenized ruler, he was considered an enemy of the Jewish tradition. At a young age he had no remorse of his misdeeds and crimes against his own Jewish brothers and sisters. However, the Pharisees ended up having the upper hand in following the Jewish tradition and the Torah, From there we notice a significant split and rivalry between the two main sects in the land.

This an important quote from *Chabad.org* by Nissan Mindel about the interactions between the young king Yannai and the dominating Pharisees. Following an unfortunate confrontation between the young king (who was also the High Priest), the Pharisees gained popularity in the Land of Israel because of their devotion to the Jewish tradition and what they esteemed to be the right way to following the commandments of the Torah. Reportedly, king Yannai who used to be aligned with the Pharisees, changed course and switched to the aristocratic circles of the Sadducees. The author describes a serious misunderstanding between the young king and his brother-in-law, Shimon Ben Shetach, who happened to be the head of the Sanhedrin.

*It is... not surprising that the young king, already from the start, failed to find favor in the eyes of the Jewish people. The people were also quite tired of all the wars which his predecessors had waged in order to extend their rule. And when King Yannai began his rule immediately with new wars, the people regarded him with even less favor. At first, there was no open split between the king and the people. Yannai had hoped that the leaders of the Pharisees would agree to compromises. His brother-in-law, brother of his wife, was the famous Tanna, Rabbi Shimon ben Shetach, the Head of the Sanhedrin (Highest Court), and one of the main spiritual leaders of the people. But Rabbi Shimon ben Shetach, understandably, refused to compromise in matters as important as Torah and Halachah. Just the opposite, he slowly removed... those members who were not worthy to hold such an important post, and who had been installed there by the king's father(Nissan Mindel in an article at Chabad.org)*

## Even before Herod, king Yannai pursued the Pharisees

This is how the author, Mr. Mindel described a serious confrontation between king Yanai and the Pharisees.

*When King Yannai saw that he could not "do business" with his brother-in-law, nor with the other spiritual leaders of the people, and not wishing to lose the support of the rich circles, he began, openly, to identify himself with the Sadducees. The result was that relations between himself and the people became extremely strained. The split came through a tragic event in the Beth Hamikdosh[the Temple] during Succoth. Yannai, as Kohen Gadol (High Priest), conducted the Service in the Beth Hamikdosh. One of the special services on [the Festival of the Tabernacles, called] Succoth, was the "Nisuch Hamayim" (Pouring of the Water) on the Altar. According to tradition, together with the pouring of wine which took place during the whole year, a pitcher of water, which had been joyfully drawn from the Spring of Shiloah, was additionally poured over the Altar on each day of Succoth...When the High Priest was handed the pitcher of water to pour over the Altar, he poured it out on the ground instead, as the Sadducees bad refused to accept this tradition. Seeing what he had done, the*

*assembled worshipers in the Beth Hamikdosh were infuriated,
and began showering him with their Ethrogim. King Yannai
became so frightened at such open rebellion, that he ordered
his non-Jewish soldiers to attack the people. This they did,
killing six thousand Jews in the court of the Beth Hamikdosh.*

## The Split in Judea and Beginning of Civil War

After this happening, the people began to hate King Yannai more than
ever. There were many uprisings against the King, and he mercilessly
crushed the rebels with the help of his paid army. This, in turn, led to further
rebellion and bitterness among the people, resulting in six years of bloody
civil warfare.

That civil war between the mercenary army of king Yannai and the
Pharisees, resulted in the self-exile to Egypt of many Pharisee leaders.
Shimon Ben Shetach, king Yannai's brother-in-law, was one of those leaders
who returned to the Holy Land only after the death of king Yannai.

Even on his death bed, king Yannai manifested cruelty by ordering the
death of the top elders of the Sanhedrin. Fortunately, his wife, Alexandra
(who was the sister of Shimon Ben Shetach, the chief of the Sanhedrin)
was instrumental in rescinding that order. This is how she saved the top
sages and scholars of Israel: In those days, an order from the king could be
done by showing the king's ring to a subordinate. After his death she did not
announce it immediately to anyone. She removed the ring from her husband
fingers and sent it to the warden who arrested those elders. She ordered him,
in the name of the king to free the elders of the Sanhedrin. Thus Queen
Alexandra saved the top judges and scholars of the Holy land. Following
their release it became known throughout the land that the king has died.
That day, the second day of the Hebrew month of Shevat (the filth month
in the Hebrew calendar) became a day of celebration for the majority of the
Jews in the land of Israel.

Consequently, the Jewish tradition of observing the commandments of
the Torah survived for generations to come after the death of king Yannai, in
the year 76 BCE. The exiled sages were able to return to the Holy Land from
Egypt and resume their holy task in maintaining their sacred duties.

## Survival of Faith Despite Hellenization

That rebellion was partly justified. The leaders of the Pharisees, guided by
Hillel, a great sage in his time, were able to tolerate the Roman occupation

as they kept their faith which taught them that the only king is the God of the Hebrews. The other religious sect, led by Shammai, the other great scholar of the time, also cooperated with the Roman occupiers for the very same reason. Faith in the God of the Hebrews was a leading motive for urging the populace to keep the peace and refrain from challenging the Roman army.

Hellenization became a world renowned culture as it influenced the Roman Empire and its dominated states. Those countries which accepted Hellenization without compromising their own culture, survived and they are still spoken about in modern History.

Those countries who rejected Hellenism as an international culture and did not combine their own culture with Hellenization only to save their own culture, disappeared as a nation.

Elias Bickerman, in his book: From Ezra to The Last of the Maccabees, makes the following observations on this critical subject of saving one's faith and culture:

> ..."Hellenism continued to be a universal power, like Western civilization in the modern world- no people could isolate itself from it if it wished to live and assert itself... With the Maccabees then, the internal Jewish reconcilement with Hellenism begins. Ideas and concepts of the new age and the new culture were taken over without surrendering native spiritual values...The recipe was very simple: the new was fitted into the system of the Torah and was employed the better to serve the God of the fathers, not to elude Him... Thus Judaism was able to enrich itself with new and foreign ideas and to be saved from the mummification that overtook the religion of the Egyptians, for example, which shuts itself off from Hellenism completely...The Maccabees preserved the Judaism of the Greek period from both dissolution and ossification. It is through their deeds that the God of Abraham, Isaac and Jacob could and did remain our God..."(Elias Bickerman, p.180-182)

Concluding this concept of survival, it was necessary for the Jewish leaders and scholars to adopt a foreign culture in order to survive within it. Adopting a foreign culture did not mean forgetting their own culture.

On the contrary, it was the best and the only way to survive within foreign influence and foreign occupation.

Many good examples of accepting the vernacular can be attributed to Moses Maimonides who wrote in Arabic for those who could not read Hebrew but also he wrote *'The Guide For The Perplexed'* in Hebrew among many other books.

For those Jews who had questions about their practice of Judaism.

Also Philo of Alexandria, a very well-known Jewish philosopher who lived in Egypt around the Roman occupation of Judea and translated the Hebrew Bible into Greek. He was well known for communicating with his intellectual contemporaries in Hebrew and Greek. His abundant philosophical works were accepted by Christians and Jewish scholars alike. His books and views, being so prolific, can be discussed in a separate subject.

Also in the Book of *Pirkey Avot* (The Sayings of The Fathers) Rabbi Hillel is featured as the champion of the Pharisees who succeeded with his colleagues and disciples to have the Pharisee interpretation of the Torah as the true interpretation,

This tradition of adapting the vernacular culture in order to practice Judaism continues to exist today as most rabbis and Jewish spiritual leaders use the same intellectual tools as their religious counterparts in order to reach their congregants (such as social media, electronic applications, faith speeches and even Artificial Intelligence which is common is all media and other means of communication).

*Therefore the survival of Judaism has developed throughout the ages as a common sense acceptance of the Diaspora culture without compromising the sanctity and the purity of the Torah.,*

# CHAPTER SIXTEEN

## JERUSALEM, FROM FAME TO HUMILIATION

*The Holy Land, especially Jerusalem, had been the center of attention for the known world, geographically and politically, since the early days of the Hebrew history.*

### Jerusalem as The Center of World's Attention

According to the book of Genesis, Ancestor Abraham was commanded by the Lord to make a sacrifice of his son Isaac at the site of Mount Moriah. That command to sacrifice his son was only an attempt to test Abraham's faith in God. Naturally Isaac was never sacrificed and God promised Abraham to have his seed as the sand of the sea and as the 'stars of heaven'

Mount Moriah is a holy spot for Moslems and Jews today and Jerusalem is the revered center for Judaism, Christianity and Islam.

We also learn from the book of Kings how King David, who exalted Jerusalem in his many Psalms, was laying the groundwork for his son King Solomon to build the most magnificent temple in the region. That temple was the envy of surrounding countries and kings and queens including the Queen of Sheba, Some fifty years after that sumptuous temple was destroyed by the Babylonians in 586 BCE. The Israelites were permitted to return to the Holy Land thanks to the decree issued by Cyrus the new Emperor of the Persian Empire.

As predicted in the book of Isaiah the Babylonians were defeated and the Holy land and neighboring countries became under the Persian Empire.

While in exile, Jewish scholars and sages in Babylonia developed and compiled the Babylonian Talmud which has become a valuable intellectual and religious asset in understanding the Torah of Moses (The Pentateuch) and the Oral Law that goes with it.

Parallel to the Babylonian Talmud, the Jerusalem Talmud was being assembled in the northern cities of Tiberias, Sephoris and Caesaria. The so called Jerusalem Talmud, although it was not created in Jerusalem, was initiated by Yohanan Bar Nappaha.

The rebuilt Temple lasted over four centuries until the arrival of Herod the Great in 37 BCE. Herod, as mentioned earlier rebuilt and aggrandized the Temple to a magnificent level.

*In sum, Jerusalem, as the capital of the Holy Land, has always attracted the attention of world powers*

What is more, the conquering leaders coveted, not only the strategic location of the Holy Land in the middle East but also the gold and the riches of the Jerusalem Temple.

Many kings and military leaders sought to build and destroy Jerusalem.

King David abundantly praised in his Psalms the walls and towers and marveled in its beauty.

Other good kings such as king Jehoshaphat, king Josiah and king Hezekiah labored to rebuild and reinforce its walls.

The evil kings of the Northern Kingdom, named kings of Israel, were not concerned about the biblical commandment to make a pilgrimage to Jerusalem. They had their own sites in Shiloh, Gilgal and Shechem.

Because of the political chaos of Northern Israel cited in previous chapters, Northern Israel ceased to exist as an independent entity.

King Omri, the sixth king of Northern Israel founded the stronghold city of Samaria as his capital. Northern Israel cities lost their independence when they were overrun and sacked by king Sargon II of Assyria in the 721 BCE.

Jerusalem remained the main focus for the conquering powers who succeeded each other.

**The Conquerors of Jerusalem since 586 BCE**

The Babylonians conquerors were followed by the Persians, the Greeks and the Romans

The conquerors sought to use their power to widen their empire in the middle eastern regions including Judea,

While subduing Judea after besieging Jerusalem, their goal was to enrich themselves with glory and gold.

Jerusalem was the center of attention when the Maccabees battled the Seleucid army in order to keep the Temple pure and intact.

The Crusaders besieged and conquered the city in 1099 and in 1187 they surrendered in the battle of Hattin to the army of Saladin from the Ayyubid dynasty. Their final battle was the battle of Jaffa in 1192 whereby a treaty was made between Richard the Lionhearted and Saladin.

As Jerusalem passed from one dominant power to another, it fell under the Ottoman Empire from 1516 to 1917 CE until the British took over after World War I.

*However, as we return to our project, the Roman occupation of the Holy Land seems to represent one of the most important chapters in Jewish history*

*as the Jewish nation was on the verge of extinction.*

*Ironically the Roman dominance of the Holy Land did not end the Jewish faith and culture as we see ahead.*

### How Roman Protection Turned Into Domination

**Roman interaction with the Holy Land was at first a protective friendship between Rome and Jerusalem which started with Julius Caesar.**

We learned that the early Roman conquerors were tolerant of the Jewish way of life. For example, the Jews under Hyrcanus (the High Priest) and Antipater(The Idumean ruler) helped the Roman forces of Julius Caesar to subdue the Egyptian army and complete its conquest of the Middle East, including Persia (today's Iran), Syria and Armenia.

> *The first decree, dated probably July, 47 B.C., registered in both Greek and Latin on a table of brass and preserved in the public records, concerns Hyrcanus, the son of Alexander, high priest and ethnarch of the Jews. Julius Cæsar, with the approbation of the senate, recognizes the services rendered by Hyrcanus to the empire, both in peace and in war. He mentions the aid given by Hyrcanus with his 1,500 soldiers in the Alexandrian war, and speaks of the personal valor of Hyrcanus. In recognition of these services he grants Hyrcanus and the Jews certain privileges (Josephus, "Ant." xiv. 10, § 2).*

**The Friendship of Rome with the Hebrew state, which started with Julius Caesar continued under Augustus, as we find an abundance of quotes by Josephus. The military might of Hyrcanus the High Priest, associated with Antipater and his son Herod, gave the Romans an opportunity to support Judea.**

> *In another decree of probably the same date, Cæsar determines "That the Jews shall possess Jerusalem, and may encompass that city with walls; and that Hyrcanus, the son of Alexander, the high priest and ethnarch of the Jews, retain it in the manner he himself pleases; and that the Jews be allowed to deduct out of their tribute, every second year the land is let [in the Sabbatical period], a corus of that tribute;*

*and that the tribute they pay be not let to farm, nor that they pay always the same tribute" (ib. xiv. 10, § 5).*

## The Good News Before The Bad News.

*The good news, as follows, show a clear support of Rome to Jerusalem, Had it continued that way, it would be very little doubt that Judea and Jerusalem would one day be destroyed and the Jerusalem Temple burned to the ground.*

*The following two decrees are of the same date: "That Hyrcanus and his children bear over the nation of the Jews, and have the profits of the places to them bequeathed; and that he, as the high priest and ethnarch of the Jews, defend those that are injured; and that ambassadors be sent to Hyrcanus, the son of Alexander, the high priest of the Jews, that may discourse with him about a league of friendship and mutual assistance; and that a table of brass containing the promises be openly proposed in the capitol, and at Sidon, and Tyre, and Ascalon, and in the temple, engraven in Roman and Greek letters: that this decree may also be communicated to the questors and pretors of the several cities, and to the friends of the Jews; and that the ambassadors may have presents made them, and that these decrees be sent everywhere" (Antiquities, chapter 10, section 3).*

*"Caius Cæsar, imperator, dictator, consul, hath granted, That out of regard to the honor, and virtue, and kindness of the man, and for the advantage of the senate, and of the people of Rome, Hyrcanus, the son of Alexander, both he and his children, be high priests and priests of Jerusalem, and of the Jewish nation, by the same right, and according to the same laws, by which their progenitors have held the priesthood" (Antiquities, chapter 10, section 4).*

## Analyzing The Forces That Played a Role in The destruction

Judea went from relative independence to subjugation to foreign rulers. To name a few figures who played a role in the gradual demise of Jerusalem and its Temple we must begin by the initial Hellenization which took place after the death of Simon, the last Maccabee and the rise of John HyrcanusI, his son.

HyrcanusI, by switching from being a Pharisee to become a Sadducee brought the first big conflict between Jewish brothers:

Saducees versus Pharisees.

Next was the influence of Antipater and Herod his son on the Hasmonean kings and High Priests.

Following the rapprochement between Rome and Herod where Herod offered bribes to Rome in order to gain power in Judea, came the weakening of the High Priesthood in the Holy Land and the gradual domination of the Herodian dynasty in Judea.

We deduct that the fights between the Hasmonean brothers, as indicated previously, was instigated by the Idumean Antipater, father of Herod

Then we learn about the Roman military expeditions in Jerusalem and the cruelty of the Roman procurators half a century after the death of Julius Caesar and we wonder why Jerusalem was destroyed and its Temple burned to the ground.

We noticed that the special friendship between Rome and Jerusalem was soured and even worsened under the various procurators of Judea and especially under to cruel procurators, Pontius Pilate during the time of Jesus and Florus, the last procurator who sparked the Jewish rebellion with his cruel actions.

As history shows, the Roman emperors who succeeded Julius Caesar did not have the same rapport with Judea as Julius Caesar did. In fact, as Julius Caesar admitted, Judea, under HyrcanusI and Antipater did well with Rome by being militarily strong and supportive of Rome.

Little did Jerusalem leaders know what was to happen in Judea when Antipater and especially his son Herod took over the reigns in Judea and committed atrocities all over Judea.

*Rome did not differentiate between Hyrcanus and the Herodian clan, Antipater, Herod and his two sons, Archelaus and Phillip the Tetrarch.*

*What the Romans wanted was gold and gifts as they were easy to bribe.*

*The power earned by Herod following his bribing Rome represented the beginning of the end of Judea's political Jewish independence and the start of rivalry between the Edumite Hierarchy (Antipater, Herod, Archelaus and Phillip) and the rest of the Jewish leadership.*

*Antigonus (grandson of Alexander Janneus, the last Hasmonean king) was murdered by order of Herod.as Herod sought to eliminate the last of the Hasmonean dynasty and gain the ultimate power of Judea.*

*Mistreatment of Jews in neighboring lands*

As Jews were mistreated by Archelaus, the son Herod, a delegation of

Jewish notables sailed to Rome in order to complain about the plight of the Jews under the Herodian dynasty. Archelaus was sent to Rome by order of Augustus.

Jews in neighboring countries to Judea were also threatened. Some rulers protected the Jews while others showed indifference. In Samaria, Roman ruler Tiberius Julius Alexander(appointed by Claudius), replaced Ventidius Cumanus, who failed to respond to murders conducted by Samaritans against Jews (in which 2000 Jews died). Cumanus was appointed by Claudius Caesar in his eighth year in Rome.

It is reported that Claudius finally settled disputes between Samaritans and Jews in the Holy Land. Following Cumanus it was Felix (Marcus Antonius Felix) who became the new procurator of Judea.

## The Main Characters Around The Demise of Jerusalem

Following Claudius Caesar it was Nero who took over in Rome. Historians report that Emperor Nero, who reigned poorly over Rome and its empire, ended up committing suicide, which brought up the Roman civil war and the arrival of Vespasian his son to become the new emperor. Under those circumstances, Titus became the new Roman military strong man in Judea.

We have indicated above how cruel was Herod, the appointed king (by Rome) of Judea.

Herod, who was suspicious of his own (other) sons had two of his sons, Alexander and Aristobulos, killed in 7 BCE, and another son, named Antipater killed in 4 BCE. We indicate here that Herod had nine wives and fourteen children.

The above mentioned children were killed because they were accused of plotting to kill their own father,

That accusation was not verified by historians. One thing is sure, Herod has been seen by some historians and archaeologists as a paranoid schizophrenic.

Herod, who was a convert to Judaism, but not an observant of that religion, made sure that the Hasmonean dynasty, that took credit for restoring Judaism to the Holy Land, was eliminated.

From here on, we are going to bring up the main figures who played a decisive role in the battle between the occupying Romans and the rebellious Jews who wanted the Romans out of Judea.

*Vespasian,* initially the brilliant military Roman commander who conquered most of Judea for Rome, became the new Emperor of Rome following the death of Nero. *Titus* would become the new military commander who would end up destroying Jerusalem and its Temple.

*King Agrippa* was instrumental in trying to exhort the zealot groups to give up their intention to fight for the Temple while, he added, God Himself Has not accepted their prayers because of sins committed against each other.

While making long and passionate speeches he asked them to refrain from defying the mighty Roman army and simply accept their rule without trying to fight them and therefore save themselves from total destruction. Furthermore, *Josephus*, after saving himself during the battle of Jotapata (Yosephta), by surrendering to Vespasian, made several passionate speeches to the rebels.

Between the harsh treatment committed by Florus the procurator and the unstable ruling of the Herodian dynasty who eliminated the seed of the Hasmonean priesthood, and finally the military might Vespasian and his son Titus, the weakening of Judea became inevitable.

To add to the crisis in Judea, it was finally the zealots headed by two major rival leader, John of Gishala, and Shimon Bar Giora. They battled each other and ended up causing the murder of hundreds of thousands of Jews who fell under the Roman legions during the rebellion.

## The Mourning on the Two Temples

The main figure who lived around the destruction of the first Tempe was Prophet Jeremiah who persistently mourned about the plight of Jerusalem and the its vanishing beauty,

The second personality who witnessed the destruction of the second Temple was Josephus who described in minute details all the phases of the destruction of Jerusalem and most cities of the Holy Land.

## Prophet Jeremiah's Mourning

Prophet Jeremiah used specific words and adjectives to depicts the tragedy of the first Temple. Here are some of his graphic descriptions

> *"How desolate sat Jerusalem....Judah has gone into exile...*
> *Her enemies became her rulers...her adversaries gloat over*
> *her demise...Indeed Jerusalem has sinned.... there is no one to*
> *comfort her...she saw foreigners enter her Temple...The Lord*
> *Has become like an enemy... The Lord planned to damage the*

*walls of Zion...My eyes became weak from weeping [and]my insides are upset... See Oh Lord and look to whom you have done so that women [are made] to eat their children...Young and old lie on the street floors...Even as I cry...He shuts out my prayer...and he set me as a target for an arrow...I became a laughing matter to my people...Let us look for our ways and examine how we can return to the Lord...My eyes overflow with tears upon the destruction of my people... The tongue of the infant stuck to his palate from thirst, young children asked for bread and no one to hand it to them...It was better to be a victim of the sword than that of famine...the hands of compassionate women cooked their [own] children in order to serve as food for them... Remember Oh Lord what happened to us and look at our humiliation...we have become orphans and no father and our mothers [became] widows... they [our enemies] have molested the women of Zion...Young men carried the mill and children staggered from [lifting] wood... You, Oh Lord shall reign forever [and] your throne for generations and generations. Turn us Oh Lord to You and we shall return, Restore our days as before ... (From the biblical book of Lamentations, Jeremiah's own words of mourning, chosen from the five chapters of the book of Lamentations)*

### The Bitter Words of Josephus on The Demise of Jerusalem

Josephus, initially a rebel himself, ended up joining the Roman army in order to save himself, in the hope of mediating between him and the attacking Romans.

Sadly the war ended in favor of the Romans and to the demise of the rebels. The rebellion caused, not only destruction of Jerusalem and its Temple and death of the rebels but also the death of the peaceful population who did not want to face the Roman soldiers. Josephus estimated that over one million people died in the war which lasted three years between 67 CE and 70 CE.

The Following two quotes of Josephus were chosen to describe the misery of the Jewish People during the rebellion and the end of independence in the Holy Land.

*Thus did the miseries of Jerusalem grow worse and worse every day, and the seditious were still more irritated by the calamities they were under, even while the famine preyed upon themselves, after it had preyed upon the people. And indeed the multitude of carcasses that lay in heaps one upon another was a horrible sight, and produced a pestilential stench, which was a hinderance to those that would make sallies out of the city, and fight the enemy: but as those were to go in battle-array, who had been already used to ten thousand murders, and must tread upon those dead bodies as they marched along, so were not they terrified, nor did they pity men as they marched over them; nor did they deem this affront offered to the deceased to be any ill omen to themselves . . . . And now the Romans, although they were greatly distressed in getting together their materials, raised their banks in one and twenty days, after they had cut down all the trees that were in the country that adjoined to the city, and that for ninety furlongs round about, as I have already related. And truly the very view itself of the country was a melancholy thing; for those places which were before adorned with trees and pleasant gardens were now become a desolate country every way, and its trees were all cut down: nor could any foreigner that had formerly seen Judea and the most beautiful suburbs of the city, and now saw it as a desert, but lament and mourn sadly at so great a change: for the war had laid all the signs of beauty quite waste: nor if any one that had known the place before, had come on a sudden to it now, would he have known it again; but though he were at the city itself, yet would he have inquired for it notwithstanding. ( The Wars of the Jews: Book 6, Chapter 5, section 1) .....*

## The Final Blow That Ended The Jewish Independence as Witnessed by Josephus

*While the holy house was on fire, everything was plundered that came to hand, and ten thousand of those that were caught were slain; nor was there a commiseration of any age, or any reverence of gravity, but children, and old men, and profane persons, and priests were all slain in the same manner; so that this war went round all sorts of men, and brought them to destruction, and as well those that made supplication for their lives, as those that defended themselves by fighting. The flame was also carried a long way, and made an echo, together with the groans of those that were slain; and because this hill was high, and the works at the temple were very great, one would have thought the whole city had been on fire. Nor can one imagine anything either greater or more terrible than this noise; for there was at once a shout of the Roman legions, who were marching all together, and a sad clamor of the seditious, who were now surrounded with fire and sword. The people also that were left above were beaten back upon the enemy, and under a great consternation, and made sad moans at the calamity they were under; the multitude also that was in the city joined in this outcry with those that were upon the hill. And besides, many of those that were worn away by the famine, and their mouths almost closed, when they saw the fire of the holy house, they exerted their utmost strength, and brake out into groans and outcries again: Pera did also return the echo, as well as the mountains round about [the city,] and augmented the force of the entire noise. Yet was the misery itself more terrible than this disorder; for one would have thought that the hill itself, on which the temple stood, was seething hot, as full of fire on every part of it, that the blood was larger in quantity than the fire, and those that were slain more in number than those that slew them; for the ground did nowhere appear visible, for the dead bodies that lay on it; but the soldiers went over heaps of those bodies, as they ran upon such as fled from them. And now it was that the multitude of the robbers were thrust out [of the inner court of the temple by the Romans,] and had much ado to get into the outward court, and from thence into the city, while the remainder of the populace fled into the cloister of that outer court. As for the priests, some of them plucked up from the holy house the spikes that were upon it, with their bases, which were made of lead, and shot them at the Romans instead of arrows. But then as they gained nothing by so doing, and as the fire burst out upon them, they retired to the wall that was eight cubits broad, and there they tarried; yet did two of these of eminence among them, who might have saved themselves by going over to the Romans, or have borne up with courage, and taken their fortune with the others, throw themselves into the fire, and were burnt together with the holy house; their names were Meirus the son of Belgas, and Joseph the son of Daleus"* (The Wars of The Jews, Book 6, Chapter 1, section 1

**In conclusion, the demise of Jerusalem in the first century was prompted by three major trends: First, it was the civil unrest which put Jews against**

*Jews. Secondly, the Herodian people who interfered in Israel's religious and political affairs. Finally it was the Roman army who finished the job of destroying the city of Jerusalem and its Temple while fighting the rebels who were themselves fighting each other.*

# Chapter Seventeen

## Comparing Israel of today to

## Historic Israel

### Are We Better off Today?

Are we better off today when comparing ancient history of Israel to today's Israel??*The short answer is a big Yes.*

There is no comparison of the Holy Land of the sixth century BCE and that of the first century CE to that of the 21[th] century.

As we know, the kingdoms of David and Solomon represented the glorious years of the nation of the Israelite around the tenth century BCE. As King David described Jerusalem as the envy of the word. King Solomon was one of the wealthiest but also one of the wisest men in his time.

However things went wrong following the death of king Solomon, as we stated before.

After the exile and the dispersion of the ten tribes of Israel to Persia and Media (based on Josephus notes) and the end of the Israelite kingdoms in 586 BCE, the Holy Land suffered occupation after occupation of the super empires. After the Babylonians, the Persians dominated the Middle East. Following the Persians, the Greeks and the Romans controlled the Holy Land and the surrounding nations.

We noticed two uprisings that restored some pride to the nation of the Israelites, before and after the Roman occupation.

The Maccabees, from the Hasmonean dynasty resisted and defeated the Seleucid army, part of the Greek Empire in 167 BCE.

The Bar Kochba rebellion against the Romans between 132 CE and 135 CE, although crushed demonstrated the desire of the Jews to be free and politically independent. It took over 1900 years of exile and suffering for the Jews to become free again. Today, Israel is a vibrant country with multiple political parties. Those parties might disagree with each other but the system of election is purely democratic. That system is not without criticism both from inside Israel and outside Israel.

Israel today gathers the majority of the world Jewish population and it is open for more newcomers.

## The Knesset, The Only Israeli Parliament

While multiple parties compete for seats to be part of the 120 seats of the Knesset, the democratic rule decides who is going to be ruling in the Israeli Parliament.

At the end of 2022, new elections in Israel resulted in a fragmented government to be composed of multiple parties to be functioning in 2023.

Previously elected several times as prime minister, *Benjamin Netanyahu* of the Likud (right wing) party has been sharing the reigns with two more right wing leaders who are considered extreme right: *Bezalel Smotrich*, representing a religious Zionist party and *Itamar Ben-Gvir* who is the head of an extreme right wing. The other religious parties who have governed since 2023 are *Shas*, a non-Zionist Haredi (ultra-religious) party and *United Torah Judaism*.

The new government has been replacing a left wing coalition government which included left wing and centrist parties which were headed by *Yair Lapid* (outgoing prime minister whose party was *Yesh Atid* (translated to: there is a future) and outgoing minister of defense, *Beny Ganz* who headed the central right *National Unity party*. To those parties who are not part of the new government.

We can add *Israel Beiteinu* (meaning Israel is our home), led by *Avigdor Lieberman*. There are three more important parties who will always be striving for participation in future governments of Israel: left wing party *Meretz* (meaning vigor), *Habbayit Hayehudi* (the Jewish Home) and finally the Arab Nationalist party *Balad*.

Naturally, in a democratic country, smaller parties burgeon and when gathering enough votes and seats, it is their choice to be added to the leading party in order to be part of a governing coalition.

As we see, today's Israel political system is composed of multiple parties. Here you have a clear proof of various patriotic factions who do not agree with each other. The huge difference between them and those of the occupied Holy Land in the first century is that in Israel there is no bloodshed between differing parties even when there is a sharp disagreement between them.

## The New Israeli Rules on Limiting The Israeli Supreme Court

As Israel does not have a Constitution just as The United States or France, after seventy five years of political existence, the need arose within the governing parties to review the extent of powers within the Supreme Court of Israel.

Although Israel and the United States are typical democracies, their Supreme Courts may be different. The US Constitution has been drawn by the founding fathers for a brand new nation, the United States of America, which separated itself from Colonial England on July 4, 1776.

On the other hand, the Israelis inside Israel. do not consider Israel as a newly born country because Israel existed for the Jewish people, on and off, for thousands of years, since the advent of Patriarch Abraham in 1812 BCE.

As Israel is evolving politically, economically and socially, the political parties and the public in general are divided as to whether or not to limit the power of the Israeli Supreme Court which has traditionally has been making the final ruling on political and social matters in the land.

In late July 2023, Israel found itself in a major political crisis as the leading coalition of the government voted by a thin majority to limit the power of the supreme court of Israel.

In Israel there is only one House of Representatives, called the Knesset which includes 120 members of all parties.

Unlike the United States where two major parties compete for the presidency, in Israel the major party has never been able to govern without forming a coalition of parties whose Knesset members would represent the majority in the parliament.

The following are excerpts of Israel's president Isaac Herzog after the first part of the Judicial reform had been voted by a thin majority of the Knesset (the Israeli Parliament). His speech has been broadcast worldwide and has been commented on by the New York Times

*"The last few weeks have been tearing us apart," the president began. "They are harming Israel's economy, security, political ties and especially Israeli cohesion. The family Shabbat meals have become an arena of struggle, friends and neighbors have become rivals. The conflicts are getting worse; The worries, the fears, the anxieties – they are all more tangible than ever," Herzog said... The president, however, said that the crisis was also an opportunity.*

*"I truly believe with all my heart that today, we are also facing a major, historic opportunity. An opportunity for balanced, smart and agreed-upon constitutional regulation*

*of the relations of the branches of government in our Jewish and democratic country," he said. "We are at a crossroads: a historical crisis or a defining constitutional moment.",,*

*"I am a person of faith, but I am not naive. I know that as soon as I finish my words, and maybe even before that, opponents will arise from all sides. I also know that there will be those who will dodge responsibility, and that there will be those who have already agreed and will suddenly deny that they did so, or retract their agreement," the president said.*

The New York Times article made a deep analysis of Israel's parties as the country is divided between the majority right wing coalition (including the religious parties), and the minority left wing. Israel's major parties have been discussed earlier.

The Israeli population, although mostly secular, is also traditional in observing or at least respecting the sabbath and the Jewish holidays (Although Mr Herzog's speech was made on February 21,2023, way before the vote in late July 2023. The New York Time analysis of Israel's political system has been updated on March 15, 2023).

## Political Divisiveness is Inevitable in Most Democracies

It is without a doubt that political divisiveness exits in the United States as it subsists in France or England or other democratic countries and especially in countries in Africa that call themselves democracies.

Some politicians and historians consider divisiveness in democracy as a good thing. The United States Congress has a problem with the make up of the US Supreme Court just as the Israeli public is divided as to whether or not to limit the Israeli Supreme Court and have the Knesset majority overrule the supreme decision.

On this subject we find an excerpt from the Baltimore Jewish

## Times editorial article (may 5, 2023)

*Over the past several months, when the topic of Judaical reform comes up in discussion, many of us think of the disturbing drama playing out in the Knesset and in the streets of Israel over the controversial 'judicial form' package being promoted by Israel's governing coalition.*

> *But here at home there is another judicial reform debate-*
> *this one relating to the absence of a formal code of ethics for*
> *the justices of the ([Unites States] Supreme Court.*

## The BBC View on Israel Judicial System -July 24 2023

## "What are people so angry about?

> *Mr Netanyahu's opponents say the reforms will severely*
> *undermine the country's democracy by weakening the judicial*
> *system, the only tool for keeping the government's use of its*
> *power in check. Underlying this is strong opposition to the*
> *kind of government currently in office - the most right-wing in*
> *Israel's history - and to Mr Netanyahu himself.*

> *Critics say the reforms will shield Mr Netanyahu, who*
> *is currently on trial for alleged corruption (he denies the*
> *charges) and help the government pass laws without any*
> *brakes.*

> *The government argues that the judiciary interferes too*
> *much with legislation, is biased in support of liberal issues*
> *and is undemocratic in the way judges are selected." (partial*
> *article by Rafi Berg, BBC News Online Middle East Editor)*

## Unusual Criticism of Israel by Silvain Cypel

*In every democracy there are issues.* Those issues which were spelled out by Sylvain Cypel, a distinguished French journalist whose book: *The State of Israel vs The Jews'* was translated into English by William Rodarmor. The title itself could be considered as an insult for Jews worldwide, as the majority of Jews, religious or secular support the basic survival of Israel.

Sylvain describes in his own details how the state of Israel discriminates against the Arab population inside Israel and he Palestinian Arabs in the West Bank.

Sylvain would be perfectly justified of his vicious attacks on the government of Israel If Israel were a normal country living among peaceful neighbors.

Unfortunately, Israel is not a normal country surrounded by peace loving states and peace loving Arab populations within its state.

Although Israel established peace agreements with Jordan and Egypt and Morocco,, there is still a menace from Lebanon, where *Hisballah* threatens the existence of Israel and *Hamas* in the South which is financed by Iran and whose constitution dictates the elimination of the state of Israel.

Furthermore, Mahmoud Ahmadinejad, one of the past presidents of Iran between 2005 and 2013 publicly and repeatedly announced to the world his intention to eliminate the 'Zionist regime' as he did not call Israel by name.

As we know, Israel, since its inception in 1948, has been attacked thousands of times from outside its borders as well as inside its borders.

Under those circumstances, our message to Mr Sylvain Cypel is simply this: You may be right to denounce Israel and its policy towards the Arab minority in Israel If Israel were surrounded by friendly neighbors who do not seek to annihilate it. On the other hand, in a democratic country as Israel, the Palestinian Arabs who live inside Israel have the right to vote and even to be elected members of the Knesset, the Israeli Parliament. In fact, the judge who sent the previous president of Israel to prison was an Arab

judge in Israel. Furthermore, Salim Joubran was the country 's first Arab Supreme Court Justice since 2003.

Since 1949, Israeli Arabs are represented in the Knesset. In fact, the past government which ended in October 2022, was composed of the left wing Israeli parties and the Arab group called Balad.

This author went through the book of Mr Cypel and read over and over several of his paragraphs like those quoting *Haaretz* which is one of the leading newspapers in Israel. Mr Sylvain chose to concentrate on those facts *Haaretz* reported which seemed damaging to the Arab minority. Just as in the United States, the New York times seems to attack this of that institution at their choosing. What I found peculiar about Mr Sylvain Cypel writing is that, in his 361 page book, I could not find one single compliment to the Government of Israel. Mr Cypel expects Israel to be as a country like France, England or the Unites States that do not have to worry every single day about their existence or survival.

Also Mr. Cypel expounded on The *Shin Bet* in Israel, which is the equivalent of the FBI in the United States and is one of the Intelligence agencies in Israel. While reading about the interrogations techniques of the Shin Bet, I could not find one single word why those interrogation techniques were applied. According to Mr Cypel every suspicious person interrogated by the Shin Bet is presumed innocent to begin with, even considered a victim (because of being interrogated).

His constant criticism of the Israeli system continues with his description of the *B'tselem* organization which claims be a neutral organization in Israel gathering information on the crimes committed by Israel and by its enemies. The chief of B'tselem is *Hagai El-Ad,* a gentle and sensible individual who does not seem to get involved in politics. El-Ad himself declared, according to the Guardian (British newspaper) when he was asked if Hamas was a terrorist organization, he said 'we are talking about armed Palestinian organizations...and we criticize their activities when they are illegal.'

In contrast Mr Cypel's story about anything that goes in Israel is wrong, leaving the reader to think that nothing is correct with the government of Israel.

In a democratic country like Israel, Hagai El-Ad is also the director of the Jerusalem Open House, Jerusalem's premier gay advocacy group. He is also involved with the Association of Civil Rights in Israel. And as free society, B'tselem has been in existence for over 25 years and has been accepted by the Israeli population as a legitimate organization, even as its aim is to criticize the government when due. I have a simple message for Mr Cypel:

Dear Mr Cypel

I understand that in your book you are trying to be the Emile Zola in the Dreyfus affair and what you think of Israel and its need for change. France may be 2000 years old if we count the years since Julius Caesar conquered Gaul in 56 BCE. The New Israel in only 75 years old as of 2023. I would give it time to find itself better.

Although the birth of the Hebrew nation begun some 4000 years ago with Abraham, Jews were subjects to various empires and exiles several times as you well know. Furthermore, in the last 2000 years, Jews were away from their original homeland as history shows. Finally, they are home since 1948.
Give them time to 'rearrange their furniture'.

## And This is Our message in French to Mr Cypel:

L'antisemitisme de 2000 ans et des millions de morts justifient le comportement d'Israel vers ses sujets de n'importe quel origine.
Accordez lui quelque temps pour ranger ses meubles.
The English translation of the above message is a s follows:

"The two thousand year old antisemitism[which resulted] in millions of dead [Jews] justifies Israel's behavior towards its subjects no matter where they come from. Give it some time to re-arrange its furniture"

## Israel And The American Jews

The following excerpt, is from the *Jewish Times of Baltimore,* Md (November 23, 2022), written by Mr Flayton who entitled his column:

*Can American Jews make demands on Israel if they don't live there?*

*Israelis will continue to be shocked and offended by shameful declarations by the U.N. Educational, Scientific and Cultural Organization (UNESCO), which has declared that Jews have no right to the Temple Mount in Jerusalem. That will compel them to vote for more radical parties. And Jews in the Diaspora will continue to voice their moral condemnations of this, which will only deepen the hostilities.*

*A solution to this quandary would be for both sides to bite the bullet. If Jews outside of Israel feel so strongly about what is happening in Israel, then they should take the advice of those with whom they most disagree and move here. They'll have a stake in the future of the nation as well as a sturdier platform when speaking for or against its policies.*

*Simultaneously, Israeli Jews should come to realize that while they are entitled to their choices, they are not entitled to be free of scrutiny and backlash, and that what the rest of the world thinks of you does make a difference. No nation has ever been able to survive moral and political isolation, especially not one whose citizens consider millions living overseas to be part of the nation as well.*

Blake Flayton is the new media director and columnist) article..
Another Jewish Times Editorial stated in its November 11, 2022, on the subject :Israel vs The Jewish Diaspora. This is an excerpt of the article:

*The irony is that if the center-right parties were willing to join the coalition, they could balance or even replace the far-*

*right parties. But each of the center-right leaders has been burned by Netanyahu before and has pledged not to join him now.*

*U.S. Jewry is overall more liberal than the steadily more conservative Israeli public. Some Jewish groups expressed distress over the election results, while others merely congratulated Israel on the election and kept silent about concerns regarding the far-right elements of the likely coalition.*

*On the eve of the election, Israeli President Isaac Herzog told the Jewish Federations of North America's General Assembly, "The results may or may not be to your liking, but the vote of the Israeli people should be respected." We agree. We need to respect and accept the will of the Israeli people. This is so even if the likely direction of several government policies could be uncomfortable for a significant segment of Diaspora Jewry. For example, no one from Netanyahu rightward supports a two state solution. And the restoration of full control of the Ministry of Religious Affairs and the Rabbinate to Haredi leadership is not likely to support religious pluralism in Israel or LGBTQ+ rights.*

*But this is the government Israel's electorate wants. As such, when it comes to the makeup of the government and the policies it pursues, the decisions aren't ours to make. We don't have to agree with every policy and decision. And we certainly don't have to support decisions with which we disagree. But we shouldn't prejudge things based upon what we think will happen. Instead, let's see what they decide to do. Let's see which ministries are given to far-right leaders. And let's see what policies are pursued. They may surprise us.*

## The Assassination that shocked the Jewish World (And the US president too)

There is also an exception within the political system in Israel: those who are considered extreme right wingers (no different than right wing militants in other countries). That exception was the assassination of an existing prime minister of Israel. a rare occasion when, Izhak Rabin, the late prime minister of Israel was shot in 1995 following the Oslo Accords (1993). The Oslo Accords included a mutual acceptance of existence between Israel and the Palestinian authority.

General Rabin died while delivering a message of hope and peace to a huge crowd in Tel Aviv.

His death triggered a national commotion and worldwide outcry from those countries and leaders who knew general Rabin just as Bill Clinton who was the President of the United States at that time who mediated between general Rabin who represented Israel and Yasser Arafat who represented the Palestinians.

Those who knew Mr Rabin recognized that he was a brilliant man who was not afraid to make war in order to protect his country but he was also a man of peace for the very same reason. Since general Rabin belonged to the left wing Labor Party who wanted to cooperate with the neighboring Palestinians, he was considered a traitor by some extremists on the right wing of the country. The killer, Igal Amir, was an extreme right law student at Bar-Ilan University in Tel Aviv who represented the fanatic trend we witnessed when we described above the rebels and the zealots who were protecting the city of Jerusalem and its Temple against the mighty Romans army.

*Winston Churchill said once about democracy that it is not the best of political system, except for all the others.*

And this is what *Rabbi Irving Greenberg* said in his "Perspectives" on the Israeli political arena.

> *The Rabin assassination threatens to unleash many of the same destructive emotions as did the murder of President John F. Kennedy: suspicion of conspiracy...fear that those who oppose change will stop at nothing...by those who want change...Jews will have to do better. They will have to prevent these developments because, to put it bluntly, Israel cannot afford to allow this to happen'*

Unlike the United States system where two major parties, Republican and Democrat, compete for the Senate and the House of Representatives, the Israeli system consists only of one governing house which contains 120 seats. The original Sanhedrin, two thousand years ago, in the Holy Land counted 71 members.

## Conclusive Difference Between Ancient Israel and Modern Israel

Comparing the existing political theater in Israel today to biblical Israel, we see a remarkable difference. The biblical Holy Land was governed by kings and aided by priests and prophets.

The Holy Land of the 70's during Josephus times was under occupation by the Romans and the rebellious Jewish factions were governed by *John of Gishala and Shimon (Simon) Bar Giora* who were fighting each other. They imposed their rules despotically over the large population of ancient Israel.

As we stated in previous chapters a lot of bloodshed took place within the kingdoms of Northern Israel and enough killing occurred during the Judean Kingdoms which began by King Saul and King David.

Fortunately, those who were under the kingdom of Judah survived despite the numerous wars we spoke about, while the kingdom of Northern Israel vanished with its ten tribes of Israel.

In today's world where the Internet and Social Media take place daily, all countries are exposed to the news even the autocratic ones.

Therefore, the events cited in the Scriptures, including in the Chronicles where leaders murdered other leaders could not take place today without being exposed to the rest of the world via social media, Television and other means of communication.

Even the events described by Josephus where rebels murdered other rebels for the sake of the country could not be duplicated today under a democratic government like Israel.

## A last Word on Democracy in Israel

As Israel democracy could not always be compared to that the United States or that of France for reasons explained before, it could take decades for the Parliament (Knesset) and the Supreme Court of Israel to find a fair system of checks and balances, leaving the power to the Parliament to be the true legislative and the Supreme Court to be the true Judicial authority

*Following the high spirited protests of the public in Israel during the summer of 2023 about the judicial reform spoken about above we find several authors who took the middle ground. The most outspoken among the well-known personalities are Professor Yaron Zelekha and Doctor Mordekhai Keydar.*

*They both believe that neither the Supreme Court of Israel nor the leading party are on the right track.*

*Professor Zelekha is a well know economist who believes that the economy is controlled by the Israeli 'Wall Street' he calls the tycoons of Israel.*

*Doctor Mordekhai Keydar is a renown political analyst who specializes in the politics of neighboring Arab countries and especially Iran which represents a threat to the existence of Israel.*

*Doctor Keydar also thinks that the Supreme Court of Israel needs to be overhauled as there is no constitution in Israel. The Israeli system works on the Basic Rules (Hukey Yesod) established upon the birth of the new Israel. Those basic rules have been periodically reviewed and revisited by the parliament (the Knesset).*

*However, as in every democratic country, there are always opposite forces that seek to outdo each other. For example: the political right wing will always face the moderate center and the left wing of Israel who want to establish a lasting peace with the Arab population of Israel. It is a complicated issue that might take years if not decades to come to an acceptable.*

***Conclusively we can celebrate the fact that modern Israel is better off today as compared to biblical Israel following the reign of King David.***

# Chapter Eighteen

## Summarizing The Complexities

## of Jewish Struggles

The following chapter deals with some details within the facts reported in the previous chapters' It delves more into the How and Why the Israelites battled each other and why the two Temples were destroyed.

It relies on biblical predictions and on the Talmud and Mishnah whose sages witnessed the tragedies of the second Temple.

It also adds additional historic events, not mentioned before, and clarifies them further.

As it is reported in history no empire or nation had ever have citizens united with each other as a way of ensuring a peaceful transition from one government to another.

Unlike some of today's existing democracies, political power is transferred via free elections from governing party to another, thus ensuring bloodless transitions of power.

In contrast, as reported in world history, Greeks battled Greeks, Persian and Babylonian chiefs battled each other in order to maintain power. Roman Emperors, for the most part, killed or poisoned each other, in order to ensure their succession.

And now to our project, which is the survival of the Jewish people throughout the ages and the struggle to keep its faith despite the savagery of its occupying power.

### Partial Tolerance of Greek Culture

As the Greek culture began to emerge in the Middle East in the fourth and third century BCE, it became harder and harder for the Israelites in the Holy Land to remain devout Jews, faithful to their Torah as prescribed by the Pentateuch.

Even before the Maccabean revolt, the Land of Israel was already overwhelmed by Hellenism.

In the Ninth Century BCE, during the first Temple era, when the Land of Israel became divided following the death of king Solomon, the Israelites ceased to be united as seen before.

While the Northern population went astray and became dispersed after the conquest of Northern Israel by Shalmaneser, the Southern Israelites remained in Judea.

Based on the Bible, those who ignored the divine prophets ceased to exist while those who battled foreign gods survived.

Consequently, even as other deities existed along the God of Israel, those Israelites who resisted and battled foreign cults survived, mainly in the Judean part of the Holy land.

A few centuries later, when the Greeks invaded and occupied the Holy land (330 BCE), Hellenism began to spread within the population.

The rules of king Antiochus IV (175 BCE-164BCE) went too far by imposing sacrifices of an impure animal, such as a pig, in the Holy Temple of Jerusalem.

However, it is also reported not all Jews of the Holy land protested against the desecration of the Temple.

## How Sadducees Were Close to Hellenism

It was only one small fraction of the devout Jews, organized by Mathatias and his five Maccabean sons who bravely achieved several victories against the occupying Seleucid armies; The Seleucids represented one branch of the Greek army which originally split into four different kingdoms following the death of Alexander the Great.

The strong influence of Hellenization in the Holy Land was responsible for the creation of a new faction called *The Hellenists* who were also close to the *Sadducees*.

The Sadducees did not believe in the Jewish Oral Law (named Halachah) and that created a certain confusion in practice of Judaism in Israel.

The Sadducees were a political force which opposed the leading religious force in the Holy Land, the Pharisees.

So, following the death of the last Maccabee (135 BCE), Simon the Hasmonean, it was his son Yohanan(John) Hyrcanus who ruled the state of Israel.

John Hyrcanus was greatly influenced by the rule of the Sadducees, who were practically the religious enemies of the Pharisees. His father, Simon was murdered by non-other than his father-law- in law Ptolemy from Egypt.

With the murder of the last Hasmonean and Maccabee, Simon, son of Mathatias, we begin to witness a violent power struggle, based on religious belief as well as cruelty and thirst for power.

This is what we learn during the reign of john Hyrcanus on the rivalry between Sadducees and Pharisees who actually occupied the majority of the population of the land of Israel.

> '*During the reign of Yohanan Hyrcanus, a growing party of law defiers came to the fore. Mainly the descendants of the Hellenists. There were the disciples of Tzadok and were therefore known as Tzadokim (Sadducees). How did the Sadducees differ from the Hellenists? Both denied the divine origin of the Oral Law and both cast off the yoke of the Commandments...The Hellenists were assimilationists who saw no reason for [the] existence of a Jewish nation....Not so the Sadducees. They were only too well aware of the spiritual achievement of the Hasmonean period. They knew that their contemporaries, who were the eyewitnesses of the miracles and divine intervention, would not easily forsake their G-d and their Jewish pride...The Sages saw them for what they truly were and tried to keep them from influencing Jewish life...according to them, the written Torah was to be taken literally...This was a declaration of war of the fundamentals of Jewish belief is that it denied the divine origin of the Oral Law and the unbroken transmission of Torah interpretation from teacher to student since Moses received it from [Mount] Sinai. Furthermore, the Sadducees denied that [Pharisee] Sages had the authority to pronounce ordinances and decrees...The Saducean courts administered justice in a particular cruel manner. The Oral Law teaches that an eye for an eye means teaches that an assailant must give monetary compensation for any wound he may have inflicted. The Sadducees, however interpreted the verse literally, if someone had blinded another man, they would blind him in retribution...in addition... the Sadducees denied the existence of the World to Come... for there was nothing after death...Much blood was shed in confrontation between the Sadducees and the loyal masses of the people and their leaders, the Sages.' (History of the Jewish People, The Second Temple Era, pages 90-91)*

From here on we are going to witness power struggle between descendants of Hasmoneans who became cruel to each other. Furthermore, since the land of Israel was not all Jewish, it was composed of converts who did not exactly care about the strict Jewish practice of religion as we spoke about before in the advent of the Herod the Great who was an Edumite who controlled the Land of Israel with Roman help.

Now we are going to witness something that could have been avoided and that could have eventually saved the destruction of Jerusalem and the destruction of the Second Temple.

In biblical times the Israelites survived the Persian massacre thanks to the intervention of queen Esther. Prophet Daniel cheated death several times because of his genius or as the Bible reports because of his faith in God and ability to interpret dreams just as Joseph interpreted dreams for Pharaoh.

Joseph and Daniel were elevated to high office and became second to royalty because of their ability to give credit to a higher power, the God of the Israelites.

The soldiers who gathered around Judah the Maccabee prayed to God before they went to multiple battles against the Greeks.

### How The Descendants of Simon Changed Course

However, the descendants of Simon, the last righteous Hasmonean, changed course and forced neighboring forces to convert to Judaism. We learn that John Hyrcanus, son of Simon, pressured the Edumites to convert to Judaism because he did not want a fifth column against his forces.

We also learn that Antigonus, his son, forced the Galileans to convert to Judaism, which made the Holy Land a mixture of Jews and non-Jews under the command of one Jewish ruler.

*We begin to understand that, after the death of faithful Hasmoneans, sons of Mathathias, something changed in the Holy Land for the worse and human life became cheaper and cheaper.*

### Temporary Victory of the Pharisees

Fortunately, there were some temporary gains amid a broken legal system conducted by the Sadducees. The arrival of Shimon Ben Shetah, brother of Shlomzion the Queen(also called Salome Alexandra) made positive changes to please the majority of the observing Jews in Israel in the last century before the common era.

He succeeded in ousting the Sadducees from the Sanhedrin during John Hyrcanus persecution of the Pharisees. Together with Joshua Ben Gamla he instituted a public educational system so all children could go to Hebrew school and continue the commandment of learning the Torah.

Here is what the Talmud teaches us on this matter. Let us state that the Talmud, which includes the Mishnah and the Gemarah, which are the scholarly interpretation of the written Jewish Law (the Torah) is a living witness to the bloody events which took place during the persecution of the Pharisees

The Talmud, we recall, was assembled by Judah the Prince (Yehudah Hannasi) after it was written between the years 200 BCE and 300 CE.

Here is a quote from the Talmud on the cruelty of the Sadducees and the advent of Shimon Ben Shetah

> *"Once a cynical, lawless man named Eleazar Ben Poera managed to convince King Yannai that the[Pharisee] Sages opposed him. Eleazar advised Yannai to test them by expressing his intention to serve Kohen Gadol [High Priest]. The Sages asked Yannai to withdraw because there was a doubt as whether he was qualified by birth for the priesthood.*

> *Eleazar Ben Poera said, 'Could a common Jew be insulted this way? You are the king and the Kohen Gadol and this is how you are treated?.' What should I do [asked Yannai]? "if you heed my advice, trample them' But what will become of the Torah,[asked Yannai]? It [the Torah Scroll] is rolled up and lying in the corner. Whoever wishes to learn, let him come and learn"*

> *Said Rabbi Nachman Bar Itzchak "At that moment Heresy penetrated the king. He should have replied :, 'That is satisfactory concerning the Written Law, but what about the Oral Law?"*

> *Immediately, the evil was unleashed by Eleazar Ben Poera, and all the Sages of Israel were killed. The world became desolate, until Shimon Ben Shetah came and restored the Torah to its former glory (Kiddushin 66a).*

The above Talmudic passage clearly shows a definite animosity between the two religious parties of the Holy Land but it also underlines the cruelty of the Sadducees and their leader towards their Pharisee brothers.

## The Regretful King Yannai, Author of Baseless Hatred

Under the reign of queen Salome Alexandra the Land of Israel knew a relative peace, away from exterior and interior threats.

But before her taking the reins of the kingdom she needed to cope with her husband's Yannai (Alexander Janneus)'s cruelty to his Pharisee brothers.

King Yannai admitted that he wrongly targeted the Pharisees as he was duped by the treachery of the Sadducees. The following words were the last he confided to his mother Salome, who reigned over Israel for another ten years.

> *"Do not fear the Pharisees, nor the non-Pharisees, but only the hypocrites, who masquerade as Pharisees. For their deeds are like Zimri but they demand a reward like that of Pinhas [grandson of biblical Aharon(Aaron) the Priest]"* (quoted from the Talmud Sotah,22b, by Yekutiel Friedner).

In order to understand the above quote, Pinhas, the grandson of biblical Aaron, brother of Moses, was credited for stopping the plague which killed 24,000 Israelites from the tribe of Shimon (Simon) for committing immoral acts.

The tribe of Simon was camped in the land of Moab at the banks of the Jordan River before the Israelites reached the Holy Land. Many people from the tribe of Simon were enticed by the Moabite and Midianite women, leading them to bow to Peor the god of the Moabites and also commit sexual acts.

Zimri was a member of the tribe of Simon. As he was influenced by the Moabites, he appeared before the multitude of the Israelites escorted by a foreign woman whose name was Cozbi daughter of Tsur, the Medianite king.

The defiant Zimri, entered a tent in the camp and began having intercourse with the Medianite woman. When Pinhas saw what was happening he took matter in his own hand, he grabbed a spear and killed both Zimri and Cozbi, the Medianite woman.

Even before that immoral act, the plague cited in the Bible was killing thousands of Israelites for their immoral acts.

When Pinhas killed both Zimri and Cozbi at once, the plague stopped, leaving 24,000 sinning Israelites dead but the rest of the people were saved.

By his action, Pinhas was rewarded by gaining priesthood as commended by God through Moses.

As written in the Pentateuch the following quote approves of the act of Pinhas who was responsible for saving the life of the remaining Israelites in the tribe of Simon who did not die in the plague.

> *"And the Lord spoke to Moses saying, 'Pinhas, the son of Eleazar, the son of Aaron the priest turned back My wrath from upon the children of Israel...and I did not consume the children of Israel in my jealousy. Therefore, tell [the children of Israel] I am indeed giving him my covenant of peace. And it shall be for him and his descendants after him a covenant of eternal priesthood because he took vengeance for his God and he atoned for the children of Israel'* - see chapter 26 in the book of Numbers

Going back to the last words of king Yannai to his Mother his mother Salome Alexandra, he regretted to have shed so much blood. He compared the evildoers to the biblical Zimri and the good people to Pinhas who saved the Israelites from the ravaging plague.

### Relative Peace Under Salome Alexandra

Under the reign of queen Salome Alexandra the Land of Israel knew a relative peace, away from exterior and interior threats.

Salome's connection to Shimon Ben Shetah, who was her brother, brought the country to the right path. Shimon Ben Shetah became the advisor to royalty. As he returned from Egypt where he fled when the Sadducees persecuted the Pharisees, his colleagues joined him and instituted biblical rules as it was the way in ancient times. The land produced abundant crops and for ten long years of the reign of Salome, the land of Israel knew peace, calm and proper observance of Jewish practices.

The Sadducees who spread trouble around the land were severely punished by order of queen Salome.

As seen before, Yannai regretted all his sinful acts in ordering the unnecessary death of 6,000 faithful Jews and another eight hundred Pharisees who died a slower death before his eyes together with their wives and children.

Unfortunately, the peaceful ten years of the reign of Salome ended in confusion. Her two sons Hyrcanus and Aristobulos ended up fighting each other for the rule of the kingdom of Israel.

While Hyrcanus the elder brother was awarded the High Priesthood and the power to rule the Holy Land, his brother Aristobulos, enticed by the emerging Sadducees waged war against his own brother.

> *"The death of Queen Shlomis[Salome] Alexandra ended the only golden era during the time of the second Temple,*

*and it ushered in a century of almost unrelieved disaster. The feared civil wars did break out, putting the two brothers, Aristobulos and Hyrcanus, against each other. The outcome of this confrontation was bloody warfare, the end of Judea's independence, the destruction of the Holy Temple and the long and still unfinished exile of the Jewish people from its homeland" (History of the Jewish People by Yekutiel Friedner, pages 101-102).*

## Religion Used as a Pretext For Domination

The Sadducees used their version of the Jewish religion as an excuse to dominate the governing parties in the Land of Israel.

As religion is being interpreted differently by those who believe in it leads us to horrific results.

Take for example the previous war between Iraq and Iran where hundreds of thousands perished on each side of the war. The Iranians are of the Shiite sect and the Iraqis are Sunnis. Both are of the Moslem religion and both believe in Prophet Mohammad.

The same divide exists between Sunni Saudi Arabia and the Shiite Iran.

In the Holy Land, the Sadducees observed the Torah as it is literally written while the Pharisees expounded on it by citing the Oral Law, which is a sine qua-non addition to the Torah in observing the Jewish religion.

Herod and his father Antipater the Edumites, who converted to Judaism used the Jewish religion as a pretext to divide the Jewish population.

Herod who often bribed the Roman occupiers of Judea could not care less about its inhabitants. His cruel acts of violence against the population in general and against his own flesh and blood did not go well with the precepts of the Torah which forbids killing and especially killing in cold blood.

The Roman way of domination included the method called *Divide and Conquer.* That strategy worked well for them in the Middle East. After defeating the Greeks they expended their empire to Syria, Judea and the neighboring countries.

The rift between Hyrcanus and his brother Aristobulos and their request for Roman intervention in their civil war worked well for General Pompeii who initiated the Roman domination of Judea.

Have we asked ourselves How the Christian religion succeeded in accounting for over the quarter of the human population in our planet? When Roman Emperor Constantine issued the Edict of Milan in 313 whereby it

> *"permanently established religious toleration for Christianity within the Roman Empire. It was the outcome of a political agreement concluded in Mediolanum (modern Milan) between the Roman emperors Constantine I and Licinius [in the East] in February 313...It granted all persons freedom to worship whatever deity they pleased, assured Christians of legal rights (including the right to organize churches) and the prompt return of confiscated property (Encyclopedia Britannica).*

Whereas Christianity split into various religions while adopting the Trinity and the divinity of Jesus Christ, the Jewish religion survived while adopting the Pharisee way of practicing Judaism.

Thanks to Shimon Ben Shetah and his sister Salome Alexandra, we have seen an initial victory (followed by some setbacks) of the Pharisee way in practicing Judaism.

Following the death of Shimon Ben Shetah, while the Sadducees continued their pressure on the Jewish population.

*The Pharisee sages decided to adopt a new policy of not interfering in government affairs but concentrate on learning the Torah, opening venues of learning and spreading Torah study and knowledge among the younger population.*

*This will be discussed in our next chapter*

# CHAPTER NINETEEN

## THE THRIVING OF JEWISH CULTURE

## UNDER DURESS

### (Ironically, Jewish Culture Grew Under The Nose of the Occupiers)

### The House of Hillel And The House Shammai

The Pharisee method of religion practice survived for generations following the destruction of the second Temple.

Fortunately, the known Sadducee influence did not persist in the Holy Land. Instead, the Pharisee scholars adopted the Oral Law, unlike the Sadducees who rejected it.

Within the Pharisees arose a multitude of scholars who followed the Oral Law which was interpreted by two schools of thought: the House of Hillel and the House of Shammai.

The House of Shammai appeared stricter in instructing its followers to adhere to the precepts of the Pentateuch, almost literally. On the other hand, the House of Hillel was more flexible in interpreting the precepts of the Torah in a more practical way. The House of Hillel prevailed in its interpretation of the precepts of the Bible and of the Oral Law and became accepted in generations to come since the destruction of the second Temple.

### Yohanan Ben Zakkai

As the second Temple was being destroyed by the Roman soldiers and as it was being besieged, arose a great scholar named Yohanan Ben Zakkai.

Yohanan Ben Zakkai, just as his learned colleagues and students, was in good terms with the Roman rulers, notably Vespasian, the general who was attacking Jerusalem before he was replaced by Titus.

While witnessing the destruction of Jerusalem and its culture (69-70CE) Rabbi Yohanan devised a plan to prolong the Jewish tradition and education of the youth and the old. Since he obtained permission from Vespasian to exit the besieged Jerusalem, he went to the city of Yavneh (near today's Tel-Aviv) and he founded the Academy of Yavneh.

He also made changes to rudimentary laws of the Bible, perhaps those rules were not fully clear but they were not deemed necessary. For example, the rule of making a woman suspected of committing adultery drink bitter waters (as it is literally written in the Bible), was abolished by Rabbi Yohanan.

Most of all, he was a pragmatist and, in other ways, he was what we call today a gentleman and a scholar. He never cursed or mistreated anyone. He was an example of goodness and kindness.

No wonder that he found out that a good heart was the best thing a human being can have. When he sent out his five students to go out and discover what was the best thing in life, the students came back with different answers. Rabbi Eleazar, one his students came out with the conclusion that a good heart was the best attribute in a human being. Therefore, Rabbi Yohanan chose a good heart as the proper answer to everyday life in a human being because a good heart included everything in life including a good eye and a good human character.

what we can learn today from Rabban Yohanan Ben Zakkai is the ability to adapt to reality and the desire to continue the tradition carried on by our forefathers. Education and study of the Torah saved a whole new generation and enabled the divine worship without the existence of the Jerusalem temple, In his eyes, God is everywhere and God continues to exist anywhere we wanted Him to be within us. A contemporary of Rabban Gamaliel II (head of the Sanhedrin), Rabban Yohanan Ben Zakkai influenced many scholars for seeking humility and never become ostentatious on account of their knowledge of the Torah. Another contemporary who agreed with Rabbi Yohanan was <u>Zadok Ben Eleazar</u> who said, 'do not make the Torah a crown for self glorification...'

## Pirkey Avot or The Saying of the Fathers

A short Synopsis: It is a Mishnaic masterpiece about Ethics and social behavior, written in traditional Hebrew and some Aramaic, between the year 300 BCE and 200 CE- This, book, which is a collection of principles from various sages who existed since the Torah was given, is quoted daily and weekly in Jewish Prayers and it is regularly read in its entirety three times each year in Hebrew Temples.

Pirkey Avot was studied by many Jewish scholars (Like Rabbi Marc Angel and Rabbi Lord Jonathan Sacks) and non-Jewish scholars (like R. Travers Herford). Incidentally, Rabbi Jonathan Sacks translated the Pirkei Avot from Hebrew (and Aramaic) to English ( Koren Publishers, Jerusalem-2015).

- There are 6 chapters in all in Pirkey Avot
- The first 5 chapters quote the wisdom of the sages around the beginning of the first millennium, roughly 200 years before the destruction of the second Temple by the Romans (70 CE) and 300 years afterward.
- The 6th chapter was added after the closing of the Talmud (500CE)
- The first chapter describes how the Torah was transmitted from Moses to his successors and their successors.
- The book contains maxims preached by the Sadducees as well as by the Pharisees. The House of Hillel was headed by the Pharisees while the House of Shammai, by the Sadducees.

> It tells us how the Torah was transmitted from Moses, down to his successors as follows: Moses received the Torah from Mount Sinai and he gave it to Joshua. From Joshua, the Torah was handed down to the Elders. The Elders handed it to the Prophets and the Prophets to the men of the Great Assembly. Simon the just was among the last members of the Great Synagogue (Hakeneset Hagedolah)

- Recapping with some more details: the Torah originated with Moses and, according to Pirkey Avot, was transmitted without interruption (following all stages mentioned above) to Rabbi *Simeon Ben Gamliel* who was under siege in Jerusalem when the Romans prepared to destroy the second Temple (year 70).
- The leaders Hillel and Shammai, who received the Torah from Rabbi Simeon(*Shimon)*, transmitted the teachings of the Torah to Rabbi Yohanan Ben Zakkai who was also under siege and who managed to get out of the besieged Jerusalem in order to open new academies and educate new disciples in the city of Yabneh (Yavneh).
- As seen above, This rabbi, Rabbi Yohanan, gets the most credit for preserving the Jewish tradition by substituting Temple sacrifices with Torah learning and prayers.
- This spiritual substitution, conceived and successfully implemented by Rabbi Yohanan Ben Zakkai stands to be the main reason for the spiritual survival of the Hebrew and the Jewish culture, if not the survival of the Jewish culture and spirit as a whole.
- Rabbi Yohanan discovered through his students that a good heart is a dominating factor. We learn that, after he sent them to research the best way one should conduct oneself under, the students came out with different choices. The choice made by Rabbi Yohanan was:

a good heart- Because, said- the rabbi, a good heart includes many aspects and therefore it is chosen over a good eye and other choices. That conclusion was made after one of the students, Rabbi *Eleazar Ben Arach* went out to the world to research only

to discover that a good heart was the best choice of what a human being should follow. The reason we underlined a good heart as a dominating factor in Pirkey Avot, is because that choice was made by one the best scholars at the time, who favored one of the brightest students mentioned in the text.

## The Importance of Pirkey Avot in Jewish Rituals

- Several parts of Pirkey Avot are used in Jewish daily prayers.
- By the 11th century CE, Pirkey Avot was read in synagogues in the Sabbath Minha services.
- Rabbi Meir, another Avot icon is featured in the 6th chapter of Pirkey Avot
- The Avot work includes icons who lived before the year 70CE (destruction of the second Temple): *Simon the Just, Shemayah and Avtatalion, Hillel and Shammai, Rabban Gamliel I, Rabbi Shimon Ben Gamliel.*
- Among the scholars who are featured in Pirkey Avot and who lived after the destruction of the Temple (year 70CE) were *Rabbi Yohanan Ben Zakkai, Rabban Gamliel II, Rabbi Elazar Ben Azariah, Rabbi Haninah Ben Dosa, just to name a few*.
- Other important figures who lived before the final rebellion against Rome, in the year 135CE, were: *Rabbi Akiba, Rabbi Tarfon and Rabbi Hananiah Ben Teradion.*
- After the rebellion and the last Jewish resistance was crushed under the Romans, two important scholars rose and were going to leave a lasting impact on the Jewish way of life: *Rabbi Shimon Bar Yohai and Rabbi Meir*. Rabbi Shimon Bar Yohai was known for his brilliance and for being the precursor of the Zohar, the Jewish Mysticism. Rabbi Meir was known for a great influence on his generation of scholars. One of his famous quotes referred to the importance of Repentance. The latter can save the world in the eyes of Rabbi Meir.

Other rabbis mentioned in Pirkey Avot but who lived between the end of the second century and the beginning of the third century were Rabban *Gamaliel Ben Yehuda, Rabbi Yehuda Ben*

*Tema, Rabbi Shimon Ben Eleazar.*

- It is important to state that among 200 tannaic scholars mentioned in the Mishnah, only 40 of them were chosen to be represented in Pirkey Avot.
- Many of the ethical remarks and recommendations mentioned in Pirkey Avot were stated as a result of the Roman occupation of the Holy Land.
- We conclude that most scholars mentioned in Pirkey Avot lived around the first century of the millennium. Nevertheless, the other 160 scholars not mentioned in Pirkey Avot remain the inspiring icons in the Talmud. We saw earlier that the Mishnah and Gemarah (the Talmud) included about 200 scholars in all.

## Who's Who in Pirkey Avot?

As we hinted before, Pirkey Avot quotes the Scriptures and the Talmud and comes to concise conclusions, based on the lengthy and heated debates between the rabbis.

The following are some pertinent remarks about several sages of the Talmud who made this book an intellectual treasure for the Jewish people and for all biblical and literary scholars worldwide.

- The following introductory remark found in the Talmud, is relevant to the survival of any nation which has parties who want to destroy each other. According to Talmud Yoma (9b), which is one the chapters of the Talmud, the Temple was destroyed as result of baseless hatred (Sinat Hinam) between brethren.
- *Rabbi Tarfon* is reputed in Kalla 9 (another chapter of the Talmud), to have been a wealthy man. A contemporary of Rabbi Akiva he was reported to stay all the night of the Passover Eve, discussing the Exodus from Egypt. His generosity to hundreds of poor women could be combined with his genial knowledge of the Torah. His famous saying was, 'the day is short and the task is great...you are not required to complete the work yet you are not free to withdraw from it.'(Avot 2:20-21).
- Rabbi Shimon Bar Yohai was the precursor of the Zohar, Jewish Mysticism. with his son Eleazar, he fled to a cave from the Romans who wanted to arrest him after the rebellion of Bar Kochba (135CE) which Rabbi Shimon supported. A student of Rabbi Akiva and a

disciple of Rabbi Meir, he devoted most of his life to the study of the Torah. He disagreed, however, with other rabbis that one must have a worldly occupation. He believed that the study of the Torah is so important that providence can help those who devote their entire life to Torah. *He* emphasized the importance of three crowns: The crown of the Torah, the crown of priesthood and the crown of kingship. Rabbi Shimon implied that, while the crown of kingship and priesthood can be transmitted from father to son, the crown of the Torah must be earned through hard study and a true way of observing its precepts and those of the Halakhah. All crowns, no matter how achieved must earn the honor of achieving a 'good name' in the words of Rabbi Shimon.

- *Rabbi Hanina Ben Hakinai* was a contemporary of Rabban Yohanan Ben Zakkai and Rabbi Akiba. He was also one of ten martyrs cruelly murdered (including Rabbi Akiba) by the Romans after the rebellion of Bar Kochbah (135 CE).

- *Rabbi Nehuniah Ben Hakanah* was a contemporary of Rabban Yohanan Ben Zakai. He was also one of the authors of the Kabala (Jewish Mysticism). Rabbi Nehuniah was a prosperous and generous person who believed that the study of the Torah 'spared the yoke of government and the yoke of worldly responsibilities.' He is mentioned in Megila 28 and Berakhot 28b (within the tractates of the Talmud).

    *Rabbi Haninah Ben Dosah* was a contemporary of Rabbi Akiba. He stressed the importance of having ten people (or more) in a congregation because then, the spirit of God resides within them. He also stressed the importance of deeds over wisdom. He taught that a person with good nature and good character is a person favored by God Himself.

- *Rabbi Elazar of Bartota* was the teacher of Rabbi Shimon Bar Yohai and Rabban Gamliel II. He professed that all and everything belongs to God. Therefore, charity is something we humans return to God by giving it to the proper people, because it is His.

- *Rabbi Yaakov* was a student of Rabbi Meir. Rabbi Yaakov was also the teacher of Rabbi Yehudah Hanasi, Judah the Prince who assembled the Talmud. Rabbi Yaakov stressed the importance of never interrupting your prayer while walking, even if you encounter a beautiful tree and a wonderful landscape. See page 202 for more on this sage.

- Rabbi Meir was a student of Rabbi Akiba. He was also a teacher of

Rabbi Yehuda Hanasi. The above three scholars are often quoted as they greatly contributed to the Jewish heritage. Talmud (Eruvin13b), states that Rabbi Meir was a new name given to Rabbi Elazar Ben Arach. We saw earlier that Rabbi Elazar Ben Arach was the favorite student of Rabbi Yohanan Ben Zakkai. This statement does not seem to be included in Pirkei Avot but it is worthwhile knowing about it.

- *Rabbi Dosa Ben Harkinas* was a contemporary of Rabbi Yohanan Ben Zakkai in the Academy of Yavneh. He did not favor sleeping late in the morning. He also advised against consuming alcohol in mid-afternoon. Although he forbade chats with children and ignorant people, that advice does not seem to hold in today's twenty-first century.

- Rabbi *Elazar the Modaiite*, was a contemporary of Rabbi Yohanan Ben Zakkai. He was against desecrating holy things and holy matters, such as Tefillin, Tallit, biblical festivals and all what is holy in the Jewish religion. One important thing that stands strong in the twenty-first century was that he was definitely opposed to one person embarrassing another person in public. This advice remains so relevant in our days. He was also against falsifying the meaning of the precepts of the Torah. He meant by that, that it was wrong to interpret the commandments of the Torah without consultation with a rabbinical authority.

- Rabbi Ishmael Ben Elisha was a contemporary of Rabbi Akiva. He, like Shammai (the head of the Sadducees), recommended that we should greet every person cheerfully. His father, Rabbi Ishmael Ben Elijah was one of the ten martyrs who were cruelly murdered by the Romans following the conquest of Jerusalem. Ben Elisha differed with Rabbi Akiva about the interpretation of the Torah. Rabbi Akiva thought that the Torah was complete and there was nothing lacking even as there were several repetitions of facts and precepts. Rabbi Elijah argued that the events of the Torah were not chronological. His school led the foundations for the Mechilta, Sifra and Sifrei (seen above) which represent the halakhic exegesis of the Torah.

- *Rabbi Akiba* was a student of Rabbi Yehoshuah and Rabbi Eliezer. He was considered a leading interpreter of the Torah around the time of the rebellion against the Romans in 135CE. Because he defied the Roman authorities who forbade all Jewish scholars to promote the teaching of the Torah, he was apprehended and tortured to death after the rebellion. He was the precursor of 'fences to the Torah'. This means, for example, if the Torah forbade committing adultery, rabbi Akiba established rules, which prevented a man from speaking in length to a woman so that it would not lead to a possible temptation and an immoral act. This idea of the 'fence to the Torah' is included in the *Halakhah* (the way to go or the way to observe the commandments of the Torah), which goes hand in hand with the Oral Torah.

Thus the Oral Torah, given along with the written Torah, served as a 'check and balance' to the written Torah. *Rabbi Akiba was therefore the master of Halachah.* He clearly stated in Pirkey Avot, that the Oral Tradition had to contain safeguards to the Torah. He also spoke about the importance of the tithes as being a fence to a person's wealth. A tithe is a contribution consisting of the tenth of someone's wealth and designed to be given to the religious authorities and designed, not only to support the Clergy but also to help the poor and the deprived.

- Silence, in the eyes of Rabbi Akiba, was the fence protecting wisdom. This does not mean that a wise scholar needs to observe silence all the time. This means that the wise person speaks when necessary while insisting on listening more than speaking. Rabbi Akiva used to say, 'beloved is the man who was created in the image of God'. He cited quotes from Genesis and Deuteronomy respectively, saying, 'because in the image of God, He made man'; 'you are the children of the Lord, your God'. Furthermore, Rabbi Akiva made a deep statement about the destiny of man and justice in the world: while everything is foreseen in life a person can make a choice to do well or choose evil ways. People's deeds are watched, whether they are good or bad deeds. Men and women can do anything they want in this world but at the end, if the good deeds exceed the bad deeds, a person may have a place in the world to come. As Rabbi Akiva puts it,

> *'the shop is open, the shopkeeper extends credit, the notebook [recording the deeds of man] is open, the hand writes. Whoever wishes to borrow can come and borrow and the collectors make rounds every day and collect payments whether a person knows it or not… the judgment is accurate and all is prepared for a banquet.'*
>
> *(Avot 3:20)*

This was how Rabbi Akiva saw how people could carve their destiny.

- Rabbi *Elazar Ben Azariah* was one of the leaders of the Academy of Yavneh, together with Rabban Gamliel. He was a descendant of Ezra the Scribe and had a deep knowledge of the Torah. Like other rabbis, he emphasized the fear of God as part of faith. However, fear of God must translate into good deeds, knowledge, wisdom, study of the Torah and especially having an occupation for sustenance purposes. No quality can exist without the other. Knowledge of Torah alone is not enough, according to Rabbi Elazar Ben Azariah. The conclusion is that deeds must exceed wisdom.

- Rabbi *Elazar Ben Hisma* was also a disciple of Rabban Gamliel. He is quoted in the Talmud (Horayot 10:1) as being well versed in Astronomy and Mathematics. Combining Torah and science he spoke about bird offerings and 'menstrual periods' to be calculated according to law. Astronomy and mathematics mean wisdom. *This the first time we see how a scholar from the academy of Yavneh speaking about scientific things we would be talking about in our century.*

- *Ben* Zoma was not titled Rabbi but he was known for being extremely bright in interpreting scriptures. His first name was Shimon and he was a student of Rabbi Yehoshua. He quoted the book of Proverbs to show that a wise man is the one who is eager to learn from everyone. He also learned from the book of Proverbs that the mighty person, is the one who can control himself. He also said, while leaning on the book of Psalms and the book of Samuel that a happy man is the one who is content with what he has or possesses. An honorable person is a person who respects other people. We can see here that learning and behaving is not necessarily a trait attributed to rabbis and scholars only.

  *Ben Azzai was* a contemporary of Ben Zoma. He taught that a minor mitzvah (good deed) was as important as a great one. People should make the same effort to perform both forms of good deeds. He also taught that performing one mitzvah leads to another mitzvah and performing one sin leads to performing another sin. He recommended being courteous to everyone. He taught people to never despise, hate or misjudge the value of anyone, 'because there is no one who does not have his hour and you cannot find a thing that does not have a place. ' He meant by that no one person should be underestimated, whether or not he or she is versed in the Torah because everyone could have a special human character regardless of Torah knowledge. *Shimon Ben Azzai was an important member of the Yavneh Academy and he was a student of Rabbi Yehoshua.*

- *Rabbi Levitas* was also a member of the Yavneh Academy. He preached about being extremely humble because our end is to be buried and be eaten by worms. Rabbi Levitas implied that humility found in our ancestors such as the one we found in Abraham, Isaac, Jacob, Moses and Aaron, is necessary for a human being in order to be close to God Himself.

- *Rabbi Yohanan Ben Beruka* was another scholar who warned people not to profane the name of God. While desecration of the name of God in public is already forbidden, Rabbi Yohanan Ben Beruka thought that some people might desecrate the name of God in secret. That is also a transgression. He meant by that, that some people could secretly do things not acceptable by the Torah or the Halachah. Such a behavior constitutes a desecration of God's name, whether it is done expressly or inadvertently

- *Rabbi Ishmael, the son of Rabbi Yohanan Ben Beruka* was a contemporary of Rabbi Meir and Rabbi Shimon Bar Yohai. He professed that teaching the Torah as a profession was acceptable on one condition: The Torah teacher must live the way the Torah instructs the person. The teacher should serve as an example to his students and his way of life should truly reflect the precepts of the Torah.

- *Rabbi Tsadok* was a contemporary of Rabbi Yohanan Ben Zakkai. His words are in agreement with what the sage Hillel said earlier: do not separate yourself from the community and do not make of the Torah a crown for self-benefit. The Torah should be learned for the sake of loving God only. It is not a means to grandeur. He also cautioned not to become one who would be among those who prepare the judges for a judicial matter. This could also be interpreted as warning people to not act as lawyers when they are sitting judges. We can definitely see here a clear separation between those who judge and those who advocate.

- *Rabbi Yose was* a student of Rabbi Akiba in the Yavneh Academy. His theme centers on the person who honors the Torah. That person is respected by all humankind. This is a departure, in that Rabbi Yose implies that Jews and non-Jews would respect a learned person who honors the Torah in all its phases. Honoring the Torah also means practicing to the fullest what the Torah prescribes. It also means that one teacher of the Torah must serve as an example to his students in practicing all the mitzvoth (the commandments) written in the Torah.

- *Rabbi Ishmael* was the son of Rabbi Yose (see above). He did not live in Yavneh but in the north of the Holy land, in another academy in the town of *Tzipori*. Although his father Rabbi Yose studied in Yavneh, he was a practicing rabbi and scholar in the academy of Tzipori. Rabbi Ishmael spoke about the responsibility of a judge. Because judges are highly placed in the hierarchy of the Torah and its laws, judges should be cautious in what they say and what they decide. They could be accused of rendering the wrong verdict or favoring one party over the other. Therefore, Rabbi Ishmael stated that if a person abstains from assuming the role of a judge he could spare himself, 'enmity, robbery and perjury.' Furthermore, a judge who is haughty in his teaching and judgment, can be considered as foolish, wicked and arrogant. This does not mean that competent judges should shy away from their task. This means that a judge has an enormous task before him and he must render justice in a manner that he could never be accused of favoritism, thus avoiding enmity. Rabbi Shimon further stated that a judge should not act alone in his decisions. He should not impose his views on his colleagues. On the contrary, his decision should be discussed, shared and the final decision should be made after careful deliberation between the members of the Court.

- *Rabbi Yonatan* was a student of Rabbi Ishmael and a contemporary of Rabbi Akiba. Rabbi Yonatan literally stated that a person keeping the Torah while in the state of poverty ends up keeping in wealth. This could make sense if poverty and wealth were a state of mind. His words can be interpreted this way: if a poor person treasures the Torah and studies it thoroughly, it gives him a sense of richness and abundance of spiritual happiness. On the other hand, if a rich man neglects the Torah, he will end up neglecting it in poverty. This can also mean that a rich man with many means may feel spiritually empty because he neglected the Torah, despite his wealth.

- *Rabbi Meir* was a student of Rabbi Akiba. They both were considered among the most original scholars of the Mishna. Rabbi Meir was also a colleague of Rabbi Ishmael and Rabbi Elisha Ben Abuya (Avuya). Although the latter became heretic, he remained a source of inspiration and learning to Rabbi Meir. Rabbi Meir is considered the most brilliant of the Tanaim, according to a Mishnaic chapter

(Eruvin 13b). His teachings and those of Rabbi Akiva became among the most quoted in the Mishnah. Later on, Rabbi Yehudah the Prince (Hanasi) gathered all the teachings of all the scholars and created the known six books of the Mishnah. Rabbi Meir preached about reducing business dealings for the benefit of Torah study. He urged humility before every person. He explained that if one neglects the study of the Torah, he would find many more people who would do the same. On the other hand, if a person works hard in studying and absorbing the Torah there is a great reward waiting for him.

- *Rabbi Eliezer Ben Yaakov* was a student of Rabbi Akiba. He was well liked in his community because of his good nature and his wisdom. He professed that a person performing a mitzvah acquires an advocate or a defender. On the other hand, the people committing transgressions trigger the existence of an accuser. As all scholars often speak in parables, Rabbi Eliezer implied that it is best for a person to do as many good deeds as possible in a lifetime. As no one is perfect and anyone, even a sage, may inadvertently commit a sin, It is preferable to have the mitzvoth (good deeds) exceed the transgressions. Repentance is a great opportunity for humans to correct themselves and redeem their soul because we know from the Bible (Jonah's story), that God has always forgiven and restored humans when they repent.

- *Rabbi Yohanan the Shoemaker (Hasandlar) was a disciple of Rabbi Akiba.* He was born in Alexandria. His remark came after the defeat of the Bar Kochbah rebellion. The Romans crushed the rebellion but the sages and scholars never lost hope. Rabbi Yohanan preached that every assembly, which is formed in the name Heaven, would be established in the end. This also implies that the assemblies existing after the Bar Kochba rebellion were not up to par with their ritual and scholastic functions because they were beaten by their enemy. Nevertheless, they functioned for the sake of God, even as they were weak and scarce throughout the land. Their intentions to continue worship of God and pursue the study of the Torah in their feeble situation would enable them to become a permanent vibrant assembly.

- *Rabbi Mathitiah Ben Heresh (the son of Heresh)* also experienced the defeat of the Bar Kochba rebellion. He consequently fled to Rome. He said, 'greet people first before they greet you. Be rather a tail to lions and do not become a head of foxes.' His quote is slightly different from the current proverb which was circulating in the Holy

Land and Rome, which was, 'Better be a head of foxes, than a tail among lions'. As Rabbi Mathitiah, lived under foreign occupation, he urged people to be cautious in what they say and what they do while facing the Roman authorities.

- *Rabbi Elazar Ben Shammua was* well qualified to be on the list of the brightest scholars in his generation. First, he was the student of the famous teacher Rabbi Akiba. When he became an illustrious teacher, he taught, among other students, no other that *Rabbi Yehudah Hanasi,* the assembler and the redactor of the entire book of the Mishnah. Rabbi Elazar Ben Shammua had a special respect for his students, his colleagues and friends, and more so for his rabbis and teachers. He viewed his teaching rabbis as those who upheld the laws of the Torah since the times of Moses himself. Therefore, proper respect was due to rabbis as well as to students who performed the enormous task of working hard in order to fulfill the biblical mitzvoth (commandments).

- *Rabbi Nehurai is a pseudonym of Rabbi Elazar Ben Arach.* We have seen earlier that he was the favorite student of Rabbi Yohanan Ben Zakkai. He was also a disciple of Rabbi Tarfon. We learned that Rabbi Elazar went away from the Academy of Yavneh and settled in Emmaus, another city in the Holy Land. He advises us that we must seek the Torah because the Torah is not going to seek us. He advises remaining with Torah associates and supporting them. By doing so, the study of Torah can flourish in the place of study. On the other hand, being away from your original place of study and staying in another place you might misinterpret some Torah precepts and that will be wrong. In another study about the title Nehurai, we learn than that pseudonym was given to other bright scholars like Rabbi Meir.

- *Rabbi Yanai is mentioned only once in Pirkey Avot and the Mishna.* Rabbi Yanai comes with a very intriguing statement about the just people and the wicked people. While we humans expect righteous people to be rewarded in this world and the wicked people to be punished, Rabbi Yanai comes with his maxim, implying that, we humans have no way of knowing while justice is not always rendered in this world. Perhaps, justice could be rendered in the world to come whereby the righteous person is rewarded and the wicked one is punished. Contemporary writers like Rabbi Kushner wrote on this subject about when good things happen to bad people and bad things happen to good people.

- *Rabbi Yaakov* was reported in the Mishnah to be one of the teachers to Rabbi Hehuda the Prince (Hanasi*)*. We recall that he warned earlier to never interrupt a prayer when one encounters beautiful scenery while walking and praying simultaneously. In this other case, Rabbi Yaakov challenges us to be extremely aware that the good deeds performed in this world will introduce us to a better place in the world to come. He named this world to be a hallway leading to an illustrious *'traklin'*, which is a non- Hebrew word, meaning a banquet hall (allusion to a special hall waiting for righteous people in the world to come). He also said that, better one hour of repentance and good deeds in this world that than the entire life in the world to come. Did he mean that the world to come is not as important as one hour of good deeds in this world? Perhaps not. He implied that a person should be busy doing good deeds in this world because he or she may not have the chance to do so in the world to come. This does not contradict what he said above, namely, that the good deeds we do in this world introduce us to other good things in the world to come.
- *Rabbi Shimon Ben Elazar* was a colleague of Rabbi Yehuda Hanassi and a student of Rabbi Meir. He was very careful in cautioning us about the timing of things. He said for example not to try to calm your friend in the middle of his anger. Do not try to console someone while his dead relative or friend is lying in front of him. Do not bother to speak about a vow to your friend while is making a vow or a pledge. He also warned people to stay away from a friend in the middle of his (her) demise. This does not mean neglecting a friend. It means that it is advisable to give space to a friend when he or she are going through a rough time. These are rules of behavior we understand in our century. They were good then and they are still valid today.
- *Samuel, the Young.* The name given to Samuel the young was *Shmuel Hakatan.* He was a precautious learner and a gifted scholar. In fact, Rabban Gamliel, head of the Assembly appointed him to compose a blessing against the heretics. That blessing is included in daily Jewish prayers, recited three times a day. Some scholars at that time turned to heresy. One good example was Elisha Ben Avuya (to be described below). at first, highly placed in the hierarchy of the Elders and scholars. He was in fact a colleague of Rabbi Akiba. He turned into heresy and became away from the circle of Jewish Scholars. He was also one of the teachers of Rabbi Meir. Because there was a scholastic connection between Rabbi Meir and Elisha Ben Abuya,

the composers of Pirkey Avot allowed his name to be included in the book. Ben Abuya said that studies done at a young age are compared to ink written on a new paper. On the other hand, studies done at an old age are compared to ink written on blotted paper. Samuel the young also spoke about how we should treat our enemies. He repeated the words of King Solomon in the book of Proverbs (24:1718) to be careful not to rejoice when your enemy falls or is destroyed. Since all humans are creatures of God, Samuel implied, being happy following your enemy's demise could make God angry.

- *Rabbi Yehuda* was also a teacher to Rabbi Yehuda Hanasi. He, himself, was a student of Rabbi Akiba. Rabbi Yehuda taught that those who study the Torah and the Halakhah must not make any mistakes of judgment. Mistakes, even if done inadvertently, can lead to rendering a false judgment and can put one of the opposing parties in jeopardy.

This briefly summarizes the short list of scholars and rabbis who contributed to the making of Pirkey Avot. More scholars and rabbis are mentioned in the Mishnah and the Gemarah, thus enriching the idea of humility, Jewish wisdom and the fear of God as best qualities down here on earth.

Pirkey Avot, as part of the Mishnah, is a most quoted masterpiece, together with the Tannakh, the Proverbs of King Solomon and the Psalms of King David.

Pirkey Avot is a proof of unity among the sages to continue and preserve the Jewish culture despite their living under civil strife and foreign occupation.

The next chapter will expound on that achievement of cultural unity.

# CHAPTER TWENTY

## HOW UNITY ACHIEVED SUCCESS

### The October 7 Israel Tragedy That Necessitated a Unity Government

October 7, 2023 is called now by the Israeli Press the Black Saturday where hundreds of young children, elderly people, young women raped and pregnant women cut open and their babies beheaded by the militant group Hamas who invaded Southern Israel after breaching the electronic 'secure' border of Israel with the Gaza Strip.

Four days later on October 11, 2023 a Unity Government was formed in order to face the threat and secure once and for all the border with the Gaza Strip.

Our project centers on unity. Despite political accusations between parties done before October 7, 2023, the Israeli people cried for a Unity Government.

This following are excerpts of articles reported by the New York Times on October 12, 2023

*'The government, approved after Saturday's attack by the militant Islamist group Hamas that governs the Gaza Strip, underlines the suspension of normal political rules during one of the most serious crises in Israel's history.*

*'This is a war for our home, it must end with one thing - in total victory, and the crushing and elimination of Hamas,"* *[prime minister] Netanyahu told parliament, calling Oct. 7 "the most horrible day for Jewish people since the Holocaust."....'*

*'After the deadliest assault on Israel in 50 years, the rightwing government and members of the centrist opposition formed a unity government on Wednesday [October 13, 2023] to navigate the crisis, while its warplanes rained destruction on the Gaza Strip and both sides braced for an escalating war between Israel and Hamas.*

*The creation of an emergency government came as the devastation of the Hamas incursion that overran dozens of towns and a military base last weekend became clearer: civilians, including children, shot dead in homes, in cars, on streets and in hiding places, with bodies still being recovered and counted..'*

American, Israeli and European Television stations reported that the toll in the attack had risen to 1,200 Israeli civilians and over 300 Israeli soldiers killed while battling the invading Hamas militants. The report also included over 3,000 civilians wounded and 240 people (of multiple nationalities) kidnapped and held hostage in Gaza.

As we recall, one month later in November 2023, the death toll was mounting on both sides (Israelis and Palestinians) as the battle raged while Israeli army sent ground troops to enter the Gaza complex.

The door to door search for enemy combatants resulted in the unfortunate death of countless Palestinians civilians who were reportedly caught in the middle.

As these lines are being written (February 2024), the battle between Hamas and Israel may take a long time to subside. In the meantime the health authorities of Hamas have reported that over 24,000 of civilians died in the battle. The Israeli military press has reported that among those Gazan civilians there were 9,000 Hamas combatants they called terrorists.

The toll on the Israeli side included 1, 400 Israeli civilians have been murdered and 4000 others wounded. Hundreds of Israeli soldiers have perished in the battle.

October 7 2023 has been considered in the Israeli press as another holocaust where women have been raped and brutally killed thereafter and children burned alive. The horrible acts committed by Hamas in the Israeli southern border have been documented by dozens of newspapers, including the New York Times and British Guardian newspapers.

Every day that passes more Hamas combatants and Israeli soldiers keep losing their lives. The Israeli military spokespeople showed to the world via videos and other means that Hamas had been using its civilians as human shields.

As the war rages on, multiple pro- Palestinian and a pro- Israel demonstrations supporting both camps have been shown daily on the television screen and the pressure had been mounting on the US government to demand a cease fire in the war.

As these lines are being written, the war continues between Israel and Hamas. Negotiations on the release of the hostages are taken place between the Israeli government and (indirectly via Qatar and the US government) and Hamas.

In the meantime, all Israeli citizens and especially the family members of the hostages are enduring a long wait for their release as well as a super anxiety mixed with sadness for those victims who were murdered on October 7, 2023.

### How Unity Can Achieve Success

One of the Israeli Opposition leaders, Mr Yair Lapid announced in early November 2023 that a new unity government was needed to overcome the Hamas challenge. He even suggested that Israelis were 'destined' to be unified in order to achieve success either military or spiritual, which brings us to the next topic.

The Israeli government, as a result of the unprovoked October 7 Hamas attack on Israeli civilians, formed a military cabinet which included prime minister Netaniahu and two of his opponents Benny Ganz and Yoav Galant, retired generals who joined the government in order to maintain security in Israel..

In time of dyer emergency Israelis united in order to confront the enemy.

### The Talmud, a Harbinger For Jewish Unity

*Going back to historical Israel, when the Israelites and their scholars worked in harmony, they achieved a remarkable success in preserving the Jewish culture for generations. When they battled each other or were betrayed by their own they failed miserably.*

The most important cultural treasure which thrived and guided Jewish scholars and non-scholars throughout history was the *Talmud,* which interprets the commandments of the Torah including its hidden secrets. It will be discussed below. the following are short statements summarizing the main events encompassing the birth and the survival of the Talmud, which has been attacked by rival scholars (often Jews who converted to Christianity) and burned over six times in history by the local authorities, including the occupying Romans and other European rulers.

On the other hand, the Talmud, for most of the time, remained preserved in the Middle Eastern and Arab countries.

The Following is a list of Important Jewish sages who greatly contributed to the survival of Jewish culture and continuous learning despite multiple hurdles in the Diaspora.

Among the most important Talmudists mentioned in the Mishnah and the *Avot* book, was Hillel the Great, who simplified and modernized some rigid and complicated laws of the Torah, such as the laws concerning the end of the Jubilee. The Mishnah and Talmud, at the time of Hillel, were not redacted yet but they were intensely discussed among scholars and their principles learned from father to son through rote memory.

*Rabban Gamaliel I (Gamaliel I), head of the Sanhedrin, was the grandson of Hillel, and teacher of Paul, according to the New Testament in the first century CE. The Mishnaic scholars greatly revered his wisdom and leadership. His death was considered a great loss for all the rabbis of his time.

Gamaliel II, was the grandson of Gamaliel I- They were both heads of the Talmudic academy.

As the original Bible influenced Christianity it also influenced Islam. When comparing the Torah to the Qur'An In Islam, the Bible corresponds to the Qur'An and some elements of the Talmud to the Hadith (which is an interpretation of the Qur'An accompanied by tales and legends).

It is important to underline how the Talmud survived under Islamic laws while it was threatened under European rulers.

The Talmud flourished in the seventh century and beyond under Islamic rule for many reasons including the fact that the Talmud and the Torah did not represent a threat to the Qur'An while the Roman occupiers linked the study of the Torah to the rebellion against Rome.

In fact, when comparing the Bible and the Qur'An many laws of the Torah are observed in the Qur'An (including some of the dietary laws).

In Europe, Justinian established harsh Roman rules in the Holy Land (527 CE). He established the code of the Roman Civil Law which established, among other things, that foreigners had no rights to property.

In the ninth century CE, legislative codes were established jointly by Moslems and Jews, under Shimon Kayyara and Moslem legislators under *Haroon Al Rashid.*

Simultaneously, within the interfaith commission, the Babylonian Geonim produced what it was called Halakhot Gedolot (great legal codes) under the Moslem governors.

The Babylonian Geonim [great scholars] established *She-Elot Uteshuvot* (questions and answers). The answers were called Responsa, which was equivalent to the Moslem Fatwa.

In 600 CE, Rav Huna and Ravah, authorized an instant Jewish divorce, without a cooling period of one year, in order to prevent Jewish divorced women from marrying Moslem men, who were able to obtain immediate divorce under Islamic law.

The Karaites in the Holy Land, just like the Sadducees, rejected the Oral Law. They only believed in the precepts of the written Torah. Although there was a constructive dialogue between the Pharisees and the Sadducees in the Talmud, the Karaite leaders were not involved in the mainstream Talmudic dialogue and debate.

Saadia Gaon, head of the Talmud academy in Babylonia, rejected the Karaite opposition to the Oral Law and considered the Karaites, apostates (928 CE).

Saadiah Gaon had a great influence in the Hebrew circles and he was instrumental in regulating and adopting the Hebrew lunar calendar. He was prolific in Arabic and Hebrew.

When the Babylonian academies lost their influence in the Jewish world, the study of the Talmud shifted to Kairouan, in the Maghreb, today's Morocco. Kairouan was a commercial city and it served as an intellectual center for Arabs and Jews.

Between 711 CE and 717 CE, the Arab armies completed the conquest of Spain and established Cordoba as their capital.

*During the eighth century, the Talmud and the Qur'An became the intellectual power in Spain under the Arab rule.

During the Golden Era in Spain, the following events took place: The Kairouan center for Jewish studies had replaced the Babylonian academies in their influence over the Jewish world. From Kairouan, there was a direct postal communication with Spain, Italy and to some degree, with some European countries like France and Germany, where a small population of Jews could be found.

*During that Golden Era, Hasdai Ibn Shaprut, a Jewish scholar, born in 915 CE, became an adviser and the top doctor in the royal court in Cordoba.

*Cordoba Academy flourished under Moshe Ben Hanoch who arrived from Baghdad (Babylon).

*In the eleventh century, however, Cordoba was destroyed by the Berbers who invaded Spain. The Jewish Center of studies moved to Malaga, Spain under Shemuel Hanagid.

*Lucena and Al Fassi were the next leading scholars. Al Fassi came from the Moroccan city of Fez to Spain.

During the Golden Era, Jewish studies and the Talmud became available for the masses with the help of the above named scholars and especially with the advent of Moses Maimonides (born in 1135 CE in Cordoba).

Moses Maimonides was unique in completing several books which helped the average person understand the Torah. Among his most acclaimed books were the Mishneh Torah (a second interpretation of the Torah) and the Guide for the Perplexed.

*Maimonides was also known for his publication of the Thirteen Principles of Faith in God. His work substantially helped the Jewish population worldwide in rediscovering their identity and pride.

*The thirteen principles of Maimonides also helped restore faith within the Jewish Diaspora. Maimonides, who was also a medical doctor and a philosopher, centered on the uniqueness of God and gave hope to those who had doubt about their faith. The presence of God is everywhere and it is up to man to obey the precepts of the Torah as it was given by God to Moses. There is also hope for the life after death. This encouraged all those who read and studied Maimonides, Jews or non-Jews, that there is a world to come and, through good deeds in this world, we have a chance to continue living in a different form after our death.

On the other side of the Middle East and Spain, the Jews of Europe who begun to flourish following their earlier ties with the thriving Jews under Islam, encountered unbearable difficulty as some European monarchs did not tolerate Jews.

When the Talmud and various Torah commentaries were introduced to England, France and Germany, they were met with the resistance of the church.

The French Edict of 846 was to remove Jewish children from their parents and place them in monasteries.

In 942 CE, Sehok, a Jewish convert to Christianity convinced the king of France to destroy the Jewish population. Furthermore, in 1007, the King of France ordered all Jews to convert of die. Since we do not have the exact details of the above mentioned edicts, we can only say that the Jewish population of France was small and details on numbers are not available.

However in 1074, under Henry IV, Roman emperor of France (not the French Henry IV, who signed the Edit De Nantes in 1598 CE), the small Jewish population had some peace and was able to pursue its tradition.

The first Jewish scholar to reconcile the Talmud with European scholars was Gershom Ben Yehuda (960 CE-1040 CE). He became the first Jewish leader of the Ashkenazi population in Europe before Rashi. He lived in the city of Maintz and he attracted scholars from Babylonia and other parts of the world.

Rashi (1040-1105), was the student of Rabbi Gershom. He is considered the most influential scholar in medieval times and the most illustrious interpreter of the Talmud and the Torah. Rashi's name derives from the full name of Rabbenu Shlomo Ben Itshak. Thanks to Rashi, the Talmud was more understood. It created a certain rapprochement between Christians and Jews as Rashi could write in ancient French as well, besides being knowledgeable in Hebrew and Aramaic. Consequently, in France and in Europe, Christian scholars began talking to Jewish scholars. They realized that there is another version of the Bible from those scholars who knew biblical Hebrew.

Rashi's grandson was Rabbi Shemuel Ben Meir (1085-1158), also named Rashbam, in short. He was a leading expert in producing additional writings to the Talmud and Torah. Those additions were called Tosaftot. His youngest brother was Rabbenu Tam. They were both the best Tosaftists (authors of Tosaftot) in the Middle Ages. Both scholars represented the European Jews called Ashkenazim.

In France, Antisemitism persisted despite Rashi's enlightened way of interpreting the Talmud. Louis IX of France(1214-1270), more than a century after the death of Rashi, offered the Jews to publicly defend the validity of the Talmud. A chief opponent of the Talmud, a converted Jew to Christianity, by the name of Donin, advocated the burning of all Jewish literature and conversion of the Jews to Christianity.

The Jews were represented by Rabbi Yehiel of France. They naturally lost the debate and all the Talmudic books, written by hand, were burned in France in the year 1242 CE. We see here a deliberate action instigated by a converted Jew under a French king who was canonized saint. It is not clear if Saint Louis wanted to have the Jewish holy books burned but it was clear than Donin, a converted Jew to Christianity, was responsible for this tragedy.

In Spain, there was a similar situation, which eventually led to the Spanish Inquisition, a tragic ending for Jews and Moslems, expelled from Spain in 1492.

Pablo Christiani, another Jew who converted to Christianity to become a Dominican friar in Barcelona Spain, asked King James I of Spain to challenge the Talmud and debate a rabbinic scholar on the veracity of the Talmud. Ramban (Rabbi Moshe Ben Nahman) was such a man. The debate took place in 1263 and ended naturally in favor of the Christian majority even as Ramban was praised by the king and rewarded for a good debate. *The Talmud was consequently burned but the Jewish spirit and culture continued the struggle for survival, leading to the Spanish Inquisition.*

In 1483, Joshua Solomon Soncino of Italy and his grandson, Gershom Soncino, revolutionized the method of studying the Torah by the first printing of the Talmud, the Torah and the Halakhah.

As King Ferdinand V of Spain managed to reconquer Cordoba, the inquisition in 1492 became a sure tragedy for all Jews and Moslems who would not convert to Christianity. It was the most tragic era for Jews who were given a choice to convert or be exiled from Spain. The chief inquisitor and executor of the Inquisition was the well-known Thomas De Torquemada, who is quoted in every history book as the person behind the Inquisition.

As half of the Jewish population in Spain was forced to convert, there was some hope from the other half of the population to never give up the Jewish religion. Fortunately, Jewish learning and traditional rituals continued in other parts of the world.

Yoseph Caro simplified the laws of the Halakhah by being the first scholar to take credit for the Shulhan Aruch (see earlier). This pattern of a prepared table of laws was followed by several more scholars who wanted their followers to have a simple set of rules on how to observe the rules of the Torah and the Halakhah (meaning the way to practice).

In the fifteenth century, several Christian scholars studied the Talmud and the Torah. For example, Martin Luther(1483-1546) wrote :*Sola Scriptura*, in which he advocated that the Bible was the only source for belief in God. Conrad Pellican (born 1478 in Alsace) studied the Talmud. Christian Reuchlin was a self- taught Hebrew scholar

Throughout centuries Christian scholars wanted to know about the Jewish Scriptures and the Jewish law. Some scholars used their knowledge of Jewish law in order to have a dialogue with other Jewish scholars. On the other hand, Those scholars who hated Jews and wanted to destroy them also studied Jewish law in order to supposedly prove how contradictory the Jewish law was to the Christian religion. This was how the persecution of Jews through medieval times culminated in the Spanish Inquisition where half of the Jewish population was forced to convert to Christianity.

Incidentally, thanks to Reuchlin the Talmud was saved from being burned when another Jew hater, Joseph Pffefercorn, recommended to Pope Leo X to burn the Jewish texts. Fortunately, Pope Leo X read the works of Reuchlin and did not burn the Talmud.

A bright spot in the history of the Talmud occurred in 1523 CE, when publisher Bomberg produced a full copy of the Jerusalem and the Babylonian Talmud with commentaries including those of Rashi, Maimonides and Asher Ben Yehiel. The new edition served as a basis for dialogue between Christians and Jews.

Unfortunately, after the death of Pope Leo X, the Talmud and protestant books were burned under the new Pope, Pope Paul IV, on October 21, 1553.

Long before the Spanish Inquisition, Jews were exiled from England in 1290 CE. Several hundred years later, in 1665, Menasheh (Manasseh) Ben Israel lobbied for their return before Cromwell of England. Manasseh, who left Spain as a result of the long campaign of exiling non-Christians at the aftermath of the Spanish Inquisition, immigrated to Holland, which was a more welcoming state to Jewish exiles from Spain. Manasseh was a prominent writer and a Talmud commentator, a bible scholar, a passionate orator and an enthusiast lobby about justice for everyone including for the Jews. After his death, the British government was set up to readmit the Jews to England as there was nothing found in the law of England which forbade immigration of Jews to their country.

The new versions of the Talmud, written in the 17ᵗʰ century and before, were admired by European scientists, and philosophers like Hobbs, Newton, Milton and Ben Johnson.

Other Jewish scholars made a difference in the world of religions and literature as they combined Talmud with science: Yehuda Halevi, from Toledo, Spain (1075-1141), was one of the greatest Jewish poets and philosophers of the 11ᵗʰ century. His passionate love for the Holy Land, which was at war between Christian crusaders and Arab rulers, caused him to arrive there in a difficult moment of his life. He died there shortly upon his arrival.

Rabbi Isserless (1520-1572) wrote his own Prepared Table for the Jews of Europe, otherwise called Ashkenazim. Thus, he completed the Prepared Table originally written by Joseph Caro (seen earlier). The Maharal of Vilna, also named Rabbenu Loew (1520-1609) combined European enlightenment with deep understanding of the Bible and the Halakhah.

Baruch Spinoza (1632-1677), was considered the most prominent philosopher of the 17ᵗʰ century. His rejection of the validity of the Bible and of the Talmud caused him to be expelled from the Jewish community of Amsterdam. He was, nevertheless, acclaimed by most Christian philosophers of his century and subsequent centuries.

The year 1648, was a bad year for the Jews in Poland. Under Bogdan Khmelintsky, the Cossack rebellion of 1648, killed many catholic poles and over 100,000 Jews in a region which occupies today's Ukraine. Poland lost three millions of its population through territory loss. Poland was subject to several invasions during its history and subsequently to many tragedies which also took a toll on the residing Jews of Poland. As Poland was home to the majority of Jews around the world, it also suffered several setbacks and victories, culminating in the concentration of most of the Jewish population in the Pale of Settlement, which harbored some five million Jews.

We all know the tragedy of the Holocaust and its outcome. **Nevertheless, Bible and Talmud study thrived in Poland** under several Jewish scholars, namely Rabbi Moses Isserles, Baal Shem Tov (1700-1760) and the rise of Hasidim, and we can never forget Shalom Aleichem, the writer of *Tevya (Tuviah) the Milkman*, after which, *Fiddler on the Roof* became a famous Broadway musical and a famous Hollywood movie.

Another significant burning of the Talmud took place in October 17, 1757 in the Polish city of Kamenets. It was triggered by rivalry among Jewish leaders and Jewish converts to Christianity. It resulted in burning of all existing books of the Talmud. The myth of the blood libel (accusing Jews of using Christian blood in order to observe Passover rituals) was not believed any longer in the 18th century. The burning took place anyway and it was authorized by the bishop of the church, Nicholas Dembowski. This tragedy resulted in an intensive rebirth of the Talmud in other parts of the world and production of multiple reprints of biblical and Talmudic books throughout Europe and throughout the Ottoman Empire.

In eighteen century Europe Jews in Lithuania, especially in the city of Vilna (Vilnus) were led by The Gaon of Vilna who was considered a Talmudic genius. He opposed the Hasidic movement which flourished in Polish Ukraine under the leadership of the Baal Shem Tov. Both leaders believed in the importance of the Talmud except that they differed in their approach to the holy book. The Hasidim (the Jews of the Hasidic movement ) looked at the Talmud from what it was called a mystical ecstasy while the Vilna Jews under the Gaon looked at the Talmud from an intellectual view point. There was no violence between the two groups but we can see here how Judaism in Europe was divided into two very different types of religious people who supported the Talmud.

Next in history was the Ottoman Empire, which dominated a great part of Europe and the Middle East from the sixteenth century to the beginning of the twentieth century. In Turkey, false Messiahs surged and confused the already baffled Jewish exiles who resided in the Ottoman controlled states, namely, the Balkan States and Middle eastern states like Egypt, Syria and the Holy Land. Jewish communities in Greece and other Balkan states enjoyed a relative freedom and were able to thrive intellectually and religiously. Following the Spanish Inquisition, hundreds of thousands of Jews settled in Europe and the Balkan states. Cases of Antisemitism were rare until the beginning of the nineteenth century when Jews were attacked by Arabs in Morocco, Tunisia and Libya. In general, Jews were able to practice their religion and trade freely. The Talmud survived this time.

Unlike in Europe, as seen above, the Talmud was no longer a threat to Christians and it certainly did not represent a threat to Islam. The Halakhah was compared to the Sharia Law and the Talmudic Aggadah (legend)was compared to the Hadith in Islam.

One important thing occurred at the end of the 19th century. May 13, 1896 was a date to remember. Solomon Schechter, a Talmudic scholar from England discovered ancient Hebrew literature buried in an ancient synagogue in the old city of Fostat, near Cairo, Egypt. Hundreds of thousands of document revealed the lives of Jews and Jewish scholars since the first Millennium. It was an important discovery which shed more light on the Talmudic era, thus showing the importance of the Jewish Heritage, which was never lost.

In concluding the Jewish intellectual and religious survival, The Talmud, the Mishnah and the Bible with numerous versions and interpretations in multiple languages have made their way to every willing reader in the 20th and the 21th century. Without any censorship or bias. the Bible, the Talmud, the Qur'An and any other religious sources of study are available today in every library in the democratic world. When comparing today's availability of the Talmud to the restrictions found in the Roman Empire and the Middle Ages and beyond, one can only say, ' was it necessary shedding 2000 years' worth of blood when the Talmud was to become one of the most eternal books, together with the Bible in all its versions.

# BACK TO ANCIENT ISRAEL

Going back to ancient Israel, the Jewish crisis dominating this project and the destruction of the second Temple can be considered by most historians as the worst and the most devastating in the history of ancient Israel.

The five factions residing in Jerusalem mentioned earlier were not united and no party agreed with the other. The causes for disunity are numerous: Hellenization, pursuit of power, baseless hatred, lack of political order, and finally a mixture of groups who did not follow the Jewish was of life and the commandments of the Torah. The Edumite (Idumean) intervention headed by the Herodian dynasty and its association with the Roman conquerors did everything to eradicate the true Jewish way of life. Under those circumstances we can say that the tragedy of 70 CE can be cited as the worse tragedy in the history of Jerusalem and its Temple.

Fortunately, the only salvation to the tragedy came from the pursuit of Jewish education as we see hereby.

**A Ray of Hope**

Throughout the Roman Empire and around the Holy land, there was a thriving Jewish population in Egypt, Syria, Persia and Babylonia (today's Iraq). We cannot ignore that the Babylonian Talmud, which represents the most prolific commentary of the Old Testament was developed by numerous Talmudic and Mishnaic sages in Babylonia.

Among the Great sages of Babylonia was Hillel the Elder (Hazzaken) who was one of the most quoted scholars in the Talmud. There was also the Jerusalem Talmud, which comprised the Mishnah and commentaries from great scholars called Tannaim, such as Rabbi Akiva (Akiba), Rabbi Meir Baal Hanness, Rabbi Shimon Bar Yohai, Rabbi Hanina Ben Teradion and The Great Rabban Yohanan Ben Zakkai.

The latter managed to exit the besieged Jerusalem and later founded the great Academy of Yavneh. He did so by obtaining permission from Vespasian as he was not a threat to the besieging Romans who were fighting the zealots of Jerusalem in the years 64-70 CE.

The Mishnah was compiled by Rabbi Judah the Prince. Without him, the Talmud would have remained a compilation of Mishanyot ( plural of Mishnah, a set of rules interpreting and expounding on the laws of Moses found in the Pentateuch).

Before we close this short paragraph on the importance of Jewish scholarship and profound knowledge of interpreting the Torah, we must acknowledge that many Jerusalem sages and scholars were limited by Roman rules to propagate the learning of the Torah.

Rabbi Akiva and Rabbi Hanina are the very well-known scholars who were tortured and burned alive by the Romans for the simple reason they were trying to teach the Torah to their students and followers.

As far as the other Jewry in surrounding countries of the Roman Empire, Josephus reported a relative stability in the growing population and practice of the Jewish religion and customs.

More often than not, Roman governors, under Roman decrees protected, the peaceful practice of the Jewish religion. That protection was not without occasional riots and murderous acts from the neighboring non-Jewish Syrian, Babylonian and Egyptian neighbors and local governors.

Because of the civil strife that took place between different factions before the destruction of the second Temple, history has taught that hatred without cause (the Hebrew words being: *Sin'At Hinnam)* can be compared to greater sins such as immorality and killing that are forbidden by the Ten Commandments.

Quoting an important comment on Ethics of The Fathers (Pirkey Avot), chosen by Rabbi Mordechai Katz in his book,' Yesterday, Today and Forever' we find the following story:

> *One of the main causes of the destruction of the second Temple was bitter hatred and animosity that one Jew showed for another.*

> *A rabbi was once visiting a certain town, and on Tishah B'Av[a day of fast mourning the destruction of the two temples] he was informed of a bitter feud between two groups. He was asked to mediate between them.*

> *"We assume however that you will not want to hear the two sides until tomorrow, since it is a fast day' they told him'*

> *'On the contrary' responded the rabbi. "The destruction of the Temple was caused by unwarranted hatred of one Jew to another. What is more appropriate than trying to promote peace and brotherhood on this very day'*

The destruction of the first Temple taught the Israelites that when the people are united by faith alone, they are be saved politically.

When Prophet Jeremiah warned the people of Judah not to join Egypt against Babylonia (as they were in war and Babylonia vowed to defeat Egypt) the Judean kings and their advisors did not heed Jeremiah's warnings. They failed. The Holy Land was invaded, the Temple of Jerusalem destroyed, the cities of the land pillaged. Those inhabitants who represented the cream of the crop were exiled to Babylonia while the rest of most of the population sold as slaves. Only the poorest of the poor remained inland.

The destruction of the second Temple was documented by Jewish historians (Josephus and the sages of the Mishnah and the Talmud) as well as Roman historians. So we learned more details on how the population of Israel was split into factions who did not tolerate each other.

Both calamities could have been avoided if unity overcame dissension.

Whether her we believe that when we leave this world, we are destined to heaven or hell is a personal belief and we will not go there for now. One thing has been sure in Jewish history: those sages, martyrs, and rebels we spoke about before who kept their faith have left us a lasting legacy.

*When comparing the Roman occupation to the Jewish plight, this author has chosen the following few words, so beautifully written and borrowed from Stephen Dando-Collins in the preface of his book* 'Conquering Jerusalem' *follows*:

> *Neither side comes out well in this story. Both [the rebels and the Roman legionaries] were at times equally heroic and often equally brutal and barbaric. In the end, the Jewish freedom fighters lost their war and lost their holy city, which has been the focus of the revolt and of the Roman military campaigns to end the revolt. Yet, today, Jerusalem is once the heart of the Jewish faith, while, thanks to Christianity, an offshoot of Judaism, the Roman Empire and its gods have long gone. It just goes to show that, sometimes, faith can have its rewards, and the tables can be turned, if you wait long enough'*

**One Short Update**

We conclude this book editing in September 2024 while the war between Israel and its neighbors is still raging. Israel is surrounded by six Iran-backed militant forces, aiming at destroying the country. Militants like Hamas in the

South and Hezbollah in the North. To them we can add Iran- backed Houtis in Yemen who occasionally attack Israel. Other Iran backed militants are found in Iraq and Syria and even in the West Bank where pockets of Hamas operate. If we add Iran, we have enumerated seven forces Israel has to deal with.

The hostage crisis is a daunting task for the IDF and Israel Security Services, whereby Hamas refuses to release those hostages unless Israel withdraws completely from the Gaza Strip.

If that was not enough, the discovery of dead hostages in Gaza tunnels august 31, 2024 by the IDF (Israeli Defense Forces) has inflamed the public opinion and the atmosphere in Israel where almost

*Israelites: Unite or Self-Destruct*

half of the population has been criticizing the unity government for 'refusing' to negotiate and accept a deal with the Hamas group.

The nation of Israel is divided in its opinion whether it is a good idea to withdraw from Gaza and allow the militants of Gaza regroup and attack Israel again

To that end it is difficult to have a clear answer and even any unity government could not solve this impasse.

Since Iran is not adjacent to Israel and since it wants to dominate the Middle East, it has backed armed groups like Hezbollah and Hamas to be its proxies against Israel.

**To that threat Israel can meet the challenge by uniting the whole country of Israel against its enemies. However, the hostage crisis is another matter.**

**Yet Israel, being a country of immigrants , has succeeded in uniting the Jewish people who came from all over the world thanks to the survival of the Jewish culture and spirit we have been describing in previous chapters of this book.**

# BIBLIOGRAPHY

1. The Fight For Jerusalem-Dore Gold (New York Times Best-selling Author of Hatred Kingdom): -Regnenery Publishing, Inc, ISBN 978-1-59698-029-7

2. Jerusalem- History of a Global City-University of California Press, Oakland, Ca, 2022.. Vincent Lemire, Katel Berthelot, Julien Loiseau, Yann Potin, Translated (from French) by Juliana Froggatt. ISBN 9780520299900(hardback).

3. The People And The Book-18 Classics of Jewish Literature, by Adam Kirsch, ISBN 978-0-393-24176-1 W. W. Norton & Company(Independent publishers since 1923)

4. Conquering Jerusalem- The AD 66-73 Roman Campaign To Crush The Jewish Revolt, by Stephen Dando- Collins- Turner Publishing Company, Nashville, Tennessee- Copyright 2021- Library Control Number: 2021937173

5. The Works of Josephus- Complete ans Unabridged – New Update Edition- Translated by William Whiston, A.M-
    Hendrickson Publishers, 1987 edition. ISBN 0-91357386-8(Hard cover)-ISBN 1-56563-167-6(Paperback edition)

6. The Holy Scriptures- Revised In Accordance With Jewish Tradition And Modern Biblical Scholarship- By Alexander Harkavy -Hebrew Publishing Company- New York (no other information on the publishing of this book- The chapter titles are written in Hebrew and the translation is in English)-

7. Tannakh (short for Torah, Neviim and Ketubbim- which means Torah, Prophets and the Writings- Mesorah Publications Ltd, 4401 Second Avenue, Brooklyn, New York(Supported by Mesorah Heritage Foundation)

8. NIV Compact Dictionary of the Bible – J.D. Douglas &Merril C. Tenney- NIV Compact Series-ZONDERVAN, Grand Rapids, Michigan 49630- ISBN-10: 0310-22873) soft Cover). ISBN 13- 978-0-310-22873-8 (soft cover), 1989.

9. Good News Bible- The Bible in Today's English Version- Old Testament-American Bible Society, 1976

10. Reflections on Jerusalem- City of David in Classical Texts- By Naftali, Rothenberg, Leora Tanenbaum. And Sara M. Silberman-

Carol Diament Editor- Copyright- 1995, Hadassah

11. Ancient Towns In Israel: by Samuel Abramsky- translated from Hebrew to English by Shimon Applebaum-
    Typography: Ernst Jacob- Printed in Israel by Publishing Department of the Jewish Agency at the Jerusalem Post Press.

12. Eichah- A Modern Commentary on The Book of Lamentations- Translation And Commentary by Leonard S. Kravitz and Kerry M. Olitzky-URJ Press- New York NY- ISBN- 13:978-0-8074-1061-5 and ISBN-10: 0-8074—1061-6

13. Perspectives- Yitzhak Rabin And The Ethic of Jewish Power- Rabbi Irving Greenberg- Published by CLAL- The National Jewish Center for Learning And Leadership.

14. Yesterday, Today and Forever- Exploring Contemporary Judaism From the Perspective of Jewish History(From the
    Creation to the Destruction of the First Temple)- Rabbi Mordechai Katz-Feldheim Publishers- Jerusalem/New York- ISBN- 087306-656-1

15. Entire Hebrew Text of the Holy Scriptures- Yavneh Publishing House- Printed in Tel Aviv, Israel, 1979 edition.

16. Hebrew Text covering the five books of the Tannakh. [the Pentateuch], based on Biblia Hebraica Sttudgartensia, 1999, by the Jewish Publication Society, ISBN 0-8276-0712-1

17. JPS Hebrew-English Tannakh- The Traditional Hebrew Text And The New JPS Translation- The Jewish Publication Society, Philadelphia, 2003, 5764.

18. Pirkei Avot – The Saying of the Fathers- Traditional Text(in Hebrew and Aramaic) on the wisdom of the sages in the Holy Land and in the Babylonian Diaspora. The quotes on morality and human behavior extend over a period of 500 years, between 300BCE and 200CE. Pirkei Avot is part of the Talmud.

19. Complete Hebrew-Hebrew Dictionary (including biblical Hebrew and accompanying Aramaic Scriptures)over 70,000 words and idioms- edited by Avraham Ben Shushan- Kiriat Sefer -Limited, Jerusalem.

20. Compendious Hebrew-English Dictionary- comprising a complete vocabulary of biblical, Mishnaic, Medieval and Modern Hebrew- compiled by Reuben Avinoam (Grossman)-Revised and edited by M.H. Segal- The Dvir Publishing Company, Tel Aviv, Israel (year of publishing, not available).

21. The New Bentam-Megido Hebrew And English Dictionary, by Dr. Reuben Sivan and Dr. Edward A.Levenston- Bantam Press: New York-Toronto-London-Sydney-Auckland. Book completely typeset in Israel-ISBN 0-553-26387-0

22. The Bible, The Power of The Word (And Between The Lines), by Asher Elkayam- ISBN 978-1-42578562-8 (Hardcover)-ISBN 978-1-4257-8554-3 (softcover) Printed in the USA, by Xlibris Corporation-2008 edition.

23. The Qur'An and Biblical Origins- by Asher Elkayam, Published by Xlibris. 2009- Book number 57417-ISBN 978-1-4455-1180-5 (Hardcover) and ISBN 978-1- 44151179-9 (softcover).

24. Whose God Is it Anyway? By Asher Elkayam. Published by Lulu Publishing Company (2011)-ISBN 978-1-257-74541-8.

25. The Holy Bible, conformable to the edition of 1611, commonly known as the King James Version, ISBN 1600810861. Printed in the United States of America.

26. Encyclopedia Judaica- Volume 9- Is-Jer- by Keter Publishing House Jerusalem Ltd. Jerusalem, Israel – Library of Congress Catalog Number 72-90254. Third printing, 1974

27. Evil Roman Emperors (The shocking History of Ancient Rome's Most Wicked Rulers From Caligula to Nero and More) by Phillip Barlag. Prometheus Books, an imprint of the Rowman&Littlefield Publishing Group, Inc- 2021-ISBN- 9781633886902

28. The Internet: various sources via Google were used to compare the accuracy of dates, names and events (including Inside Science, Encyclopedia Britannica and Wikipedia).

29. Et Tu Brute? (Deaths of the Roman Emperors) by Jason Novak-W.W. Norton & Company Ltd (New York and London)- 2018- ISBN 9780393635737 (hardcover).

30. TWELVE CAESARS (Images of Power From The Ancient World To The Modern) -By Mary Beard- Princeton University Press (Princeton and Oxford)- 2021- ISBN 9780691222363(hardcover) ISBN9780691225869(ebook).

31. Sefer Yosippon (A Tenth Century History Of Ancient Israel) Written in Hebrew by David Flusser ans translated to English Steven B. Bowman. ISBN 978-0-8143-4943-4 (paperback). Library of Congress catalog number 2021951020. Copyright 2023 by Wayne State University Press, Detroit, Michigan, 48201

32. Nissan Mindel, commentator on historical events and associated with Chabad.org. His work was published and copyrighted by Kehat Publication Society.

33. History of the Jewish People (The Second Temple Era)- Hebrew text by Yekutiel Friedner and translated by Dr. Eliezer Ebner to English-Hillel Press by Menorah Publications, ISBN 0-89906-454-X (hard cover) and ISBN 0-89906-455-8 (paperback)-Eighth impression October 2000.

34. From Ezra to The Last of The Maccabees(Foundation of Postbiblical Judaism), by Elias Bickerman, Schocken
    Books, Inc,1962 edition. ISBN 0-8052-0036-3

# CHART 1: KINGS OF JUDAH

Note: Although King Saul was the very first anointed king of the Holy Land, the story of the kings of the Holy Land begins with King David who was reported to be the most revered and the most quoted king in the land of Israel (and for that matter, a most quoted king and poet in the Judaeo-Christian rituals).

1. KING SAUL-1038-1012 BCE. First king of Israel – He reigned over Israel and Judah.
2. ISH BOSHET-1012-1010 BCE. He was Saul 's son and he was appointed by Abner, Saul's military leader and, replaced by David
3. KING DAVID -1010-970 BCE- considered best king of all kings (of Judah as well as king of Israel) as he worshiped God faithfully and inspired the nation in instilling faith in God.
4. KING SOLOMON- 970 931- second best as he deviated towards the end of his life
5. REHOBOAM- 931-913 BCE -reigned 17 years. He was considered a weak king.
6. ABIJAH- 913 -911 BCE- (almost) 3 years. in power- He was a good king-
7. ASA- 911- 870 BCE- -41 years. He was considered a good king
8. YEHOSHAFAT-870- 848 or 849- BCE-25 years. By far he was considered a better king since King David and king Solomon as he followed the words and principles of the Torah.
9. YEHORAM-849-842 BCE-(almost) 8 years. He was reported to be cruel by killing his brothers and prevent them from claiming power. There was a connection between him and Ahab and Ataliah (originally in the Israel camp)
10. AHAZIAH-842-841 BCE- 1 year. He did evil as his father Yoram (Yehoram).
11. ATALIAH(queen) -841-835 BCE-6 years- Very cruel and murderous-
12. YOASH-835-795 BCE- 40 years reign. He survived Ataliah 's murder – He did well at first, he became evil toward the end of his life.
13. A possible break in government between 796 BCE and 795 BCE.
14. AMAZIAH- Son of Yoash. 796-767 BCE- 29 years of reign- He did right first, then evil in old age.

15. UZZIAH- 767 -740 BCE-27 years of reign and 52 years in power. However. He was a co-regent with his father Amaziah for 24 years. He did right.
16. YOTAM-740-732 BCE-8 years. In total, he reigned for 16 years as a co-regent with his son Ahaz. Yotam did well as a king (see below Ahaz)..
17. AHAZ-732 -716 BCE-16 years. He was a co-regent with his father Yotam. Ahaz did evil.
18. HEZEKIAH-716 -687-BCE- 29 years. Hezekiah was considered a good king.
19. MANASSEH-687-642- BCE- 45 years. In another source he reigned for 55, which can be explained by the fact that he became king at the age of 12 and he was a co-regent with Hezekiah (above).
20. AMON 642- 640 BCE- 2 years. He did evil
21. JOSIAH- 640-609 BCE- 31 years. Contrary to his father Amon, he did right.
22. YEHOAHAZ-609 BCE- 3 months (only). He did evil.
23. YEHOYAKIM-609- 597 BCE- 11 years (almost 12 years). As his father, he did evil.
24. YEHOYAKHIN 597 BCE- 3 MONTHS- He did evil- He was replaced by the son of Josiah by Nebuchadnezzar( see next king)
25. ZEDEKIAH- 597 -586 BCE. He was not totally in charge of the Holy Land as he was under the rule of Nebuchadnezzar, king of Babylon who overthrew his predecessor, Yehoyakhin. He reigned until the destruction of the temple of king Solomon in 586 BCE.

## CHART 2: KINGS OF ISRAEL

As a remark for the kings of Israel. They all did evil except for Jehu, who did well in some cases (as explained above) but he exceeded his authority in killing and authorizing multiples killings.

1. JEROBOAM 931-910 -21 YEARS (almost 22 years) -was reported to be no good king-
2. NADAB (NADAV)-910-909- almost 2 years
3. BAASA-909-885BCE- 24 years
4. ELAH-886-885 BCE (almost 2 years)
5. ZIMRI- 885-885 BCE- (7 days only)
6. OMRI- 885-874 BCE- 12 years

7.  AHAB- 874-853 BCE- He was considered to be the nastiest and the worst kings of Israel.- He reigned 22 years over Israel..
8.  AHAZIAH-853-852 BCE- 2 years
9.  YORAM-852-841 BCE- 12 years
10. JEHU-841-814BCE- almost 28 years
11. YEHOAHAZ-814-798 BCE- almost 17 years
12. YEHOASH-798-782 BCE- - 16 years
13. JEROBOAM II(Jeroboab II) - 793-753 BCE- 41 years of reign of which his co-regency with father Yehoash was from 793- to 782.
14. ZECHARIAH-753 BCE- six months
15. SHALLUM-752 BCE- one month only
16. MENAHEM- 752-742-BCE- 10 years
17. PEKAHIAH- 742- 740-BCE- 2years
18. PEKAH- 740-720 BCE- 20 years
19. HOSHEA- 732-723 BCE- 9 years

The historical dates in this book may vary in their accuracy depending on their historian source: For example: according to Encyclopedia Britannica, King Saul only reigned from 1021BCE to 1000BCE. Other historians (see Bibliography) state that his reign was between 1038 BCE to 1012 BCE (see page 230). Per biblical count it is stated in Time Line (see Page 234) that he reigned 40 years (1050 BCE to 1010 BCE). Nevertheless all BCE historical dates mentioned in this book are approximate and they are not intended to confuse the reader because they are sufficiently close to each other in historic time.

# Historical Highlights From Abraham to the Destruction of the Second Temple

The following chronological dates depict timeline events from the advent of forefather Abraham, father monotheism until the destruction of the second Temple in the Holy Land.

The dates below are marked to the best of historical accuracy. As some dates in ancient history may be approximate because of varying estimates from historians.

We are including the chronology of the kings of Israel and Judah, within the general chronology and also by themselves (see below chart)who were responsible for the unification and the welfare of their people. Unfortunately, not all kings followed justice. They were divided into kings who did 'well' and those who were 'evil in the eyes of the Lord'. Those who were considered bad worshiped foreign gods and, in the process, allowed for promiscuity and lewdness in the land.

Fortunately, there were also some good kings who made up for the sins of the bad ones.

The more recent and more modern dates are more accurate because of their proximity to exact documentation by modern historians.

We have also included below world events leading to our time. The early Hebrews, were later called Israelites and later in history they were called: Jews. Jews lived everywhere throughout history.

1812 BCE - Birth of Abraham

1725 BCE - Birth of Ishmael: Born 13 years before Isaac

1712 BCE- Birth of Isaac (Abraham was 100 years old when Isaac was born: Genesis)

1652 BCE- Birth of Esau and Jacob

1561 BCE- Birth of Joseph

1394 BCE – Estimated birth year of Moses.

1313 BCE: The Exodus from Egypt( 1 year earlier: 1314 BCE, Moses stood before Pharaoh, as the Bible reports, he was 80 years-old)

1312 BCE- Torah Given

1079 BCE –estimated date of king Saul's birth. Saul was the first king of Israel. Saul reigned 40 years (1050 to 1010 BCE). His death was self-inflicted.

1010-970 BCE-The reign of King David, second and most famous king of Israel

970-931 BCE: Forty (plus) years of reign of Solomon, king of Israel, son of David. Solomon, builder of the First Temple in Jerusalem.

954 BCE: First Temple built

BCE- estimated death of King Solomon—The nation split into Judah and Israel.

931-913 BCE- Reign of King Rehoboam, considered a sinning king in Judah

931-910 BCE- Reign of Jeroboam in the kingdom of Israel. He was also considered a sinning king.

913-911 BCE- Abiyah (also called Abijah in English) succeeded Rehoboam in Judah.-Considered a sinning king.

910-909 BCE- Nadav (Nabab in English) succeeded Jeroboam in the kingdom of Israel. He was another sinning king.

911-848 BCE- Two good kings reigned in the kingdom of Judah: Asa ( 911-870BCE) and Jehoshaphat (870-848). They followed the path of King David.

909-852 BCE- Five bad kings reigned in Israel: Baasha (909-886), Elah (886-885), Zimri (seven days only in 885 BCE), Omri (885874 BCE), Ahab (874-853 BCE), and Ahaziah (853-853 BCE)- Ahab (Ahav) was considered one of the worst kings of Israel(mainly because of bad influence by his wife, Jezebel).

848-841 BCE- Jehoram (Yehoram) reigned in the kingdom of Judah- During this reign Yoram (Joram) ruled the kingdom of Israel between 852BCE and 841 BCE. He was a sinner.

BCE-Ahaziah reigned in Israel for one year. He was considered a bad king.

841-835- Athaliah was the queen of Judah, after murdering her own relatives. She was considered the second most cruel woman in the Bible after her mother Jezebel, wife of Ahab, king of Israel. At the same time Jehu was the king of Israel (841-814 BCE)-

**835-732 BCE: Simultaneously, Five** good kings ruled the kingdom **of Judah and nine bad kings ruled the kingdom of Israel.** Their reign spread for over 100 years where, for a change, there was more faith in the Lord and more observance of the Torah. **The Judean kings were:** Joash ( 835-796 BCE), Amaziah (Amatziah) (796-767 BCE), Azariah (767-740 BCE), and Yotam ( 740-742 BCE)-

**During the same time the kings of the kingdom of Israel who were all considered bad were**: Jehohaz (Yehohaz) 814-798 BCE,

Jehoash (Yehoash) 798-782BCE, Jeroboam the second (782-753 BCE), Zechariah ( 753-752 BCE) Shallum (reigned only one month in 752 BCE), Menahem (752-742), Pekahiah (742-740), Pekah (740-732) and Hosea (732-721 BCE)

**Note: At this point Israel became captive to Assyria- So there were no more kings to be added to the kingdom of Israel.**

**However, the kingdom of Judah, after the fall of Israel, kept the Israelite nation independent until the eventual destruction of Jerusalem and the exile of the most important, intellectual and professional Israelites from Judah to Babylon under the command of Nebuchadnezzar. The following is the chain of events leading to that demise.**

740-732 BCE- Jotham (Yotam) reigns in Judah for 8 years.

732-716 BCE- Accession of Ahaz who reigned in Judah for 16 years

716-687- Hezekiah, considered a righteous king reigned over Judah and tried to follow God's rules despite the foreign trends in the Holy Land.

687-642 BCE- **Manasseh,** considered one of the worst kings of Judah was believed, as other bad kings, to have done 'evil in the eyes of the Lord'.

642-640 BCE- Amon, considered a bad king, reigned over Judah.

**640-608 BCE-** *Josiah reigned for 31 years in Judah. He, for a change, was considered a righteous king.*

608-597BCE- The last kings of Judah (Judea) named below were the last kings to rule Judea before the final capture of Jerusalem and Judea: Jeoahaz briefly ruled Judah before Jehoiakim took over the command of Judah for a period of 11 years. **This was the last, longest reign of a Judean king before the fall of Judea (Judah) and Jerusalem**

**in the hand of the Babylonians**. The last king, mentioned briefly in the Bible was *Yehoyachin*, who briefly reigned over Judah in 597 BCE, before the fall of Judah and Jerusalem in 586 BCE.

586 BCE- First Hebrew temple destroyed

245 BCE: Torah translated into Greek

2 -6 BCE – Jesus 'estimated year of birth

32 BCE – Hillel and Shammai: Two imminent leading Rabbis represented the two leading schools of thought in the Holy Land. Rabbi Hillel was considered more pragmatic and more liberal than Shammai.

1 BCE (March 1)- Julian Calendar begins in Rome after it is revised.

70 CE – Second temple destroyed by the Romans-

www.ingramcontent.com/pod-product-compliance
Lightning Source LLC
Chambersburg PA
CBHW071731120626
46550CB00002B/474